The Social Context
of Language

The Social Context of Language

Edited by
Ivana Marková

Department of Psychology
University of Stirling

JOHN WILEY & SONS
Chichester · New York · Brisbane · Toronto

Library of Congress Cataloging in Publication Data:
Main entry under title:

The social context of language.

   Based on a conference on language and the social context, sponsored by the Social Section and Scottish
Branch of the British Psychological Society, held at the University of Stirling, Jan. 10–11, 1975.
   1. Sociolinguistics—Addresses, essays, lectures.
2. Psycholinguistics—Addresses, essays, lectures.
3. Children—Language—Addresses, essays, lectures.
I. Marková, Ivana.   II. British Psychological Society. Social Section.   III. British Psychological Society.
Scottish Branch.
P40.S54   301.2   77-3861

ISBN 0 471 99511 8

*Typeset by Computacomp (UK) Ltd., Fort William, Scotland
and printed by Unwin Brothers Ltd., The Gresham Press,
Old Woking, Surrey.*

CONTRIBUTORS

BRUNER, J. S. — *University of Oxford, Department of Experimental Psychology, South Parks Road, Oxford OX1 3PS, England*

DORE, J. — *The Rockefeller University, Psychology Laboratory, New York, N.Y. 10021, U.S.A.*

EDWARDS, D. — *Loughborough University, Department of Social Sciences, Loughborough, Leicestershire LE11 3TU, England*

FIELDING, G. — *University of Bradford, Undergraduate School of Studies in Social Sciences, Bradford, West Yorkshire BD7 1DP, England*

FRASER, C. — *University of Cambridge, Social and Political Sciences Committee, Syndics Building, Mill Lane, Cambridge CB2 1RX, England*

MARKOVA, I. — *University of Stirling, Department of Psychology, Stirling FK9 4LA, Scotland*

MCNEILL, D. — *The University of Chicago, Department of Behavioral Sciences, Committee on Coition and Communication, Beecher Hall, 5848 S. University Avenue, Chicago, Illinois 60637, U.S.A.*

ROMMETVEIT, R. — *University of Oslo, Institute of Psychology, Blindern, Box 1094, Oslo 3, Norway*

SINHA, C. — *University of Bristol, School of Education, 19 Berkeley Square, Bristol 8, England*

SUGARMAN-BELL, S. — *University of California, Department of Psychology, Berkeley, California, 94720, U.S.A.*

WALKERDINE, V. — *North East London Polytechnic, Department of Educational Studies, Longbridge Road, Dagenham, Essex RM8 2AS.*

CONTENTS

CONTENTS

PREFACE

This book has arisen out of a conference on Language and the Social Context, sponsored by the Social Section and Scottish Branch of the British Psychological Society, and held at the University of Stirling, 10–11 January 1975. The purpose of the conference was to support the growing interest in the social psychology of language and to identify the new spheres of research in this field. The essays included in the book are either based on papers presented at the conference or are contributed by invited authors. I am grateful to Iain Macfarlane for his part in organizing the conference and thus making the book possible.

The essay by J. S. Bruner is reproduced, with very slight changes, from his article 'From communication to language—a psychological perspective', published in *Cognition*, 3, 1975, 255–287, by courtesy of Elsevier Sequoia, Lausanne. That by D. McNeill is based on chapter 3 of his forthcoming book *Speech and Thought*, to be published by Laurence Erlbaum Associates. Acknowledgement is also made to the following for permission to reproduce passages from the works named: The Belknap Press of Harvard University Press for quotations from *The Collected Papers of Charles Sanders Peirce*, ed. by C. Hartshorne and P. Weiss; Penguin Books Ltd for quotations from R. F. Cromer, 'The development of language and cognition: the cognition hypothesis', in B. Foss (ed.), *New Perspectives in Child Development*, p. 234, both in the chapter by D. McNeill; University of Miami Press for quotations from E. Benveniste, *Problems in General Linguistics*, in the chapter by J. S. Bruner; Cambridge University Press for quotations from J. Ryan, 'Early language development', in M. Richards (ed.), *The Integration of the Child into a Social World*; and The American Psychological Association Inc. for quotations from K. Nelson, 'Concept, word and sentence: interrelations in acquisition and development', *Psychological Review*, 81, 1974, 267–285, both in the chapter by J. Dore.

The editing of a book of original essays involves a great amount of work and I would like to thank Colin Wright for sharing this task with me.

I.M.

1

INTRODUCTION

Ivana Marková

At the very beginning of the history of modern psychology René Descartes sanctified the 'I'. The stage for this, of course, had already been prepared by the Renaissance. Imitating and renewing the culture of ancient Greece, the intellectual movement of the Renaissance elevated the importance of the individual which, for the second time in the history of Western culture, reached its highest point. Paul Valéry comments on Descartes' individualism:

> Never before him had any philosopher so deliberately displayed himself upon the stage of his own thought, showing himself off, daring to use the first personal pronoun throughout whole pages. And never, as Descartes above all did ... had any philosopher so gone out of his way to convey to us the details of his mental debates and the inward workings, ... that least personal of *Me's* which must be the same in all men, the universal in each of us. (Valéry, 1948, p. 17)

The use of the first personal pronoun, the 'I', in Descartes' philosophy is not just a matter of grammatical expedience: neither is it primarily an attempt to continue and complete the humanistic spirit of the Renaissance tradition; nor is it an exuberant celebration of the achievements of the seventeenth-century mind. Descartes' 'I' is, in the first instance, the result of a painstaking effort to find rock-bottom certainty: the method of critical doubt and the attitude of distrust towards everything we think we know led Descartes to question the evidence of the senses, the sciences of physics and astronomy, and even mathematics. Where does he find this ultimate certainty?

> afterwards I noticed that whilst I thus wished to think all things false, it was absolutely essential that the 'I' who thought this should be somewhat, and remarking that this truth '*I think, therefore I am*' was so certain and so assured that all the most extravagant suppositions brought forward by the sceptics were incapable of shaking it, I came to the conclusion that I could receive it without scruple as the first principle of the Philosophy for which I was seeking. (Descartes, 1637, p. 101)

Knowledge, therefore, begins with awareness of one's own existence, which is founded upon the 'I think', and on this in turn is founded our knowledge of other minds and of the physical world. All the philosophy, including psychology, which descended from Cartesianism, was therefore individualistic and subjectivistic, whether it drifted towards *rationalism* or towards *empiricism*.

On the rationalistic side individualism culminated in Leibniz's *windowless monads*. According to this conception the universe is constituted of totally isolated individuals or monads. Each monad contains within itself the history and future of the world of monads which progressively unfolds with time; they differ only with respect to the perspective from which this history is perceived and the loss of distinctness that develops as the images of other monads recede from view. They retain their absolute individuality, but only by being totally independent of one another, without contact or interaction: their histories remain synchronized by a harmony pre-established by God. They are 'windowless' individuals wandering lonely in the world.

On the side of empiricism individualism started with Locke's assumption, which he shared with Descartes, that direct awareness was only of ideas. Some of these were objective, corresponding to features of the world like number, size, shape, solidity, texture, and motion. Others were only subjective like colours, sounds, and smells, and though caused by the world acting on our senses, did not directly correspond to anything in the world. In this case individualism reached its highest point with Berkeley who, without in any way denying its reality, *identified* the world with the ideas in the mind of the individual perceiver, but preserved its objectivity by insisting that these ideas emanated from God. And for Kant, the synthesizing unity of the *individual consciousness* became the condition of any kind of knowledge.

Cartesian Man, however, was more than just a thinking being, in our sense of the word 'think', for from the security of the Cogito Descartes could go on to say that the I that thinks is also an I that understands, affirms and denies, desires and feels. It was this conception of Man that took the centre of the stage in *the first rationalistic phase* in the history of cognitive psychology and, though somewhat changed, it was still man, basically in this sense, who was at the centre when *the empiricist phase* commenced half a century after Descartes. And individualism has persisted in cognitive psychology right up to the present. The Cartesian conceptions of innate ideas and of individualism have been revived, more than anywhere else, in Chomskyan linguistics, a branch of cognitive psychology (Chomsky, 1968, p. 1). According to Chomsky, the particular grammar of any language reflects a *universal grammar* that is rooted in certain innate human intellectual capacities (Chomsky, 1968, p. 24). Children have *a priori* knowledge of certain grammatical structures and this knowledge is actualized when certain special conditions obtain. How else, rationalists argue, could we explain a child's ability to acquire grammar so quickly in his individual development, to create sentences he has never heard before, and to express such a wide variety of different ideas?

The problem, however, has been to discover whether the linguistic abilities of a child originate in cognition, or whether they are the result of a special linguistic capacity. McNeill (1970) suggests that it is the knowledge of certain basic grammatical categories, such as noun and verb phrases and the grammatical relations between them, which is innate. Schlesinger (1971) on the other hand is more cautious. He suggests that it is the child's *cognitive* capacity that is innate and that there 'is nothing specifically linguistic about this capacity' (Schlesinger, 1971, p. 70). Clark (1973) is concerned with the investigation of *how* the child's innate knowledge of language enters into the acquisition process through learning mechanisms, memory constraints, perceptual abilities, motor abilities, etc. Clark's particular interest is in the way in which the child acquires the expressions for space and time. He sees this as the problem as to how the child, given his perceptual apparatus and biological make-up, learns to apply the expressions for space and time to the prior cognition of the properties of space and time that arises from his interaction with his physical environment.

The existence of a universal grammar implies the existence of language independent of any actual use. Bever says of judgements distinguishing sentences from nonsensical strings of words, that 'It is ... clear that adults can make sophisticated phenomenological judgments about the sentences in their languages ... All of these judgments require that the adult have the concept of the languages as a system independent of any actual use' (Bever, 1970, p. 285).

Innateness and independence have also penetrated semantics. This applies in particular to the semantic theory derived from Chomsky's work and concerned with semantic features (or semantic markers). Bierwisch (1970), for example, elaborates the idea of 'innate basic elements of semantic structure' first produced by Postal. He assumes that semantic components represent categories according to which objects and situations are structured and classified. These categories or principles are not, however, discovered in the external world, but are the means by which human beings process their physical and social environment. And this leads, in his view, to the 'extremely far-reaching, though plausible, hypothesis that all semantic structures might finally be reduced to components representing the basic dispositions of the cognitive and perceptual structure of the human organism' (Bierwisch, 1970, p. 181).

The investigation of the role of language in verbal reasoning which stems from Chomskyan linguistics also assumes that the rules of reasoning can be discovered by inspection of natural language without appeal to actual use. Lakoff (1970) maintains that a great part of reasoning is carried out in natural language. After discussing the various ways in which the rules of grammar and the rules of natural logic coincide, he concluded that 'natural logic taken together with linguistics, is the empirical study of the nature of human language and human reasoning' (p. 254). Natural logic in Lakoff's account is concerned with the logical structure of sentences and with the regularities governing reasoning in natural language, and in this sense Lakoff considers it to be a theory about the human mind. The basic assumption of natural logic is that the logical rules are linguistically adequate and the linguistic rules are logically correct. Symbolic logic and the grammatical analysis of language are not, Lakoff argues, at present able to cope with the complexities of natural language: first, symbolic logic has been over-concerned with techniques neglecting the subject matter itself and generative grammar is preoccupied with global grammatical rules. Second, there is a discrepancy between the developments of different topics. For example, the already well-developed logic of quantifiers can have linguistic significance only in relationship to the yet undeveloped logic of scalar predicates (i.e. words such as 'fascinating', 'interesting', 'uninteresting', suggesting different points on a scale). The consequence of such a discrepancy in development is that we cannot be sure whether or not in fact 'we have an adequate analysis of the logical forms of quantifiers' (p. 255).

In psychology verbal reasoning has been investigated within the tradition of individual cognition. The philosophy of the eighteenth and nineteenth centuries has upgraded the *Cartesian* I THINK to the *logical* I THINK. For Kant logic became the 'science of the necessary laws of thought' (Kant, 1800) and for him the I THINK 'necessarily accompanies all our ideas of objects' (Paton, 1936, vol. I, p. 207). Similarly Boole (1854) in his *The Laws of Thought* undertook 'to investigate the fundamental laws of those operations of the mind by which reasoning is performed'. Psychology of reasoning developed under the safe wing of philosophy and took the Kantian and Boolean positions seriously. Fully in accord with the rationalistic tradition, its main task has become an investigation of deviances from the ideal of pure reasoning as defined by the laws of thought. In Greek philosophy the laws of thought consisted of three principles: the principle of identity (everything is what it is); of contradiction (a thing cannot both be something and not be that something at the same time); and of excluded middle (a thing is either something or is not that something and there is no third possibility). Since Leibniz another principle has sometimes been added, that of sufficient reason (there is nothing which cannot be explained). For the Greek philosophers, and for Aristotle in particular, the laws of thought had *ontological* significance, that is they were descriptive of the nature of existence as such. For Aristotle the principle 'that the same attribute cannot at the same time belong and not belong to the same subject and in the same respect' (Aristotle, *Metaphysica*, Book 3. 1005^b, 18–20) is the ultimate commonsense belief on which 'all men base their proofs' (Aristotle, *Metaphysica*, Book 2, 996^b, 28). Common sense is quite often the basis for Aristotle's theorizing and we may say that the laws of thought in this respect are the laws of man's survival on this earth. They are the conditions of *existence*, indeed the *sine qua non* of *being* itself, and as such they are entirely *a priori* and incapable of empirical investigation. There are no proofs for these principles as they are the principles of human existence itself. If these principles are disobeyed, that is, if a man contradicts himself, for example both believing and disbelieving something at the same time, or trying to do something and avoid doing it at the same time, then a conflict arises and if it proceeds too far and long enough then the man's very existence is threatened and his destruction as a living organism will eventually follow.

While for Aristotle the laws of thought were in the first instance the laws of existence as such and only secondly the laws of correct thinking, for Kant, on the other hand, they are primarily the laws of correct thinking. But they are not only prescriptive, concerned with how we ought to think, but are the laws by which the understanding employs itself, so that they constitute the *sine qua non* of any understanding (Kant, 1787, B76). In so far, therefore, as the rules of thought do not obtain under actual empirical conditions, there can be no true knowledge or understanding. They are therefore completely general, and apply irrespective of the subject matter, though *not apart from any subject matter*: for Kant as for Aristotle, the form of thought can no more be empirically abstracted from its content than the shape of a statue can be empirically separated from the stone out of which it is formed.

The science of the laws of thought for Kant is *pure* general logic. It is entirely *a priori*, which in this sense means non-empirical, and cannot therefore be discovered by any empirical means. It is not only not concerned with the *content* of thought, but also confines itself to the ideal, ignoring all the subjective conditions under which reasoning actually takes place. In it

> we abstract from all empirical conditions under which our understanding is exercised, *i.e.* from the influence of the senses, the play of imagination, the laws of memory, the force of habit, inclination, etc., and so from all sources of prejudice, indeed from all causes from which this or that knowledge may arise or seem to arise. (Kant, 1787, B76)

It is only *applied* general logic which deals with the way we think under the various actual subjective conditions and may, therefore, be subjected to empirical investigation by psychology. 'It treats of attention, its impediments and consequences, of the source of error, of the state of doubt, hesitation, and conviction, etc.' (Kant, 1787, B79). According to Kant the laws of thought cannot be investigated empirically because they are the subject matter of pure logic which is 'a body of demonstrated doctrine, and everything in it must be certain entirely *a priori*' (i.e. independently of any experience) (Kant, 1787, B76). Pure logic 'is the necessary science of the laws of thought' and is true of correct thinking *a priori* and irrespective of the content of the propositions involved.

Psychologists of verbal reasoning, on the other hand, have set out to investigate the laws of thought experimentally, and to escape from the effect of subjective factors by investigating the ability of untutored subjects to perform operations in formal logic. The bases for such investigations have been certain well-formed formulae in the propositional calculus, that is formulae formed according to the syntactic rules of the calculus, that correspond to the laws of thought:

Law of identity: $P \rightarrow P$
Law of contradiction: $-(P \ \& \ -P)$
Law of excluded middle: $P \ v \ -P$

In these formulae 'P' is a *propositional variable*, '$\rightarrow$', '$\&$', and 'v' are *logical connectives*. Propositional variables can stand for any proposition in the same way as 'x' or 'y' in algebra can stand for any number. Propositions are therefore replaced by symbols, which can be subjected to formal operations in accordance with precisely formulated syntactic rules. This programme requires that the laws of thought also be treated in this manner. Although, as we have seen, Kant considered that the laws of thought could not be treated apart from some subject matter or other, in order that reasoning might be investigated in its pure state, uncontaminated by any interfering factor, it has become necessary to remove all content, or at least to make it so insignificant, ambiguous or irrelevant that its effect can be discounted.

> The advantage of a formal calculus is that it brings order to a great variety of inferences, and that it allows the specific content of an inference to be ignored .... The essential logical point about such inferences is that validity depends purely upon the position of the propositions within their framework of logical connectives .... Once the form of the inference has been ascertained there are simple mechanical procedures which will reveal whether it is valid. (Wason and Johnson-Laird, 1972, pp. 40–41)

The consequences of this programme are, however, serious. In so far as these symbols are treated only as marks on paper, they no longer signify anything. We can start with a proposition such as 'it is impossible for a man to have his cake and eat it' and symbolize it as follows: $-(P \\& -P)$. In this case the symbols *symbolize* a proposition and have content. If, on the other hand, we start with a formula, then the supposed symbols in fact symbolize nothing. The laws of thought lose the physical, biological, and social significance they were given by the Greeks. And the result is that while adults or children are completely capable of utilizing the laws of thought as a commonsense guide in their lives, they fail to utilize them in logical and psychological tasks, make errors and, apparently, behave illogically.

Social psychology in general, and *cognitive social psychology* in particular has taken it for granted that the investigation of thought was the preserve of individual cognitive psychology. It has found its own role instead in the investigation of *influence*, for example, of suggestion, persuasion, conformity, the group mind, and so on, rather than of those aspects of thought which transcend the individual, that is of thought as communicated and objectivized in speech, of language as a socially created system which is itself an object of thought. While individual cognitive psychology has been concerned with the investigation of intellectual and rational man epitomized in the Cartesian I THINK, social cognitive psychology has, until very recently, been concerned primarily with those processes by which man has been dragged down to a state of irrationality under the influence of other people, and therefore with the degradation of the I THINK. Investigation of the process of communication has been mostly concerned with the process of *persuasive communication* with the main emphasis on opinion and attitude change within the tradition of the 'Yale Communication Programme'. The exploration of such topics as: source, message, recipients, techniques of persuasion, selective exposure, public opinion change, and resistance to persuasion have led to considerable progress in the understanding of this whole general area. Textbooks of social psychology have, in addition to such topics, usually included a chapter entitled 'Language and Social Communication' and discussed a limited number of topics such as Whorfian linguistic relativity, denotation and connotation, Osgood's semantic differential, and perhaps a few others. But the more essential issues such as, for example, the problems of achieving intersubjectivity in person-to-person communication, differences between 'what is said' and 'what is meant', the analysis of silences, the acquisition of communicative competence, and the ability to take the attitude of the other person have not been the focus of interest.

It was this state of affairs which led Moscovici to complain in a recently published book on *The Psychosociology of Language* (1972) that 'linguists are not interested in the psychosociological aspect of language and psychosociologists are not concerned with the linguistic aspect of social behavior'.

This comment characterized the situation as it was a few years ago. We must not forget, however, that even at a time when only a very few researchers doubted that Chomskyan linguistics could solve all the basic problems in the psychology of language, some important studies signalling a new development were initiated. Thus Rommetveit's book on *Words, Meanings and Messages* (1967) was both a criticism of the various reductionist tendencies in the psychology of language and a creative consideration of problems which the prevailing theories could neither account for nor even recognize because of the limitations of their conceptual systems. Similarly the work of the few sociolinguists, for example Hymes's exploration of communicative competence and of the interaction of various aspects of language and social setting, as well as Labov's concern with sociolinguistic structure and the role of social factors in linguistic evolution, can now be seen as indicating the new developments in research into language and communication.

In consequence of its weaknesses 'the initial optimism that grew out of Chomsky's formulation of a generative–transformational grammar has not been sustained by the torrent of work that it provoked' (Bruner, this volume) and this has finally led to a profound criticism and a search for alternatives, both in psychology and in linguistics.

Such an effort in psychology is perhaps most pronounced in Rommetveit's *On Message Structure* (1974). In contrast to the Yale Communication Programme message structure is not concerned with the exploration of the 'I' as degraded under the influence of other people, but treats the I in the WE THINK and WE SAY of the temporarily shared social world. Such an approach leads to the point of departure for an analysis of communication and intersubjectivity. Message structure is an alternative conceptual framework for the study of language and communication, and the case for it involves a criticism of the Chomskyan notion of the deep structure of a sentence. In the initial Chomskyan account it was assumed that the meaning and structure of a sentence can be analysed *in vacuo*. A sentence, however, is only the medium for an assertion and as Rommetveit has demonstrated can be the medium for various assertions or messages, depending upon the context in which it is uttered and the intention of the people who utter it. Thus, 'the full message potential of a given sentence ... might be conceived of as *the entire set of assertions that can be mediated by that sentence within a certain range of plausible communication settings*' (Rommetveit, 1974, p. 104). The meaning of a sentence *in vacuo* is therefore indeterminate, and Chomsky's revised programme (1972) does not alter this fundamental objection for variations of focus and intonation can only affect the meaning of a *message*.

As Rommetveit shows, the sentence

'The old man is poor'

might, in Chomsky's tradition, be decomposed into the two constituent assertions
'The man is old'   and
'The man is poor'.

Such an analysis, Rommetveit argues, is a gross simplification. It artificially treats 'The old man' as a proposition ('the man is old') with a truth-value when it certainly is not true or false in the same manner as 'The man is poor'. Moreover it attributes actual propositional content where there is only *message potentiality*. What is made known by the word 'poor', for instance, is contingent upon what has been intersubjectivity: the I-You relationship in the here-and-now is the focus of attention. *established social realities* might be, for example, economic poverty with respect to Western standards of living, but they could also be poor artistic talents or, perhaps, poverty in the third world. Message structure, therefore, aims to go beyond *what is said*, that is, the utterance of the speaker, to consider *what is made known*, that is what is understood by the speaker and hearer *when a sentence is uttered in the context of some intersubjectively agreed social reality*.

The key concept which opposes that of the Cartesian individual mind is that of intersubjectivity: the I–You relationship in the here-and-now the focus of attention. But *hermeneutic philosophy of language* (see Habermas, 1968; Apel, 1965) is also concerned with I–You relationships and with the here-and-now in the act of speech. In his analysis, however, Rommetveit points out the crucial difference between the hermeneutic position and the message structure approach. Habermas's and Apel's individuals are individuals in the very sense of this word, they are not a *sharing*, i.e. a communicating You and I. In hermeneutics 'what is made known during a dialogue cannot ... be accounted for in terms of an interaction between two people, each of whom is imprisoned in a *here-and-now* as defined by his own *individual* bodily engagement, interest and intention' (Rommetveit, 1974, p. 43). The notion of sharing is also embodied in *complementarity*. Rommetveit endorses Birdwhistell's contention that 'what is preserved in typed transcripts of face-to-face dialogues is in fact only "the cadaver of speech"' (Rommetveit, 1974, p. 62). What is omitted from the fully-fledged act of communication when language is conceived as only a system of signs is the *complementarity* of the speaker–listener relationship, and the whole framework of intersubjectivity within which the participants contract to communicate with one another. 'We are writing on the premises of the reader, reading on the premises of the writer, speaking on the premises of the listener, and listening on the premises of the speaker' (Rommetveit, 1974, p. 63), and each one of us is constantly oscillating between these complementary roles of the *speaking I and the listening You*. It is the speaker's privilege to select the particular social reality in which any act of communication takes place, and the listener's obligation, under the contract into which he has entered, to decode the message on these premises. It is the speaker's obligation, for his part, to monitor what he says on these same premises.

The full-fledged act of verbal communication is thus under normal conditions based upon a reciprocally endorsed and spontaneously fulfilled contract of complementarity: *encoding* is tacitly assumed to involve *anticipatory decoding*, i.e. it is taken for granted that speech is continuously listener-oriented and monitored in accordance with assumptions concerning a *shared* social world and convergent strategies of categorization. Conversely—and on precisely those premises—*decoding* is tacitly assumed to be speaker-oriented and aiming at *a reconstruction of what the speaker* intends to make known. (Rommetveit, 1974, p. 55)

The social reality within which two people contract to communicate may be selected by certain signs or standard phrases which, because they are institutionalized, are interpreted unconsciously as a matter of habit. Such signs may, in the case of verbal communication, be such things as facial expressions and tone of voice, and the novelist has his own recognized means for conveying the settings of his story. Institution and habit also play an important part with respect to the form of discourse in which a sentence is presented: it may, for example, make a great deal of difference if a sentence appears in a poem instead of in the more conventional medium of a newspaper report (Rommetveit, 1974, p. 104), or in the setting of a laboratory experiment.

Such cases of the endorsement of conventional contracts and of complementarity may be seen, for example, in Orwell's *Nineteen Eighty-Four* (1949). When a child reads such sentences as

WAR IS PEACE
FREEDOM IS SLAVERY
IGNORANCE IS STRENGTH

he is probably puzzled because what he has learned about the meanings of such words as WAR, PEACE, and FREEDOM, conflicts with what is said about them. The child does not have the ability for what Piaget calls decentration; the words are taken literally as defined in a dictionary. The adult reader, on the other hand, will accept the game and will tentatively endorse a contract between himself and the author in the belief that what is not understood immediately will become clear in the course of further reading. The common meanings of WAR, PEACE, and FREEDOM vanish, and we read them as if we already know the new meanings which the author wishes to convey to the reader. Gradually we learn the Orwellian rules of Newspeak and can assess backwards the meaning of WAR IS PEACE.

What is initially unknown to the listener is made known to him in terms of a progressive expansion and modification of an actual or intersubjectively presupposed shared social world. (Rommetveit, 1974, p. 95)

The notions of encoding and complementarity also play an important role in the psychology of problem-solving and reasoning. In individual cognitive psychology, since Duncker's pioneer work (1945), problem-solving behaviour has been viewed as a sequence of steps consisting of the gradual narrowing and final closing of the gap between the initial data and the goal. Attention has been focused on the types of method by which the subject achieves his goal. His activity has been most commonly described in terms of elementary information processes, such as, for example, elementary manipulations with symbols (Feigenbaum and Feldman, 1963).

Elementary information processes constitute either the plan of a human being's action or the program in a computer. In Newell, Shaw, and Simon (1960), General Problem Solver program strategies consist of the sequential solution of sub-goals of the original goal. The solution of the sub-goal at each step is algorithmically dependent on the solution of the sub-goal at the previous step, so that the solution must proceed in a determined sequence of decisions. The sequence of decisions is complete when the gap between the initial data and the goal is closed.

Our Orwellian situation might also be interpreted from the point of view of the gap-filling theory. The encoding of WAR IS PEACE might be considered as the initial data and the author's intention could stand for the final goal. Reading of the novel would gradually contribute to a narrowing of the gap between the original understanding of the sentence and the author's intention. The complementarity approach, however, requires the sequence of sub-goals to be reinterpreted in terms of progressive understanding of the writer's intentions. This process is admirably described by Wellek as a circle of understanding (discussed by Rommetveit, 1974). It proceeds from a partial understanding of some detail in a problem to an anticipatory partial understanding of the whole, and back to a greater understanding of this and other detail.

> In reading with a sense for continuity, for contextual coherence, for wholeness, there comes a moment when we feel that we have 'understood', that we have seized on the right interpretation, the real meaning .... It is a process that has been called 'the circle of understanding'. It proceeds from attention to a detail to an anticipation of the whole and back again to an interpretation of the detail. It is a circle that is not vicious, but a fruitful circle. (Wellek, quoted by Rommetveit, 1974, p. 89)

Just as we communicate on the premises that we understand one another, so the person in a psychological laboratory who is presented with a verbal reasoning problem solves it on the assumptions that he understands the experimenter's expectations. The experimenter, for his part, in the same way as he does outside his laboratory, when talking to his colleagues and his family, should attempt to understand what the subject is thinking, not for the purpose of manipulating his reactions, but in order to determine the premises of the communication. What Rosenthal (1969) describes as an 'expectancy effect', should not be conceived of as an obstacle to experimenting, to be overcome by devising new techniques by which to deceive the subject. On the contrary, we should accept that this so-called 'expectancy effect' is an essential aspect of communication, and that if we don't provide a context of social reality for our experimental tasks, the subject will invent his own. So rather than attempting to eliminate expectancy, an aspect of complementarity, we should make it a positive feature of our investigations and incorporate this entirely natural feature of human behaviour into the experimental design.

In linguistics the disappointment with Chomskyan linguistics has led to the establishment of a new discipline with an old name—*pragmatics*—which has been defined as the study of linguistic acts and contexts relevant to linguistics acts.

Stalnaker (1970, p. 275) points out two basic types of problem which should be solved by pragmatics: 'first, to define interesting types of speech acts and speech products; second, to characterize the features of the speech context which help determine which proposition is expressed by a given sentence'. Attention to context is prominent in pragmatics, for example in the analysis of that notion of the 'presupposition'. Thus Keenan suggests (1971, p. 49) that the notion of a presupposition should be defined on the basis of 'the relation between the utterance of a sentence and the context in which it is uttered'. By the utterance of a sentence Keenan means an actual act of speaking performed at a certain point in time and space. By its context he means the actual individuals involved in the speech act, as well as its physical and cultural or social setting. Similarly Stalnaker (1970, p. 279) claims that 'any participant in a linguistic context (a person, a group, an institution, perhaps a machine) may be the subject of a presupposition. Any proposition may be the object, or content of one'.

The notion of 'context' has thus become central in most of the work in the investigation of language. But context may mean different things to different investigators. In pragmatics, it is the stage set for an act of communication. In Rommetveit's conception of message structure, on the other hand, context enters the act of communication only if it is cognized as such by the participants of the act. Physical context may serve to induce certain presuppositions, but unless a shared *here-and-now* is established by the common presuppositions of speaker and hearer, no external context as such is relevant. This means that the physical context, and much of our shared knowledge, beliefs, and attitudes may be utterly irrelevant for a particular act of communication. They become significant if and only if they influence what is made known by being tacitly taken for granted or by directly invading the awareness of the participants, thus providing part of the context of a dialogue. And what is made known is dependent on common pre-established social realities or social fictions and without it communication is impossible. This becomes obvious when, under certain circumstances, we suddenly become aware of presuppositions we do not share. A number of children's trick questions are based on the deliberate breaking of our shared social world. For example, the likely answer to the question

Why do birds fly to a warm country in winter?

is that they do so in order to escape the coldness of the British winter. The child's 'No' to such an explanation and his own joking reply

Because they cannot walk there

makes us only too aware that our answer was embedded in a certain tacit presupposition.

The notion of context and its various roles in the developing field of the social psychology of language is the main unifying feature of the essays included in this book. In addition, the essays have certain conceptual themes in common:

(1) Language is a means of communication rather than a system of signs which can be analysed in its own right.

(2) Psychology of language has taken a new role: while in the Chomskyan tradition psychologists were seeking the psychological correlates of linguistically defined

structures, now the question is how linguistic structures develop from psychological processes or how the two interact. Moreover, although the term 'pragmatics' is used both by linguists and psychologists, the content of this concept is different. For Bruner and others who use this notion in accord with him, pragmatics is concerned with the activity of the participants, while for linguists it is concerned with description of the stage set for communication.

(3) Adult concepts and adult language are not the standards according to which child's reasoning and language are to be assessed. Previous psychological investigation was inclined to attribute adult meanings to the child's words. It therefore followed that a child either knew the meaning of a word or he did not, and either had a concept or did not: when a child, for example, failed to accomplish the conservation of volume task it was usually assumed that he/she has 'the' concept of water but does not have 'the' concept of volume. Analysing the Piagetian theory of conceptual development Hamlyn (1971) argues against this all-or-none approach to the acquisition of concepts: 'such knowledge is not and cannot be an all-or-none affair, and ... it is not formed out of fixed and constant units of understanding, so that we can without qualification speak of identical or similar structures, as Piaget does' (Hamlyn, 1971, p. 10). Hamlyn points out that we have no right to assume that a child operates with the *same* concept of water as an adult; rather we should think of a child who fails the conservation test as having a conceptual system in which both of the concepts of water and volume are different from those to which adults are accustomed.

The attribution of adult meanings to children may be one of the reasons why child logic is considered to be defective when compared with adult logic. Rommetveit (this volume) has coined the expression 'negative rationalism' for this approach to the cognitive processes of a child. As the title of the book *The Growth of Logical Thinking from Childhood to Adolescence* (Inhelder and Piaget, 1958) indicates, Piaget's conception of cognitive growth is defined as growth from non-logicality to logicality. But is it right to characterize the child's way of thinking as a-logical because he seems to be unable to solve the problems which we have created for him? The child may see the world *in his own way* and not just in a defective version of the adult's way. As Hamlyn (1971, pp. 10–11) remarks,

It is only our final conception of how the world is, the one which constitutes the norm of how the world really is, the one that is agreed, that makes the child's thinking appear just a stage in the development to that goal. It may, however, be both less and more than this. It may be less in that it does not constitute a state in a process towards that goal; it may be more in that given the child's needs and interests it serves his immediate purposes admirably, and is in that respect not defective at all.

The essays included in this book either explicitly state or they imply that the use by a child of an adult word to label an object or action does not necessarily mean that the word has the same meaning for the child.

In addition to these conceptual themes which are common to most of these essays, we can distinguish three themes of content. The first of these is concerned with precursors of language, which are manifested in the child's social and cognitive development, and in his ability to make references and to express intentions. The problem is to discover how the transition from pre-speech communication to language occurs, and which skills in his pre-verbal behaviour are necessary for the appearance of language. This theme is represented in the chapters by Bruner, Sugarman-Bell, Dore, and Edwards. Bruner's chapter, which is a follow-up of his previous work (1975), sets the tone of this section. It demonstrates 'that one can establish continuities between pre-speech communication and language, and do so without recourse to inappropriate reductionism' (p. 17). Understanding of such a transition is based on 'taking into account the uses of communication as speech acts' (p. 44). Bruner investigates four precursors of language: the expression of intentions in an infant's communication with his mother and the mother's interpretations of such expressions; aspects of early reference; examination of the means the infant uses to communicate his wishes and needs in order to achieve *joint action*, i.e. demand, request, exchange, and reciprocal modes of interaction when participating in a *common task*; and prerequisities for predication, i.e. topic-comment in the pre-verbal child. Sugarman-Bell's chapter explores general communicative and intentional marking in the pre-verbal child. It is shown that the child's transactions with objects and persons are at first mutually exclusive and repetitive, then they differentiate and lastly they are integrated into a person–object schemata. Edwards is concerned with the analysis of three sources of early meanings: these are the child's comprehension of the *structure* of the physical world of objects and the social world of people, the child's relationships with other people, and finally reference. Dore's paper is an attempt to assess the contribution of conceptual and communicative skills *and* grammatical knowledge to the acquisition of language. Language development is viewed as 'the integration of these distinct inputs within some pragmatic-grammatical unit of language behaviour', (p. 88). Such a unit, enabling us to study *'the whole language of the whole child'*, is the speech act (p. 107–109).

A language and reasoning theme is central to the chapters by Rommetveit, Walkerdine and Sinha, McNeill, and partly in that by Marková. While Rommetveit's *On Message Structure* is a *programme* for future research, his contribution to this book is message structure in *practice*. From a discussion of 'negative rationalism' in the work of Piaget we are led into a consideration of the WHY of communication. 'Piaget's "why" is ... often apparently a request for explanation of some physical event or state of affairs'—but *is it* for a child? The chapter includes a theoretical and empirical exploration of semantic competence and identifying reference in Piaget-type problems. Walkerdine and Sinha's paper is concerned with the neglect of context in Piagetian experiments. They present some empirical evidence showing that the child's interpretation of a task is dependent on the context of the task, so that this factor must not be overlooked in any investigation of child language and reasoning. David McNeill presents here his new conception of the relationships between language and thought discussed in the terminology of the American pragmatist, C. S. Peirce. The relationships of thought and speech are discussed in terms of the process of 'semiotic extension' consisting of the extension of 'the sensori-motor concepts introduced through interiorization of the first process to more abstract conceptualizations'. Two aspects of semiotic extension, ontogenetic and functional, are compared and analysed. Heider's attribution theory and Rommetveit's notion of semantic potentialities form the conceptual framework of Marková's chapter which is concerned with the effect of dispositionality and episodicity in verbal reasoning tasks. This chapter thus forms the transition to the third content theme in this book, i.e. to problems of interpersonal relationships and language. Fielding and Fraser's contribution explores both theoretically and empirically the dependence between social relations of participants (defined in terms of liking, superiority and familiarity) in conversation and the speech they use. The main finding is the nominal–verbal distinction in speech style which is a function both of the structure of the task and of the interpersonal relationships between the participants.

In conclusion, the approaches of individual and social cognitive psychology represent different approaches to reality and knowledge. The acceptance of one approach commits one to asking certain kinds of question, even questions which have no meaning with respect to the other approach. They are not, however, mutually exclusive. More likely, they each represent only a partial conception of man, in somewhat the same way that the particle and wave models are only partial conceptions of the electron. The truth is probably represented by some synthesis of the two positions. Meanwhile discussion and argumentation between the two sides can be very productive.

References

Apel, K. D. (1965), Die Entfaltung der 'sprachanalytischen' Philosophie und das Problem der 'Geisteswissenschaft', *Philos. Jahrbuch*, 72, 239–289.

Aristotle (1928), *Metaphysica*, trs. Ross, W. D., Oxford: Oxford University Press.

Bever, T. (1970), The cognitive basis for linguistic structures. In Hayes, J. R. (ed.), *Cognition and the Development of Language*, New York and London: Wiley.

Bierwisch, M. (1970), Semantics. In Lyons, J. (ed.), *New Horizons in Linguistics*, Harmondsworth: Penguin Books.

Boole, G. (1854), *An Investigation of the Laws of Thought*, republished New York: Dover Publications, 1961.

Bruner, J. (1975), The ontogenesis of speech acts, *Journal of Child Language*, 2, 1–19.

Bruner, J. (this volume), From communication to language: a psychological perspective.

Chomsky, N. (1968), *Language and Mind*, New York: Harcourt, Brace & World.

Chomsky, N. (1972), *Studies on Semantics in Generative Grammar*, The Hague: Mouton.

Clark, E. V. (1973), What's in a word? On the child's acquisition of semantics in his first language. In Moore, T. E. (ed.), *Cognitive Development and the Acquisition of Language*, New York and London: Academic Press.

Descartes, R. (1637), *Discourse on the Method of Rightly Conduction the Reason and Seeking for Truth in the Sciences*. In Haldane, E. S., and Ross, G. R. T. (eds), *The Philosophical Works of Descartes*, vol. I, Cambridge: Cambridge University Press.

Duncker, K. (1945), On problem solving, *Psychological Monographs*, 58.

Feigenbaum, E. A., and Feldman, J. (1963), *Computers and Thought*, New York: McGraw-Hill.

Habermas, J. (1968), *Erkenntnis und Interesse*, Frankfurt a.M.: Suhrkamp.

Hamlyn, D. W. (1971), Epistemology and conceptual development. In Mischel, T. (ed.), *Cognitive Psychology and Epistemology*, New York: Academic Press.

Inhelder, B. and Piaget, J. (1958), *The Growth of Logical Thinking from Childhood to Adolescence*, London: Routledge & Kegan Paul.

Kant, I. (1787), *Critique of Pure Reason*, trs. Smith, N. Kemp, London: Macmillan; New York: St Martins Press; 1929 and 1933.

Kant, I. (1800), *Logik*, English edition 1885, trs. Abbott, T. K., *Introduction to Logic*, London: Longmans, Green.

Keenan, E. L. (1971), Two kinds of presupposition in natural language. In Fillmore, C. J., and Langendoen, D. T. (eds), *Studies in Linguistic Semantics*, New York and London: Holt, Rinehart & Winston.

Lakoff, G. (1970), Linguistics and natural logic, *Synthèse*, 22, 151–271.

McNeill, D. (1970), *The Acquisition of Language: the Study of Developmental Psycholinguistics*, New York and London: Harper & Row.

Moscovici, S. (1972), *The Psychosociology of Language*, Chicago: Markham Publishing Company.

Newell, A., Shaw, J. C., and Simon, H. A. (1960), Report on a general problem-solving program for a computer. In *Information Processing: Proceedings of the International Conference on Information Processing*, Paris: Unesco, 256–264.

Orwell, G. (1949), *Nineteen Eighty-Four*, New York: Harcourt Brace.

Paton, H. J. (1936), *Kant's Metaphysics of Experience*, London: Allen & Unwin.

Rommetveit, R. (1967), *Words, Meanings and Messages*, New York & London: Academic Press.

Rommetveit, R. (1974), *On Message Structure*, London and New York: Wiley.

Rosenthal, R. (1969), Interpersonal expectations: effects of the experimenter's hypothesis. In Rosenthal, R., and Rosnow, R. L., *Artifact in Behavioral Research*, New York and London: Academic Press.

Schlesinger, I. M. (1971), On linguistic competence. In Bar-Hillel, Y., *Pragmatics of Natural Languages*, Dordrecht-Holland: D. Reidel Publishing Company.

Stalnaker, R. C. (1970), Pragmatics, *Synthèse*, 22, 272–289.

Valéry, P. (1948), Descartes. In Valéry, Paul, *The Living Thoughts of Descartes*, London and Toronto: Cassell.

Wason, P., and Johnson-Laird, P. N. (1972), *Psychology of Reasoning: Structure and Content*, London: Batsford.

2

FROM COMMUNICATION TO LANGUAGE: A PSYCHOLOGICAL PERSPECTIVE

Jerome S. Bruner

Whatever view one takes of research on language acquisition proper—however nativist or empiricist one's bias—one must still come to terms with the role or significance of the child's pre-speech communication system. What is the nature of that system and does its very nature aid the passage from pre-speech communication to language? What makes for linguistic difficulty in answering such questions is that since the child's communication before language is not amenable to conventional grammatical analysis, efforts to trace continuities often seem little more than a hunt for analogies of 'grammar' in early action or gesture. On the psychological side, the difficulty inheres in the tradition of such research—usually to explain away language as 'nothing but' the concatenation of simple conditioning, imitation, or other mysterious simplifications. I shall try in the following pages to show that one can establish continuities between pre-speech communication and language, and do so without recourse to inappropriate reductionism.

The resurgent nativism that followed upon the work of Chomsky (1965) nurtured quite falsely the hope that this first step could be by-passed—although there is nothing in Chomsky's own writing that would lead necessarily to such a conclusion. The reasoning seems to have been that, if language grows from its own roots, it suffices to study the beginnings of language proper if one wishes to understand the nature of its early acquisiton. The programme, in effect, was the linguists' programme: gather a corpus of speech, with due regard for context (unspecified), and subject it to grammatical analysis. Or, to add an experimental dimension, contrive experimental situations to tap the child's capacities for producing and comprehending speech in particular contexts, and draw inferences from the child's responses concerning his underlying linguistic competence.

There can be little doubt that this programme has deeply enriched our understanding of early language and of the course of its early development. The work of Brown (1970, 1973) and his group, of Bloom (1970), of McNeill (1970a, 1970b) of Slobin (1973), of the Edinburgh group (for example Donaldson and Wales, 1970) all attest to the enormous progress of the last decade.

But the early language for which a grammar is written is the end result of psychological processes leading to its acquistion, and to write a grammar of that language at any point in its development is in no sense to explicate the nature of its acquistion. Even if it were literally true (as claimed by Chomsky) that the child, mastering a particular language, initially possesses a tacit knowledge of an alleged universal deep structure of language, we would still have to know how he managed to recognize these universal deep rules as they manifest themselves in the surface structure of a particular language. Even an innate 'language acquisition device' would require a programme to guide such recognition and it would fall to the psychologist to discover the nature of the programme by investigating the alleged recognition process (Chomsky, 1965, p. 27). For Chomsky, the child's problem is 'to determine which of the (humanly) possible languages is that of the community in which he is placed'. If there were no such recognition problems, the child would obviously learn language immediately and perfectly—at least those portions of it to which he was exposed. This is so far from what happens that we generally agree that it is eminently worth studying what might be called the prerequisites necessary for learning a language or for progressing in the mastery of that language. At the most general level, we may say that to master a language a child must acquire a complex set of broadly transferable or generative skills—perceptual, motor, conceptual, social, *and* linguistic—which when appropriately co-ordinated yield linguistic performances that can be described (though only in a limited sense) by the linguists' rules of grammar. Such rules of grammar may bear no closer resemblance to the psychological laws of language production, comprehension, and use than do the principles of optics bear to the laws of visual perception—in neither case can the one violate the other.

If we are to concentrate upon the prerequisite sensory, motor, conceptual, and social skills whose co-ordination makes language possible, we must alas abandon in large part the powerful grammar-writing procedures of the developmental linguist. For it no longer suffices to collect a corpus of spoken language for which successive grammars may be written, though these grammars may yield valuable hypotheses about the antecedent psychological processes that brought them into being. Instead one must devise ways of investigating the constituent skills involved in language. And typically one begins well *before* language begins, following the communicative behaviour of particular children until a particular level of linguistic mastery is achieved, testing as well for other, concomitant indices of growth. Not surprisingly, then, there are few such studies available, most still in progress: Trevarthen (1974a, 1974b), Sugarman (1974), Bates, Camaioni and Volterra (1973), Lock (1972), McNeill (1974), Dore (1974, 1975), Urwin (1973), and Bruner (1975), though more are starting up.

What is peculiarly difficult in conducting such studies is that their design depends upon more or less explicit decisions concerning what beside language should be studied, decisions derived from hypotheses about the precursors and prerequisites of early language. Typically, in such work, an investigator starts by selecting a 'target' process in later speech and explores its precursors in pre-linguistic communication, concentrating upon forms of communication later realized by linguistic means but earlier fulfilled (partially or fully) by gestural or other expression. Studies of this kind explore the continuity between functionally equivalent forms of communication before and after the onset of speech proper. The investigator, for example, may study the pre-linguistic devices a child uses for making a *request* or for establishing a *joint referent* before these can be handled through such grammatically appropriate means as interrogatives or demonstratives. Inevitably, such an approach shifts emphasis to functions of language use, to pragmatics and communicative competence (Campbell and Wales, 1970) and away from syntactic competence in the sense employed by Chomsky (1965) and McNeill (1970a, 1970b).

If one pursues this course, one is tempted to look for the 'grammar' inherent in certain forms of social interaction, the emergence of 'proper' grammar then being conceived of as the child gaining insight about how to *express in language* an idea previously held but expressed by other than linguistic means. Both Sugarman (1974) and Bates *et al.* (1973), for example, use non-linguistic behavioural indicators to infer the presence in pre-speech behaviour of such concepts as *Agent* and *Instrument* (when the child signals an adult to help him do something that he wishes to accomplish). They see these prelinguistic accomplishments as precursors of case-grammatical categories like *Agentive* and *Instrumental* in Fillmore's (1968) sense of case grammar (of which more will be said later).

But this procedure inevitably brings the investigator to the psychological question: what makes it possible for the child to progress, say, from a pre-linguistic form of expressing the demonstrative or agentive to a more advanced linguistic form of expression? It is at this point that the second side of this type of research emerges: the search for the constituent skills relevant to linguistic mastery. The commonest practice is to turn to Piaget (for example Sinclair-de-Zwart, 1969). According to his well-known view, language is facilitated by the development of sensorimotor schemas, that represent the joint outcomes of perception and action. These undergo orderly changes that are nourished (though not shaped) by continued experience in acting on the world. In time, for example, the child comes to separate thought from action in his schemas, and his concepts of objects and events in the world become independent of the actions to be performed on them. Sensorimotor schemas also come with experience to transcend space and time, so that the concept of an object is no longer tied to particular contexts, but becomes somewhat more context-free. The acquisition of language is seen as somehow emerging from these developments. Thus a concept of objects that is independent of action on the object should aid the child in mastering such linguistic distinctions as Action and Object in case grammar, or even Noun Phrase and Verb Phrase in the more usual generative grammar. Bates *et al.* (1973), for example, attribute pre-linguistic progress in signalling imperatives and declaratives to the child's maturing Piagetian sensorimotor schemas, though their basis for doing so is partly by appeal to coincidence between the times of appearance of different forms of signalling and the dates usually cited in Piagetian norms and partly to their presence in the sample studied.

Sugarman does somewhat better in this regard. She notes Piaget's observation (1952) that the child, in organizing a sensorimotor schema, will first go through a phase of dealing separately with particular objects before he is able to subordinate the use of one object to the other, as in using one as a tool for getting the other. She likens this to the process of early skill development which progresses by the combining of skilled routines that have first developed separately (Bruner, 1973). With this as background, she postulates that the child will first go through a stage in which he treats persons and objects independently, developing schemas for each, will then elaborate these, until finally he will combine them into a unified schema: person-as-agent-to-help-obtain-object. As this schema develops, the child will acquire signalling techniques appropriate to his level of growth. And, indeed, her data indicate that the child first addresses himself separately to objects or to the mother, and finally learns to signal the mother to get her help in obtaining an object, with an intermediate stage in which there is elaboration of signalling toward mother and object separately.

My principal concern with the Piagetian approach of these authors and of Sinclair-de-Zwart (1969) is that it concentrates almost exclusively on the formal aspects of language at the expense of the functional, the emerging structure of the child's language without due regard for the uses to which language is put in different contexts. It will be clearer in the following pages why I think this is a serious and distorting difficulty. But in general, one can only applaud the aim of such efforts, for they do indeed represent the kind of 'middle way' between extreme nativism that sees no problem because it is all there in advance, and extreme empiricist reductionism that sees no problem because it dismisses what is in fact already there by way of readiness to use language in a particularly structured way.

Whoever studies pre-linguistic precursors of language must, I believe, commit himself to what Cromer (1974) has recently called the 'cognition hypothesis'. The cognition hypothesis has two parts to it. The first holds that 'we are able to understand and productively to use particular linguistic structures only when our cognitive abilities enable us to do so' (Cromer, 1974, p. 246). The second holds that when our cognitive abilities allow us to grasp a particular idea, we may still not have grasped the complex rule for expressing it freely but may none the less express it in a less complex, if indirect form. He provides as an example the perfect tense and the conceptual idea of completed action: a child who has not yet grasped the perfective device embodied in such sentences as

Have you peeked?

can none the less express the same meaning by using the simpler rule of combining a known form with the word *yet*, yielding utterances like,

Did you peek yet?

Presumably, this capacity to express a cognitive insight by means short of the fully realized linguistic rule can be pushed down in age to the point where one asks whether the child is able to use pre-linguistic devices for expressing a cognitive insight even before sentential grammar is present in his language.

Both parts of the cognition hypothesis presuppose the doctrine of functional substitutability or at least of continuity. Neither is a doctrine to be facilely accepted. In semantics, substitutability is represented by Bloomfield's (1933) 'fundamental postulate' that in any given speech community one can find formal and semantic equivalents of certain sentences that serve as 'glosses' of each other. The transformational grammarian usually handles these matters by invoking 'a common "underlying" structure for semantically equivalent "surface" syntactic arrangements' (Silverstein, 1975). But while in Cromer's example of the more and less compact versions of the grammatical perfective, one can arguably make the case for a gloss, it becomes progressively more difficult to do so as communicative devices become more separated in ontogenetic time. What is the relationship, for example, between a gestural sign of pointing to an apple and the uttering of the word *apple*? They are plainly not glosses of each other in any formal sense. Yet, one is prepared, if only intuitively, to grant that they may be continuous with each other. We say that the two serve the same function of indicating, or at least *some* aspect of this function. If we make a further separation in time and compare a gestural indication with a simple sentence, *That apple* (whether or not we assume that the existential copula is absent because of a deletion rule), then the gap becomes so great as to seem discontinuous. For example, the predicational form of the more advanced utterance makes it amenable to truth testing, the word *that* already presupposes deictic marking, etc.—none of which are remotely attributable to ostensive pointing. Yet, again we assume there is *some* continuity. In what does it consist?

I would suggest that continuity can be attributed for two reasons: the first is by a principle of incorporation, that in achieving competence to utter a simple sentential indicative the child necessarily incorporates prior knowledge implied in his mastery of the ostensive indicative. But this is surely a weak form of continuity by incorporation, no stronger than the indubitable claim that an infant must stand before he can take his first step. It is strengthened by two additional considerations, one treated below in examining some bases for attributing continuity, the second being the following. If we can show that the child's prior grasp of ostensive indicating by pointing provides knowledge that permits him to 'crack the code', say, of lexical indicating, that it is in fact a stepping stone in a line of prerequisites leading to the use of a simple sentential form of indicating, then incorporation ceases to be merely logical and becomes psychological. The stronger form would be, then, that lexical indicating occurs if and only if the child has previously grasped a more primitive device of indicating and can be shown to use that device instrumentally in the acquisition of the more advanced form. In a word, for a precursor utterance to become psychologically and linguistically interesting, it must be shown to be an instrumental prerequisite to a more evolved utterance.

A second basis for attributing continuity is provided in a more comprehensive view of the nature of language use within any given culture, a subject too readily overlooked in our headlong pursuit of structural regularities in grammar. Stated at its most banal, it is that speech is meaningful social behaviour. But at the same time, it is crucial to bear in mind that articulate phonetic speech is only one of the devices by which meaning is transmitted in such social behaviour. Whatever the device employed, 'this functional sign mode always involves some aspect of the context in which the sign occurs' (Silverstein, 1975). This pragmatic aspect of sign use is dependent upon a mastery of cultural conventions and it is the linkage of signs to conventions that assures the 'meaningful' use of any signalling system, language included. It is not surprising that Cohen (1974) has recently lamented that, in applying speech-act theory, it is very difficult to decide where linguistics ends and where the study of 'manners' begins. For, as we shall try to show, many of the conventions that underlie the use of language are learned prior to the onset of articulate phonetic speech. Silverstein (1975), proposing to extend the tradition of pragmatics in the line from Peirce to Jakobson and beyond, puts the matter as follows:

> To say of social behavior that it is meaningful implies necessarily that it is communicative, that is, that the behavior is a complex of signs (sign vehicles) that signal or stand for something in some respect. Such behavioral signs are significant to someone, participants in a communicative event, and such behavior is purposive, that is goal-oriented in the sense of accomplishing (or failing to accomplish) certain ends of communication .... In general, then, we can say that people are constituted as a society with a certain *culture* to the extent that they share the same means of social communication.

He then goes on to point to various of the properties of communicative events— notably the nature of the relationships that prevail between communicator and recipient. These relationships, interchangeability of roles being one of the most obvious, are highly structured by some subtle mix of human endowment and cultural convention. Silverstein is not concerned directly with the ontogenesis of these role relations, but they lie at the base of the concern of much of what follows in this paper. These are the functioning communicative acts that give shape to the infant's discourse with adults in his immediate environment: referencer and recipient, demander and complier, seeker and finder, task-initiator and accomplice, actor and prohibitor, etc. A close analysis of the first year of an infant's life provides not only a catalogue of the joint 'formats' (see below) in which communicator and recipient habitually find each other, but also provides a vivid record of how roles developed in such formats become conventionalized. The infant is not only learning, as we shall see, what constitutes indicating something to another, or having something indicated to him, but he is also learning how to substitute new means for doing so in order to achieve less uncertain outcomes by the use of more ritualized techniques. When, finally, he reaches a stage at which lexical indicating is psychologically within his reach, he already knows a great deal about the nature of indicative contexts and conventions for dealing with them.

It is in this second sense that continuity becomes of special importance. For if the child, say, already knows (as we shall see) many of the conventions for give-and-take exchanges and how to conduct them by appropriate non-linguistic signalling, he is equipped better to interpret or 'crack the code' of linguistic utterances used as regulators of such exchanges. We too readily overlook the fact, perhaps in celebration of the undoubted generativeness of language, that speech makes its ontogenetic progress in highly familiar contexts that have already been well conventionalized by the infant and his mother (or other caretaker). In this sense, it is not extravagant to say that initial language at least has a pragmatic base structure.

Let one matter, finally, be made abundantly clear. The point of view that has been set forth in this introductory section is in no sense to be interpreted as a rejection of the role of innate predispositions in the acquisition of language. In the opening paragraphs of this section I commented in passing that there is nothing in Chomsky's writings that would in any sense deny the role of pre-linguistic precursors or prerequisites in aiding the acquisition of language. Indeed, it would be absurd to imagine that the Chomskyan Language Acquisition Device could operate without considerable pre-tuning achieved during the period that precedes the use of articulate phonetic grammatical speech. Chomsky comments (1965, p. 58), 'The real problem is that of developing an hypothesis about initial structure that is sufficiently rich to account for acquisition of language ....' Surely, part of that richness is the representation built up of communicative requirements established over the long period of interaction between infant and caretaker. I have argued in this section, and will develop the argument further in what follows, that these representations help the child crack the linguistic code. As I have stated elsewhere (Bruner, 1972), there is a long evolutionary history that has shaped human immaturity and many of the elaborated forms of mother–infant interdependence are sufficiently invariant in our species to make inescapable the conclusion that they are in some crucial measure based on innate predispositions, however much these predispositions require priming by experience. What other forms of innateness must be present for the child to acquire language proper—its grammar and phonology particularly—I cannot debate, though it is worthwhile pointing out that until we discern more clearly the contribution of pre-linguistic concepts it is premature to conclude that *innate or even acquired ideas about grammar* are all that operate. Grammar may itself be a product of the evolution of joint action in the species and one does well, therefore, to examine how the human ontogenesis of joint action contributes to the mastery of that grammar.

This chapter is an attempt to throw some light on some of the persistent problems that are encountered in the study of the transition from pre-speech communication to early language. There are, as this introduction hopefully makes plain, many such problems. I have chosen four of them as illustrative. In a concluding section I shall try to formulate a general conclusion about the role of the three branches of semiotics in such work: syntax, semantics, and pragmatics (Morris, 1938). The four topics are: (1) the inference of communicative intent, (2) the nature of early reference, (3) the use of language in the regulation of joint action, and (4) the precursors of predication.

1. Communicative Intentions

Communication, as Silverstein (1975) has already noted, presupposes intent or purpose in communicating in the sense that a communication succeeds or fails in its objective. Grammarians usually take intent for granted but one does so at one's peril. To underline the intentionality of language, linguistic philosphers like Austin (1962), Grice (1968), and Searle (1969) have been particularly insistent on drawing the distinction between the performative or illocutionary functions of utterances, judged both by their conventional felicity and their efficacy in achieving desired results, and the locutionary function, to be judged against such criteria as well-formedness or truth-value.

But intent in communication is difficult to deal with for a variety of reasons, not the least demanding of which is the morass into which it leads when one tries to establish whether something was *really*, or *consciously* intended. Does a pre-linguistic infant *consciously* intend to signal his displeasure or express his delight? To obviate such difficulties, it has become customary to speak of the *functions* that communication or language serve and to determine *how* they do so. This has the virtue, at least, of postponing ultimate questions about 'reality' and 'consciousness' in the hope that they may become more manageable.

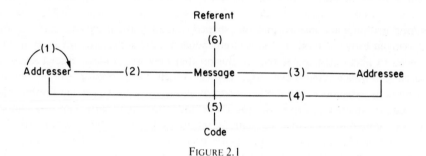

FIGURE 2.1

Jakobson (1960) proposes an analysis of language functions based upon the familiar 'information' diagram, functions being noted by numbers. Function 1 is *expressive* and is made up usually of accompaniments to the addresser's feelings. In a primitive sense, its 'success' or 'failure' depends upon innate or early learned recognition routines. In time, the form and the recognition of expressions of state become increasingly conventionalized. Function 2 is *poetic* and involves modes of structuring messages to achieve the illuminative or exhibitive effects of an art form. Again, it comes increasingly to use the conventions and devices of a language community (Gombrich, 1975). Function 3 is *conative* and is concerned with forming messages in such a way as to produce desired behaviour in the addressee. It encompasses the philosophers' illocutionary force. Function 4 is *phatic* and relates to the maintenance of a channel of communication between addresser and addressee. Its conduct, too, may be governed by standard procedures as represented by permissible pause lengths, etc. Function 5 is *metalinguistic* and it serves to explicate, usually by reference to a code, for example,

Why do you call it *meta*linguistic?

Oh, because it is talk about talk itself.

Function 6 is *referential* and its use is to make clear the referent of a message by clearing up the context for interpreting an utterance. In the stringent terms of the philosophers of language, we may say that 'If a speaker refers to an object, then he identifies or is able on demand to identify that object for the hearer apart from all other objects' (Searle, 1969, p. 79). But it is usually much sloppier than that in practice, viz.

What did you mean, in front of the house?

It's right in front of the house, by the wall.

Any linguistic community has, as noted, conventions for dealing with the functions of language. So do sub-communities. Scientists in communication follow conventions of appearing to 'avoid' conative, poetic, and expressive functions by the use of meticulous declaratives, passive voice, and words of compact rather than diffuse associative value, etc. The sociologist Garfinkel (1963) notes that in virtually all communities excessive request for metalinguistic clarification in ordinary discourse is often taken as a sign of hostility or disbelief in one's interlocutor. To be felicitous requires learning a great many such conventions and rituals.

To characterize these conventions Grice (1975) invokes conversational postulates that govern discourse, from which rather loose-fitting maxims are derived—maxims of relevance, of quantity, of quality. Speakers in conversation are expected to stick to the point, to give not too little and not too much information about context, to speak the truth as they see it. When they depart from these maxims, it is expected that they will do so in a patterned way, with specific intent—irony, humour, or some effort at manipulation. The pre-linguistic child is probably not much under the sway of such maxims. The postulates governing their communication cannot be taken for granted. But we as their tutors in communication very soon learn their speech proclivities and very early try to shape them to those of the adult community. Unfortunately, there are no studies that have investigated the ways in which this is done, although work on social class differences seems to be making a start (Bernstein, 1960; Hess and Shipman, 1965; Schoggen and Schoggen, 1971; Howe, 1975).

Generally (and often unconsciously) adults impute communicative intent to the utterances of infants and children—intent with respect to all the Jakobsonian functions. Indeed, Macfarlane (1975), in studies of birth 'greeting behaviour', finds mothers irresistibly imputing intent to the cries, gestures, expressions, and postures of newborns. And there is often a strikingly moralistic approach to the imputations. Infants are seen to be showing off, to be asking more than their share, to be 'buttering up' mother, to be 'going on too much about it'. Let us postpone for a bit the question whether these inferences about intent are 'correct' or even 'consistent'.

Joanna Ryan (1974) puts the issue of a child's communicative intent and its interpretation by an adult in a useful light. She notes 'that much of what a child utters in the early stages is difficult to understand, if not unintelligible', though the 'child's speech and other vocalizations take place within a context of interaction with adults who are motivated to understand the child's utterances' (p. 199). She continues: 'Many young children experience extensive verbal interchanges with their mothers. During these the mother actively picks up, interprets, comments upon, extends, repeats, and sometimes misinterprets what the child has said', a point which our own observations would certainly confirm as characteristic of even the 3-month-old and his mother. Ryan properly complains that the grammarian's emphasis on well-formedness and semantic sense obscures the role of these interpreted exchanges in preparing the child for language use. Not only do mothers interpret the child's gestures and vocalizations in conative terms—what he wants—but also in terms of Grice-like maxims like 'sincerity' ('He's really faking when he makes that sound') and 'consistency' ('Won't you please make up your mind what you want'). Our own observations during the first year of life point to the importance of the creation of what Garvey (1974) has called 'formats', habitual exchanges that provide a basis for interpreting concretely the intent of the communications of the child and of the mother. We shall have more to say in a later section about the nature of such formats and their transformations. It suffices to note here that they serve not only to concretize but to socialize and give pattern to the child's communicative intentions as well as providing the adult with a basis for interpreting them.

There is, of course, a great deal of variation in the attitudes of mothers toward their children's communicative intent, variation that produces considerable disparity in the manner in which mothers interact and talk with their young children. Howe (1975) has shown the extent to which middle-class mothers conceive their role toward their infants as being more 'instructive', not only responding more to their infants' efforts to vocalize by speaking in return, but also attempting more often to initiate exchanges. The working-class mothers in her study were more often *laissez faire* in their approach. By the time, then, that he is $2^1/_2$ or 3 years old, the middle-class child is on average not more *competent* to handle more advanced forms of utterances—propositions of state and of action—but in fact is using such advanced forms more often. For their mothers continued to *interpret* their child's utterances as having to do with state and action (in contrast to propositions of naming only) until the child explicitly replied with such propositional forms. The mother's interpretation of the child's communicative intent is what seemed to keep the verbal interaction going and it keeps going until the child conforms or the mother gives up. While Howe's data begin at 18 months, when holophrases and early two-word utterances were appearing, the same principle can be shown to govern the mother's persistence even when the criterion the mother is applying relates to pre-linguistic communicative exchanges.

In interpreting the infant's communicative intent—correctly or incorrectly—the mother has a rich variety of cues to use. So, too, the child, for if the mother is at all consistent, he gives forth cues that come increasingly to have a predictable consequence as far as her behaviour is concerned. In this sense, they are in a transactional situation; their joint behaviour determining its own future course. Ryan (1974) adapts a classification of the cues used by the mother prepared originally by John Austin (1962) for the analysis of performative aspects of speech. (1) *Aspects of the utterance* itself including intonation patterns that suggest insistence, pleasure, protest, request, etc. As Ryan puts it, 'what is important is that adults interpret children's use of intonation in a systematic way, thus allowing children to learn what is conventional usage'. Wolff (1969) was one of the first to indicate that the early cries of infants were interpretable by parents. Ricks (1972) has shown even more convincingly that cries of normal babies obtained under controlled conditions (expressing greeting, pleased surprise, request, and frustration) were correctly identifiable—although the cries of the parent's own children included in the sample were not reliably identifiable. And Dore (1975) has suggested that intonation contours may be the first carriers of primitive illocutionary force in the child's utterances. (2) *Accompaniments of the utterance* provide a second set of cues for interpretation—'pointing, searching, playing with specific objects, refusing'. These are evident enough and need no comment here. We shall meet them again in a later section. (3) And finally, *circumstance of the utterance* constitutes the third source of cues, the context of the communicative event. Families of the children in our present study at Oxford typically classify their infants' vocalizations by context; babbling contentedly in his cot on first waking up, calling for attention on waking from the afternoon nap, hunger-fretting before feed time, annoyance at not being able to reach an object, etc. For what it is worth, we have also found distinctive voicing patterns in these calls as early as 4 months, suggesting that it may not be context alone that is being used as a cue.

When, then, does the infant come to 'intend consciously' to communicate? Early students of pre-linguistic communication were given to classifying pre-speech utterances of children into expressive (early cries of discomfort and pleasure), stimulative (producing reactions in others), and representational (Bühler, 1934). The process of going from expressive to stimulative was conceived much as Piaget's (1952) secondary circular reaction for producing or prolonging a desirable state of affairs previously produced inadvertently. Was intent involved in going from the expressive to the stimulative, and could one tell that the trip had been made? That debate does not seem worth a repeat performance, for we surely have no better basis for deciding than did our forbears. Rather, I think we would do better to concentrate instead on the description of particular intention-imputing situations and their outcomes to determine the child's and the mother's course in learning to deal with Jakobson's communicative functions. How indeed do the child and mother cope with the joint reference requirements in communicating? How is the phatic link maintained? How do the child and mother handle misunderstandings and their disambiguation? How do the child and mother express and recognize states of feeling? Is there an early poetic function and, if so, which well-turned babbles are rewarded by smiles? Can one discern a systematic trend in the conative devices a child uses to produce desired behaviour in his listeners?

If only for methodological reasons, I would propose that we avoid *a priori* arguments about 'conscious intent' and 'when' it is born. For questions whose answers are not in principle recognizable are rarely useful, and it is likely that 'consciousness' and 'intention' are opaque in this way. The issue, rather, is how communicative functions are shaped and how they are fulfilled. In fact, when one examines the development of specific communicative functions, the issue of conscious intent and its dating seems to wither away. An example is provided by one of our own subjects, Jon A., and the development of a signal pattern involving reaching outward bimanually while in a sitting position, hands prone. It had usually been interpreted by the mother as a signal that Jon wanted some familiar, hand-sized object beyond his reach's terminus, and she generally provided him with it, often heightening his anticipation by advancing the object slowly or 'dramatically' toward his hand with an accompanying rising voice pitch. At 8 months, 1 week, Jon used the signal; M interpreted it as calling for her hand, since there was no object close by, and performed her 'walking hand' body-game format, with the fingers walking up Jon's front to his chin. He tolerated it, though not entering as exuberantly as usual.

That over, Jon then reached out again. M interpreted it as a request for repetition. He participated even more reluctantly. M, on completion, then repeated the game though Jon had not signalled. He averted his gaze and whimpered a little. She repeated again and he was totally turned off. Pause. Then, 27 seconds after Jon first reached out, he reached again, this time pulling M's hands to a position where he could take hold of the ulnar edges and raise himself to a standing position. There was a following sequence of fourteen episodes extending for slightly over 9 minutes in which M and Jon played a game of alternating irregularly between the two 'formats'—M's hand either walking on fingers to tickle position, or M's hands in stand-supporting position. Under M's control, it was made into a 'surprise' evoking, alternating format, with her alternative interpretations of his reach gestures being rendered explicit.

In the course of such exchanges, as Ryan (1974) has already noted, 'The child is developing skills that are at least as essential to speaking and understanding language as the mastery of grammar is supposed to be'. Much of that learning is based upon the mother interpreting the child's intent, the child sometimes conforming with the interpretation, sometimes not, but learning, *en route*, what interpretations his efforts evoke and how these may be modified.

We shall return to these issues in a more general way in the concluding section. Here it suffices to say, with Dore (1974), that any theoretical framework for understanding language development requires a consideration of pragmatics, and a theory of pragmatics must have some way of coping with the communicative intentions of speakers. Dore proposes that communicative intent be defined as the inducement in a listener of the speaker's expectation. In this section, we have looked at intent as being realized in a transactional situation, with mother providing an interpretation to which the infant 'speaker' can conform, dissent, or which he can attempt to modify by correction or persistence. In the following sections we shall deal with more specific communicative intents—referring, regulating joint action, and predicating.

2. Reference

The issues raised in traditional philosophical discussions of reference have often been introduced into the debate by invoking the example of a hypothetical infant learning that a given sound, word, or gesture 'stands for' something in the extra-linguistic environment. Though such exercises are logically stimulating—else they would not have continued over the centuries—they are, alas, principally empty or irrelevant in explicating psychologically the infant's real problem in mastering reference. I find myself strongly in agreement with Harrison's (1972) contention that the psychological (and even arguably the philosophical) problem of reference is how the child develops a *set of procedures for constructing a very limited taxonomy* to deal with a limited set of extra-linguistic objects with which he traffics jointly with adult members of the linguistic community. What adults do for the child is to teach him or help to realize how these taxonomic procedures operate in assuring joint reference in relatively well-established situations until, finally, the child can go on quite on his own in coping referentially with larger arrays of objects in novel situations. The procedures of reference, I believe, are generative. The issue is how to differentiate among a set of objects, and how to refer precisely to any single one. I am quite prepared to accept Wittgenstein's (1953) demolition of empiricist associationist theories of naming based on pointing or other forms of ostension on his grounds: that ostension, even with negative feedback, can never specify what it is that a sign refers to in the complex welter of properties that any object necessarily displays. The negative feedback, moreover, is rarely in evidence in the data on language acquisition and when it does occur (for example Nelson, 1973), it is usually followed by the child abandoning his effort to use a name to indicate an object. Moreover, associative theories of naming or reference are beleaguered by the presuppositon that uttering a sound or making a gesture in the presence of a referent somehow evokes a nascent or innate recognition in the child that the name is associated with some feature of something that is at the focus of the child's attention, so that any concatenation of sign and referent is as likely as any other to be learned, and that is plainly not so. Whatever the reference triangle is (Ogden and Richards, 1923), it is plainly not an isolated bit of mental furniture produced by the linking of a sign, a thought, and a referent. The objective of early reference, rather, is to indicate to another by some reliable means which among an alternative set of things or states or actions is relevant to the child's line of endeavour. Exactitude is initially a minor issue. 'Efficacy of singling out' is the crucial objective, and the procedures employed are initially quite independent of the particular nature of objects and their defining or essential properties. If what I have boldy asserted here is even arguably so (and for a more carefully reasoned presentation of the same argument, the reader is referred to Harrison's 1972 discussion), then we would do well to avoid falling into the classical empiricist trap of the theory of naming or referring (even Quine's (1960) seductively commonsense version of it in *Word and Object*) and look instead at the procedures earliest used by the infant and adult in indicating and differentiating the very limited set of objects with which they traffic.

I shall want to deal with three separate aspects of early reference, and for convenience I shall give them labels. The first we may call *indicating* (if only to avoid the term ostension!), and it refers to gestural, postural, and idiosyncratic vocal procedures for bringing a partner's attention to an object or action or state. The second is *deixis* and refers, of course, to the use of spatial, temporal, and interpersonal contextual features of situations as aids in the management of joint reference. The third involves the development of standard lexical items that 'stand for' extra-linguistic events in the shared world of infant and caretaker and I shall call the process *naming*. Our task, as already indicated, is to explore the procedures employed in all three of these considerable linguistic accomplishments.

Take indicating first. Studies by Collis and Schaffer (1975), by Kaye (1976), and by Scaife and Bruner (1975) all point to a highly primitive form of indicating early in the child's first year. Collis and Schaffer have shown the extent to which the mother's line of regard follows the infant's, she constantly monitoring and following where the child looks as an important feature of inferring what is at the focus of his attention—better to interpret his demands, to elaborate upon what he is attending to, etc. Kaye has shown the extent to which mothers, asked to teach their child a simple task of taking an object from behind a transparent barrier, actively enlist the child's attention by 'marking' the target object in various ways—touching it, shaking it, etc. Strikingly, such manoeuvres occur far in excess of chance expectancy when the infant *looks away* from the task. In sum, she follows his line of regard, and when it diverges from where the task requires it to be, she uses effective procedures of indicating to re-establish joint attention. The findings of Scaife and Bruner provide the final piece in this picture. Not only, as indicated by Collis and Schaffer (1975), does the mother follow the child's line of regard as an indicator, but in this experiment the infant seems able as early as four months to follow and increasingly does follow an adult's line of regard when it is turned toward a locus removed from the child. We do not yet know what the processes are that bring this accomplishment about, but there are some tantalizing indications of the kinds of factors that are involved and that will have to be unravelled by experiment and close observation. What Scaife and Bruner (1975) have found is that as early as 4 months in some children and with high frequency by 9 months, the infant turns his regard in the same direction as a facing experimenter turns his. To what extent imitation is initially involved is difficult to say, but it can be said that there is no confusion among their young subjects as to which way to turn, though imitation might lead to head turning in either direction. Work is continuing at Oxford on these tangled issues by Scaife and by Churcher, and hopefully a clearer indication of the origins of this behaviour will emerge. Qualitative analysis of the responses of Scaife and Bruner's babies seems to suggest that the head turns of the infants are not of a magnitude to match imitatively the degree of head turn by the adult. Yet, it is quite possible that initial imitative turning might lead the child to 'pick up' an interesting object and thereby provide a perceptual reinforcement to the child's head turning. Again, this would very likely depend upon the density and discriminability of targets available to the child who orients in the direction of an adult's gaze. In any case, what we can say at this early juncture is that there is present from a surprisingly early age a mutual system by which joint selective attention between the infant and his caretaker is assured—under the control of the caretaker and/or of the child, eventually managed by joint pick-up of relevant directional cues that each provides the other.

Plainly, such devices for assuring a joint focus are insufficient for indicating what feature of a focus of attention is being abstracted—by the mother or by the child. That, of course, is the shortcoming of all ostensive indicating. But it is far more to the point to note not this shortcoming, which in a practical sense seems trivial in terms of what the child is actually doing, but the nature of the accomplishment (whether it be innately primed or somehow learned). What has been mastered is a *procedure* for homing in on the attentional locus of another: learning where to look in order to be tuned to another's attention. It is a discovery routine and not a naming procedure. It is totally generative within the limited world inhabited by the infant in the sense that it is not limited to looking at oranges or dolls or rattles. It has also equipped the child with a basis for dealing with space that transcends egocentrism, or, in any case, the child's egocentrism does not prevent him from following another's attention. For the child is able to use both a second origin of reference, another's line of regard, as well as various forms of marking or highlighting of objects (as in the Kaye experiment). These accomplishments would surely qualify as precursors of Piagetian decentration, their earlier occurrence being attributable perhaps to the more personal, less object-orientated testing situations used in Oxford. In this sense, these accomplishments guarantee the first bases for spatial, interpersonal deixis.

There is a further procedural accomplishment implied by Kaye's (1976) study of the 'implicit pedagogy' of mothers, their use of 'marking' in indicating an object or event to be attended to. Without going into the details, it is plain that mothers of 6-month-olds succeed in getting their infants to attend to and capture the object intended, in spite of the barrier. They not only mark the object, but evoke the action either by a process of tempting—putting the object nearer and at the edge of the barrier—or by modelling the behaviour themselves. The marking involves a combination of 'highlighting' features and exaggerating the structure of acts to be performed. They do both in a manner that is highly contingent on the child's state, his attentional deployment, and his line of activity. (For a fuller account of earlier implict pedagogies concerned with such 'marking', see Wood, Bruner, and Ross, (1976).)

We may now profitably introduce the concept of 'natural categories' so interestingly expounded in a recent series of papers by Rosch *et al.* (1976). She argues that in development, categories of objects are built on the basis of a common sharing of 'motor programmes' and of those perceptual features required for their execution. In this sense, they are 'practical' objects that are marked by features of use and their structuring into equivalence classes is based upon that use. In this sense, jointly managed activities provide an essential contextual basis for parent indicating to child and child to parent. As Nelson (1973) notes, categories of use are the first to develop and the childish definition 'a hole to dig' is to be taken as something more than quaint. But what is apparent is that indicating in either direction—child to mother or mother to child—occurs in situations where *both* are involved jointly in the act of digging or of reaching or of knocking down. The indicating that is used by each is based on the joint knowledge of the course of these actions and initially takes the form of exaggerating or 'marking' some phase of the action as a signal (often accompanied by ancillary vocalization and gesture, as in the child indicating a target of reaching by exaggerating the reach toward an object and making an 'effort' or 'fretting' vocalization, or by the mother shaking or vocally marking by 'C'mon' a proferred object). Note again that the procedure is independent of the conventional defining properties of the objects involved and relates instead to the programme of use.

Generative procedures for indicating undergo three striking changes over time: *decontextualization*, *conventionalization*, and increased *economy*. Decontextualization involves the development of indicating strategies that are not so closely linked to the specific action patterns in which they are embedded. Rather than indicating by exaggerating a feature of the reach (like extension) and fretting, the child now uses a more peremptory reach toward the object. This manoeuvre appears to signal more the child's line of regard and less the next step in his line of activity. *The extended hand becomes an external pointer for noting line of regard rather than direction of activity.* It is probably this crucial fact that leads to an increase in economy in indicating. For by 8 months, and often earlier in 'comfortably familiar' joint action formats, the child holds his hand out toward the object in a non-grasping directional gesture. By a year, when he is presented with pictures on the page of a book, he rarely 'grasps' at the picture, but touches it, and eventually touches it only with the index finger.

With respect to conventionalization, its basis is somewhat problematic. Its origin may be in the phenomenon of visual 'cross checking' between mother and infant: each looking at the other *en face* while in the process of indicating (present from the start for the mother, but increasingly evident for the child after 6 months in our own observations as well as in those by Sugarman, 1974, and by Bates *et al.*, 1973). They appear to be seeking agreement on a referent. The term 'conventionalization' may, perhaps, be inappropriately grandiose for such a minimal sign. I use it none the less to indicate that mother and child seem increasingly in the second half of the first year to be checking whether their gesturing or marking is 'getting through' to the other, as if there were mutual recognition of a correct way to signal.

It is after all of this prior learning that holophrastic 'naming' comes into the picture. Again, it seems highly unlikely that naming is what in fact is at issue. For as I have argued in a previous paper (1975), and as Bloom (1973), Greenfield and Smith (1976) and others, I think, abundantly illustrated, the child's holophrases are grammatically contextualized in a Fillmore-like (1968) case form that highlights some aspect of who is doing what with what object toward whom in whose possession and in what location and often by what instrumentality: Agent, Object, Recipient of Action, Location, Possession, Instrument. And it is not surprising, as Eve Clark (1973) has pointed out, that from a sheerly referential point of view, the child's usage is highly over-generalized, since he is still grouping objects and actions in terms of function rather than properties—a point well made in Greenfield's (1973) paper on 'Who is "Dada"?' In this sense, the emphasis is upon a rough taxonomic procedure rather than exactitude of response.

Equipped with such useful and generative procedural rules, the child may then get on with the Augustinian business of learning to refer—but in no sense can it be taken as claimed by St Augustine (cf. Wittgenstein, 1953) as learning language through naming *ab initio*. For if the child now fails to be able to discern the properties to which 'orange' or 'rattle' or 'Dada' refer, he has an extensive repertory of procedures available for disambiguation—though, to echo Wittgenstein's critique again, there is no set of ostension procedures that can ever *uniquely* determine reference or meaning.

We may now turn to the issue of *deixis* and its development. Recall that from the fourth month there is already some basis for spatial deixis in the line-of-regard following of mother and infant and, probably, this implies some appreciation of deixis of person—at least the recognition that it is another's line of regard which is being followed. Much of the 'reality of discourse' depends upon the establishment of what Benveniste (1971) calls a locution-dependent I/You concept. Adult speech would be impossible without it and Lyons (1974) has argued that reference is dependent for its growth upon it to deal not only with the shifters *I* and *You* but with spatial and temporal indicators like *here* and *there*, *now* and *later*, etc. Benveniste's point is worth quoting (1971, pp. 217–218):

> Between *I* and a noun referring to a lexical notion, there are not only the greatly varying formal differences that the morphological and syntactic structure of particular languages imposes; there are also others that result from the very process of linguistic utterance and which are of a more general and more basic nature. The utterance containing *I* belongs to that level of type of language which Charles Morris calls pragmatic, which includes, with the signs, those who make use of them. A linguistic text of great length—a scientific treatise, for example—can be imagined in which *I* and *you* would not appear a single time; conversely, it would be difficult to conceive of a short spoken text in which they were not employed. But the other signs of a language are distributed indifferently between these two types of texts. Besides this condition of use, which is itself distinctive, we shall call attention to a fundamental and moreover obvious property of *I* and *you* in the referential organization of linguistic signs. Each instance of use of a noun is referred to a fixed and 'objective' notion, capable of remaining potential or of being actualized in a particular object and always identical with the mental image it awakens. But the instances of the use of *I* do not constitute a class of reference since there is no 'object' definable as *I* to which these instances can refer in identical fashion. Each *I* has its own reference and corresponds each time to a unique being who is set up as such.
>
> What then is the reality to which *I* or *you* refers? It is solely a 'reality of discourse,' and this is a very strange thing. *I* cannot be defined except in terms of 'locution,' not in terms of objects as a nominal sign is. *I* signifies 'the person who is uttering the present instance of the discourse containing *I*.' This instance is unique by definition and has validity only in its uniqueness. If I perceive two successive instances of discourse containing *I*, uttered in the same voice, nothing guarantees to me that one of them is not a reported discourse, a quotation in which *I* could be imputed to another. It is thus necessary to stress this point: *I* can only be identified by the instance of discourse that contains it and by that alone. It has no value except in the instance in which it is produced. But in the same way it is also as an instance of form that *I* must be taken; the form of *I* has no linguistic existence except in the act of speaking in which it is uttered. There is thus a combined double instance in this process: the instance of *I* as referent and the instance of discourse containing *I* as the referee. The definition can now be stated precisely as: *I* is 'the individual who utters the present instance of discourse containing the linguistic instance *I*.' Consequently, by introducing the situation of 'address,' we obtain a symmetrical definition for *you* as the 'individual spoken to in the present instance of discourse containing the linguistic instance *you*.' These definitions refer to *I* and *you* as a category of language and are related to their position in language. We are not considering the specific forms of this category within given languages, and it matters little whether these forms must figure explicitly in the discourse or may remain implicit in it.

This constant and necessary reference to the instance of discourse constitutes the feature that unites to *I*/*you* a series of 'indicators' which, from their form and their systematic capacity, belong to different classes, some being pronouns, others adverbs, and still others, adverbial locutions.

If we can interpret Benveniste as implying that psychologically a grasp of reciprocal roles in discourse is the essential prerequisite for deixis of person, place, and time, then some very interesting questions arise about the development of reference. For one thing, the Benveniste hypothesis places pragmatics—the relation of language to those who are speaking it—at the heart of the problem of reference.

Again, the beginnings of a locution-dependent reciprocal concept emerges in action well before it is ever used in formal language. Established and reversible role relationships obviously provide a primitive base for later linguistic deixis. The universal pre-linguistic game of 'peekaboo' is a striking example (Bruner and Sherwood, 1976; Greenfield, 1972) of such reversible role structures, bound as it is by rule constraints with respect to who is the recipient and who the agent of coverings and uncoverings and how these may be reversed. Give-and-take routines, early established between mother and infant, again with reversibility of roles, and often marked by distinctive vocalizations for marking the giving and the receipt of an object (Bruner, 1975) provide another example. In such games, once developed, the child looks mother directly in the eye for a signal at crucial pauses in the play, as if to calibrate his intended actions with hers and to check which one is playing which role. In the first year of life, then, the child is mastering a convention—checking procedure not unlike that of adults—indeed, even using eye-to-eye contact for determining intent, readiness, and whose 'turn' it is (Argyle and Ingham, 1972).

But there is a big step from 'behavioural' to 'linguistic' deixis. In the latter, the context is contained in the message, in the former in the behavioural field of the speakers. Are there any small steps that help the child scale the heights from extra-linguistic to intra-linguistic deixis?

Perhaps one such step is through early phonological marking. One of the children we are studying showed at 6 months a difference in range of pitch for vocalizations accompanying the manipulation of objects in hand and those accompanying his interactions with his mother. Vocal 'comments' or babblings while manipulating objects were higher pitched than those accompanying exchanges with the mother. The mother was observed to look back to the child when the pitch of his vocalization dropped, to check whether he had redirected his attention toward her, though pitch difference did not develop as a systematic calling device to which the child and mother had recourse. The same child used a sharper onset of voicing when reaching toward out-of-reach objects than when taking one in hand that was within easy reach, a distinction akin to Lyons's (1974) second-order deictic marker, proximal/non-proximal. When the child did use sharper onset voicing the mother responded by moving an out-of-reach object toward him. It may well be, to be sure, that the sharper onset was an accompaniment of the effort of reaching for the more distant object—and in this sense be 'expressive'—but the fact remains that the distinction provided a *vocal* cue to the mother as to the topic of the child's attention. We cannot know whether the child 'deliberately' used the distinction for signalling purposes, but the mother responded as if it were deliberate and he continued to use such signalling in appropriate situations. In one other instance the same child, again at 6 months, was observed to use a distinctive vocalization that soon was able to produce a particular act by the mother. The situation was the familiar one in which mother 'looms' an object toward the child, the termination of the looming being to touch the object to the child's chest or hand or forehead. It is a standard body-game play 'format' for this child–mother pair. The child responded to looming with a pharyageal fricative, shifting to velar stop, and terminating with the achromatic vowel, 'aah'. When the mother delayed looming, the child used this call. If mother delayed too long, the vocalization shifted to a fretting call. This signalling was observed over two observational sessions separated by 3 weeks.

Kaplan and Kaplan (1971) have set out a plausible case for such phonological marking as a beginning of a semantic referential system that may precede or operate independently of syntax. Cromer's (1974) admirably concise summary of the Kaplans' position will serve:

[They] propose that the child's semantic position develops out of the early distinctions present in his communication system. They feel that with adequate data one will be able to identify a set of semantic features and chart the developmental order of their emergence. For example, when the infant makes the early distinction between human and non-human sounds, the Kaplans suggest the feature ' ± human' has become operative. When the infant differentiates himself from others, as observable in the effect of delayed auditory feedback on crying (i.e., indicating that the infant can distinguish between his own voice and other sounds), he is credited with the feature ' ± ego.' As the child develops his knowledge of object properties he adds such features as ' ± existence' and ' ± presence'. Other later acquisitions would include ' ± agent', ' ± past' and the like. These semantic features would place constraints on the child's language acquisition.

May not such devices provide the beginnings of the idea of vocally marking different positions of play in the relation between mother and child? I am all too aware that such instances do not provide a proper 'tracing' of the course from behavioural to linguistic deixis, yet I would urge that an effort be made to examine the small steps that might, in combination, provide the big insight that must be involved in learning to handle the classical deictic 'shifters'—those expressions whose interpretation varies as a function of which member of a pair uttered them, ranging from 'you' and 'me' to 'in front of' and 'behind'. We shall pursue this matter further in the following section.

With respect to naming proper, finally, there is ample evidence that well before language the *idea* of the word or label as an instrument of reference becomes firmly fixed. Indeed, Nelson's (1973) study of language acquisition indicates that one of the two 'styles' of language acquisition is referential—exercises in labelling being at the centre of certain mother–infant verbal interactions. (The other style, expressive, will be considered in the following section.) It takes the form, prior to word *production*, of playing: 'Where's your nose', or 'Show me your eyes'. Thus, the *concept* of a label must be a very early feature of language competence. Indeed, it too may have a deictic element as evidenced by the very common phenomenon of labelling both the infant's mouth, eyes, nose, etc., and the infant then indicating the mother's corresponding parts.

How early a start the lexical concept or label may get is indicated in some recent work by Ricks (1972). He distinguishes at 11 to 18 months three classes of vocalization: babble sounds with no evident referent, 'dada' words with a loose referent, and 'label' words. He lists seven properties of the last of these (like 'bow-wow'): they are not found in babbling, they are used only in the presence of a particular object or event, they are not modified toward conventionality but rather are adopted by the parents, they are frequently generalized and over-generalized (Clark, 1973), the expression of the 'word' is often accompanied by excitement, mention of the label word alerts the child to searching and also leads the child to repetition of the word. Ricks's data start at 11 months. By 18 or 20 months, some children have even introduced a word that stands for 'label-lacking' objects as with Matthew in Greenfield *et al.* (1972) who uses 'Umh' for unknowns and Bloom's (1970) Allison whose 'widə' is even more ambiguous.

We know very little about the onset of labelling as an instrument of reference. It seems highly likely that, at least later and possibly earlier as well, it is related to IQ, for after 3 or 4, the single best indicator of a child's measurable intelligence is the size of his vocabulary (Raven, 1948). Surely, if we are to understand the origins of and the later elaboration of reference, we shall have to explore more fully the kinds of phenomena reported by Ricks as they begin to manifest themselves in the first year of life. They may be a natural outgrowth of the phonological labels mentioned earlier or may indeed be an elaborated and later accompaniment to mutual pointing and joint gaze direction. All of these phenomena point to the early existence of means for managing joint reference. Yet none of them moves very far along the line toward discourse-sensitive, deictically dependent reference of the kind so carefully described by Benveniste. We turn next to a form of development that may explicate the early phases of such reference.

3. Language and Joint Action

As we have already noted, emphasis upon linguistic competence can easily distort the study of acquisition of or preoccupation with syntax. Joanna Ryan's critique (1974, p. 185) is doubtless correct:

Recent psycholinguistic work has neglected the earliest, presyntactic stages of language development, concentrating exclusively on the details of the child's later mastery of grammar. This approach can be characterized as exclusively cognitive, in the sense that it regards language as something to be studied as the *object* of the child's knowledge, and ignores all the other skills that determine actual language use. This neglect of what has come to be known as 'communicative competence' (Campbell & Wales, 1970) is not only serious in itself, but has also led to a distorted view of the child's grammatical abilities.

Perhaps the best antidote to syntactic preoccupation is to examine closely how the infant masters the task of communicating to others his needs, wishes, and objectives in order to assure either assistance or joint action. It is this that constitutes the beginnings of the more elaborated speech acts that are developed to 'get things done with words'. Rejecting as incomplete Chomsky's definition of the task of linguistics as the specification of rules that relate sound and meanings, Searle (1975) comments:

> I don't think that his picture is false, so much as it is extremely misleading and misleading in ways which have unfortunate consequences for research. A more accurate picture seems to me this. The purpose of language is communication. The unit of human communication in language is the speech act, of the type called illocutionary act. The problem (or at least an important problem) of the theory of language is to describe how we get from the sounds to the illocutionary acts. What, so to speak, has to be added to the noises that come out of my mouth in order that their production should be a performance of the act of asking a question, or making a statement, or giving an order, etc.?

To the beginning of this process we turn now.

From the start, the child is well-equipped with communicative routines in what we shall call the *demand mode*, many derived from innate patterns of expressing discomfort. By the third or fourth month of their baby's life, most mothers claim to be able to distinguish forms of demand calling as well as two or more forms of satisfaction expressed by vocalization. The demand cries almost always include pain or physical discomfort, hunger, demand for social interaction, and fatigue-frustration. Whether these cries have a universal phonological pattern or are idiosyncratic is not clear. Alan Leslie and Christopher Pratt at Oxford are currently carrying out analyses of changes that occur in such cries recorded in the child's familiar home setting.

'Pleasure' vocalizations usually include 'chatting' upon awakening and then playing by oneself and also the gurgling accompanying 'happy' interactions with a familiar caretaker. We can say little about these as yet save that they are recognizable to the mother and do not sound 'troubled' to the naive listener. Characteristically, 'trouble' demand cries, on the other hand, are insistent, with no pauses in anticipation of response, are 'wide spectrum' in their distribution of energy across a range of audible frequencies, and if unattended are followed by uncontrolled scream-crying. In practice, they are usually responded to, with the effect of establishing an expectancy of response. When such expectancy is established, at least three changes occur, marking the beginning of what I call a *request mode*. One major change is moderation in the wide-band intensity and 'insistence' of initial calling. Its wide-band spectrum is reduced. A second change is condensation of the call to a more limited time span with a pause in anticipation of response. If the response is not forthcoming, the infant reverts to the demand mode. There also ensues an increasing 'stylization' of initial calling with each infant developing a more recognizable 'signature' call. Studies of crying and fretting (for example Sander *et al.*, 1970; Ainsworth, 1975) point to the important role of a consistent caretaker in effecting this transition from demand to request.

There next appears a distinctive *exchange mode*. It begins with indicating a demand for an object gesturally and often with vocal accompaniment. By 8–10 months the child not only calls for and receives an object, but hands it back, calling again, receiving it, and handing it back again. As noted in the discussion of deixis, he reverses roles with himself first as recipient of action, then as agent. Indeed, exchange may make an even earlier appearance at the gestural level, for at as early as 2 weeks of age an infant will imitate facial and manual gestures (Moore and Meltzoff, 1975). If the child's imitation of the mother is then imitated in turn by the mother, the rate of the child's responding with matching gesture can be raised (Rheingold, Gewirtz, and Ross, 1959). Meltzoff (1975) has preliminary results indicating, moreover, that if the mother responds to the child's imitative gesture with a non-matching one, the child will either start imitating that gesture or will stop and may show distress or gaze aversion. It is difficult to say whether this early gestural exchange has any role in supporting the later exchange patterns first described, for the later pattern involves tasks with objects rather than directly interpersonal ones.

The exchange mode is gradually transformed into what we may call a *reciprocal mode*. Interactions are now organized around a *task* that possesses *exteriority*, *constraint*, and *division of labour*. The two participants enter upon a task with reciprocal, though non-identical, roles. It may involve nothing more complex than the mother holding steady the ever-present toy pillar box into which different shapes can be inserted. Elsewhere (Wood, Bruner, and Ross, 1976) we have referred to this as 'scaffolding' activity by the mother on the child's behalf. In time, and with the development of anticipatory schemas, the child's conception of the task is elaborated. He may now hold up a form to his mother's view before placing it in the pillar box. The mother may hand him one to put in. He may hand her one to insert. Much intermittent eye-to-eye checking and vocalizing accompanies these variations. The task is gradually being structured into reciprocating roles, the roles defined into rounds, each composed of turns, often with turns interchangeable (Garvey, 1974). The *task* and its constituents have become the objects of joint attention. Betimes, more complex tasks emerge and task formats are combined, with a strong quality of play and pleasure. But however playful, the striking thing about such task formats is that they are rule bound and constraining.

The progress from demand to request to exchange to reciprocity during the first year is, I believe, of central importance to the development of speech acts (or, more properly, communicative acts) and, as well, to the establishment of a ground work for the later grasping of case in language. An unexpected source of information about the elaboration of communicative acts comes from Ainsworth and Bell's study of mother–infant pairs (1974). They report that as 'crying and fretting'—what we would call the demand mode—recedes, more subtle forms of communicating increase, and those children who persist in the demand mode are slow in developing communicatively. More directly relevant are contextualized observations of my own (Bruner, 1975) and of Edwards (this volume).

The first example is from the Oxford corpus: Ann had learned between 8 and 10 months to play a well modulated exchange game involving the handing back and forth of objects. When, at 13 months, the game was well organized, Ann picked up her mother's receiving 'Thank you'. She used it both when giving and when receiving an object. After 2 weeks the expression dropped out of the giving position, nothing at first taking its place, but remained in the receiving position. Meanwhile, the demand demonstrative 'Look' was appearing in Ann's lexicon, used in referential situations, as when looking at pictures in a book. At the end of the thirteenth month, 'Look' was transposed as well into the position at which Ann handed her mother an object. 'Look' was later replaced by 'There' in the giving–taking format.

I would interpret Ann's performance in terms of Searle's (1975) earlier quoted comment on how we go 'from sound to illocutionary force'. Initially, she accompanies both roles in the exchange format by a single expression, in recognition of the compact of exchange. In time, each role is appropriately and conventionally accompanied by differentiated vocalizations, one of them borrowed from a demonstrative speech act ('Look'), but shortly replaced by one more appropriate to the act of bestowal. One is reminded of Cohen's (1974) discussion of 'markers' used for characterizing such semantic force properties as imperative, optative, interrogative, exclamatory, or performative. He goes on to raise the issue of whether there might not also be markers used for differentiating the uses to which performatives are put: indicating explicitness/implicitness, noting intention/inadvertence, whether a verdict, commitment, or promise is being made, etc. One has the impression in examining protocols that something of this order is occurring, and in the present case, the final shift on the 'giving' end from 'Look' to 'There' is a subtle recognition by Ann that exchange and demonstration involve different accompanying performatives.

The second example illustrates a somewhat different point: that a joint-action format provides, as already noted, an opportunity for the child to master major elements of case grammar as it relates to specific and familiar action formats. Edwards (this volume) shows how a child's knowledge of a 'prohibitive' format— having to do with objects she was not to touch—provided an opportunity for her to develop grammatical concepts. Initially, she used the simple negative 'No' to characterize situations in which she was not to touch an object. This was followed, in comparable formats, by the introduction of possession, 'Yours' or 'Mine' for objects she was forbidden to touch or play with. Still later, a verb form was inserted into the format—'Leave it' for what was prohibited. And finally, again in the same format type, the adjectival form appeared: 'hot' or 'sharp' for the object that was prohibited. Edwards's Alice was learning not only grammar, but learning it as an adjunct to social situations whose structure she was having to learn and to manage. The case variants were all embodiments of a self-directed imperative—to keep clear of the object in question.

We turn next to predication and its pre-linguistic precursors and prerequisites.

4. Predication

Looked at in its linguistic sense, 'predication involves affirming or asserting something of or about the subject of a proposition' (Wall, 1974, p. 9). It might seem then somewhat jejune to enquire about the precursors or even the prerequisites for predication in the pre-linguistic child, for surely he can in no sense be thought to be dealing in propositions. What has made the issue of pre-propositional predication a persistent and interesting one, however, was the early insistence of DeLaguna (1927) that the single words of holophrastic speech could profitably be treated as compacted sentence forms, and that single words could be conceived within that framework as comments upon extra-linguistic topics inherent in the contexts in which the child found himself. The primitive topic, then, was implicit rather than explicit. This interpretation of early one-word utterances persisted in the literature—cited principally in general reviews of language development—until picked up again in McNeill's (1970a, 1970b) work, and then further developed by Bloom (1973) and more recently in a rather widely circulated manuscript by Greenfield and Smith (1976) who were specifically concerned with interpreting the run-up in early speech development from single-word utterances to the patterns that are found when M.L.U.s approach two morphs. Like DeLaguna, these investigators were interested in the manner in which the 'unmentioned' topic finally found its way into explicitness to be represented by a nominal or other grammatically interpretable form that could carry language development beyond dependence on unspecified context—DeLaguna's famous claim that language development could be conceived as a process of decontextualization.[1]

McNeill (1970a, 1970b) carried the argument one step further. Arguing from the existence of the predicational postpositions in Japanese, *ga* and *wa*, indicating respectively extrinsic and intrinsic predicates, the latter being habitual or essential and the former temporary or transitory, he proposed that initial predication with unmentioned topic could be conceived of as the intrinsic form, while extrinsic predication was more of the *ga* type. In Japanese, the postpositions could be noted by the contrast: 'The dog-wa has hair' versus 'The dog-ga is on the chair'. He found that for both Japanese- and English-speaking children, early sentences contained about twice as many intrinsic as extrinsic predications, and that subject noun phrase topics that referred to the speaker were particularly rare. This led him to conclude that 'holophrastic utterances consist largely, if not exclusively, of intrinsic predicates .... Children would add subjects to predicates ... when the predicates become extrinsic. Such an event appears to happen first when the children are 18 to 24 months old' (McNeill, 1970b, p. 1093). To this interesting finding (or contention) should be added two others. Quite counter-intuitively, Wall (1968) found that the mean length of dialogue between children and parents was *shorter* than dialogues between the same children and strangers. Chafe (1970) had, meanwhile, urged that one must make the contrast between 'new' information and 'old' or shared information, that the two are handled grammatically in different ways. Wall (1974, pp. 232–233) makes the point that

It seemed possible that the difference in utterance length might well be explained on the basis of presence or absence of shared information between participants in the conversations. That is, it is necessary for relative strangers to state explicitly whatever it may be that they are trying to communicate verbally for efficient information transfer, whereas among friends and close associates remarks are often greatly abbreviated with little or no resulting loss of information transferred.

Vygotsky (1962, p. 139) has made the same point (*en route* to presenting his argument that the nature of inner speech is condensed predication, with topical subject left implicit): 'Now let us imagine that several people are waiting for a bus. No one will say, on seeing the bus approach, "The bus for which we are waiting is coming." The sentence is likely to be an abbreviated "Coming," or some such expression, because the subject is plain from the situation.' And, indeed, in Wall's (1974) study, too, her 18 to 30-month-olds conformed to the rule in an interesting way. She compares the number of constituents in sentences given in response to a question (where the topic, of course, is shared in advance) and sentences spoken spontaneously. Just half of the spontaneous sentences contained two or more constituents, but only 18 per cent of those in reply to a topic-setting question.

We may now, in the light of the foregoing, consider afresh the significance of established, mutual-action formats discussed in the preceding section. They constitute the implicit or shared topics on which comments can be made by the child without having to be mentioned. These are the implicit topics about which comments can be made. And as these formats become differentiated into reversible or complementary roles during the growth of exchange and reciprocal modes, implicit topics become that much more contextualized in the action that adult and child share. I used the three terms, 'division of labour,' 'exteriority,' and 'constraint' to characterize the nature of the shared action formats that developed during the onset of the reciprocal mode—terms borrowed, of course, from Durkheim's (1933) characterization of the requisite properties of social norms—to specify the manner in which formats seemed to take on a shared existence binding the two partners in discourse. And it is this development that is, in my view, crucial to the course of pre-linguistic predicational activity to which we now turn—particularly to the development of intrinsic predication in McNeill's (1970b) sense.

What, we may first ask, are the forms of 'comment' that can be made pre-linguistically (or pre-propositionally) on such shared topics as the joint-action patterns described in the preceding section? Before we can answer this question, we must first consider the function of predication in a communicative act. Its functions are three in number: (1) to specify something about a topic that is explicit or implicit, (2) to do so in such a way that topic and comment can be rendered separable (for example, *John is a boy* and *John has a hat*), and (3) to specify something in a way that is subject to truth testing or, more simply, negation. I do not know whether pre-linguistic 'comments' (in forms we shall consider) upon implicit topics fulfil all three of these functions, and I should prefer to leave out of consideration the last of these (since it is now just in process of being studied by Roy Pea in our laboratory), to treat the second rather lightly, and to concentrate principally upon the first function.

The first and perhaps simplest form of comment is, I think, giving indication that a topic is being shared in joint action, and it is principally revealed in the child's management of gaze direction. Typically in our own protocols, the child, when involved in a transaction over some object or activity, looks up at some juncture and makes eye-to-eye contact with the mother, often smiling as well. The topic is the joint activity, the comment is the establishment of 'intersubjective' sharing in connection with that activity, after which the activity goes on. A good example is provided in the account of glance management in an exchange game reported by Bruner (1975). The 'comment' consists of noting whether both partners are 'with it', engaged in the game. Similarly, when one of our mothers uses a toy such as a clown that disappears inside a cone, when the clown had disappeared and then reappeared, the child will usually then turn from the clown to the mother for gaze contact. I would interpret this 'joining' as an act of reasserting the joint action, a primitive version of the 'interpersonal concept' in respect of which Benveniste (1971) was cited in a previous section.

This form of confirming comment is supplemented and extended at around the ninth month by the emergence of a form of vocalization we have dubbed 'proclamative'. It occurs at two points during joint-action sequences: first, at a point where the infant is about to undertake his part of a jointly attended action, seemingly as an accompaniment to intention; second, when the act is complete. The vocalized babbling may be coincident with the child looking back at the mother or may precede it. The vocalization, in short, appears to be initiating or completive with respect to an act embedded in a jointly attended task. In this sense, it may be considered as a 'candidate-comment' on an implicit topic. In time, the pattern becomes further elaborated, and the child may not only vocalize in these positions and make gaze contact, but also hold up an implicated object to show the mother, as when picking up a brick and placing it on a pile.

Elsewhere I have commented on the fact that attentional deployment as revealed in eye-movement records (Bruner, 1975; Mackworth and Bruner, 1970) may itself predispose to topic-comment structures in the very organization of information processing. For typically, large saccades that move attention to a sharply defined focus in the visual field are followed by smaller inspection saccades that play around features of this focus. Coles, Sigman, and Heywood in our laboratory are now exploring this feature of early attention, and while it is too early to say anything definitive about the onset of these focus-inspecting eye-movement patterns, their stabilization might surely be thought of as a further predisposing factor to topic-comment communication—linguistically or pre-linguistically.

Finally a word about the separability of topic and comment achieved in predication. It is by now a common observation that the child's play with objects takes one of two forms (a point also noted for chimpanzees by Köhler, 1926, and commented upon by Bruner, 1972, 1973). An *object* is successively placed into as many different action-patterns as the child can manage: a ball is successively mouthed, squeezed, banged on the table, thrown down, called for, etc. Or an *action* is fitted to as many different objects as it will accommodate: successively a cup is banged, then a spoon, then a doll, then any other loose object to hand. These play patterns, while in no sense direct precursors of propositional predicating, are none the less striking examples of separation and variation of comments on topics, with either the object serving as topic and actions-upon-it as comments, or the action serving as organizing topic and a variety of fitting objects as comments. Typical of the play of both higher apes and children (Loizos, 1967), this focus-variation pattern should not be overlooked as a factor that predisposes action, attention, and eventually language to the pattern that at the propositional level we call predicational.

In conclusion, I find myself in strong agreement with Lyons (1966, p. 131) when he comments:

> By the time the child arrives at the age of eighteen months or so, he is already in possession of the ability to distinguish 'things' and 'properties' in the 'situations' in which he is learning and uses language. And this ability seems to me quite adequate as a basis for the learning of the principal deep-structure relationship between lexical items (the subject–predicate relationship), provided that the child is presented with a sufficient amount of 'primary linguistic data' in real 'situations' of language use.

Before he reaches 18 months, indeed during the second half of his first year, he is well on the way toward conceptual mastery of these concepts in the extra-linguistic sphere.

5. Conclusion

The developmental psychology of language is currently in a rather confused state. The initial optimism that grew out of Chomsky's formulation of a generative–transformational grammar has not been sustained by the torrent of work that it provoked. His was a powerful idea, one that will want a revisit after other aspects of language acquisition become clearer. The central notion—that the child in some sense 'has a knowledge' of the rules of language and that he is attempting to generate from this knowledge hypotheses about a local language—while boldly suggestive, is plainly insufficient.

Principally as a result of the studies of Brown (1973) and his students, it has become increasingly apparent that language acquisition is enormously aided by the child's pre-linguistic grasp of concepts and meanings that make it easier for him to penetrate grammatical rules. In a closely reasoned and provocative paper published in 1972, Macnamara formulated the case well, arguing that syntactic rules are discovered by the child with the aid of meaning. His view was that the child roughly determined the referent of principal lexical items in a sentence and then used previously acquired knowledge of these referents to decode the grammar of the sentence. Sinclair-de-Zwart's (for example 1969) work, too, has alerted the psycholinguist to the link between development and the child's emerging, extra-linguistic knowledge of the world. And Bloom's most recent work has also dealt a strong blow in favour of the early semantic origins of single-word utterances. She concludes that 'children develop certain conceptual representations of regularly recurring experiences, and then learn whatever words conveniently code such conceptual notions' (1973, p. 113). The effect of this recent work has been to put the semantic element back into the developmental picture and make more attractive such ideas as Fillmore's (1968) semantically relevant case categories.

But neither the syntactic nor the semantic approach to language acquisition takes sufficiently into account what the child is trying to do by communicating. As linguistic philosophers remind us, utterances are used for different ends and use is a powerful determinant of rule structures. The brunt of my argument has been that one cannot understand the transition from pre-linguistic to linguistic communication without taking into account the uses of communication as speech acts. I have, accordingly, placed greater emphasis on the importance of pragmatics in this transition—the directive function of speech through which speakers affect the behaviour of others in trying to carry out their intentions. I find myself in sympathy with Dore's effort (1975) to understand the process whereby 'primitive forces' or 'orectic intentions' are gradually conventionalized and 'grammaticalized' so that they can be reformed into communications with illocutionary force. I am not dismayed at all by Jonathan Cohen's (1974) warning that the conventionalizations by which illocutionary force is achieved are often, strictly, extra-linguistic 'manners', for perhaps, as Silverstein (1975) suggests, there is not so sharp a boundary between social convention and grammatical devices. Dore's account of how illocutionary skill is augmented by the acquisition of such 'grammaticalizing devices' is interesting. He defines a primitive speech act 'as a rudimentary referring expression plus a primitive illocutionary force' (such as requesting, answering, etc.) so that the child 'communicates *what* it is he means or wants' through referential tricks and, through prosodic pattern initially and then by other means, '*that* he intends or wants something'. How the child gets from the primitive to the grammaticalized is left to rather mysterious processes like 'emergence' and 'grammaticalization' that may do no more than paper over the discontinuous course of language acquisition with some new words. Yet, my sympathies are with Dore's effort to examine how the requirement of 'getting different things done with words' constantly alerts the child to appropriate devices and conventions and, in an evolutionary sense, may even have equipped him with special sensitivities for picking these up. Yet, for all that, I hope I have not seemed to deny that syntactic and semantic precursors can also be explored fruitfully: grammar-like principles underlying reference, predication, privileges of occurrence, etc. But if there is one point that deserves emphasis, whether one is searching for syntactic, semantic, or pragmatic precursors of early language, it is that language acquisition occurs in the context of an 'action dialogue' in which joint action is being undertaken by infant and adult. The joint enterprise sets the deictic limits that govern joint reference, determines the need for a referential taxonomy, establishes the need for signalling intent, and provides a context for the development of explicit predication. The evolution of language itself, notably its universal structures, probably reflects the requirements of joint action and it is probably because of that evolutionary history that its use is mastered with such relative ease, though its theoretical explication still eludes us.

Acknowledgements

This research was supported by a grant from the Social Science Research Council of Great Britain, and parts of this paper have been presented at the Universities of Stirling and London and at the University College of Swansea. I am particularly grateful for criticism to Mr Churcher, Mr Leslie, Dr Scaife, Ms Caudill, and Ms Garton of Oxford, as well as to Dr Richard Cromer, Dr Elizabeth Bates, and Susan Sugarman-Bell. I gratefully dedicate this paper to Professor Roman Jakobson in honour of his eightieth birthday.

Note

1. With respect to the issue of the sentential or predicational status of the holophrase—still a very lively theoretical issue— the reader is referred to Bloom (1973), whose conclusions are taken up in the final section, and Dore (1975) who reviews the arguments for and against sentential status for the holophrase and ends by opting for the view that holophrases represent a first step along the hard path from primitive force to grammaticalized illocutionary force, a path one traverses by successive mastery of grammaticalizing devices such as using word order, intonation, etc., in the spirit of Harrison (1972).

References

Ainsworth, Mary D. Salter (1975), Social development in the first year of life: maternal influences on infant–mother attachment. Paper presented in Geoffrey Vickers Lecture, London.

Ainsworth, Mary D. Salter, and Bell, Sylvia M. (1974), Mother–infant interaction and the development of competence. In Connolly, K., and Bruner, J. S. (eds.), *The Growth of Competence*, London and New York: Academic Press.

Argyle, M., and Ingham, R., (1972), Gaze, mutual gaze and proximity, *Semiotica*, IV, 32–49.

Austin, J. L. (1962)., *How To Do Things with Words*, Oxford: Oxford University Press.

Bates, Elizabeth, Camaioni, L., and Volterra, V. (1973), The acquisition of performatives prior to speech. Technical Report no. 129, Consiglio Nazionale delle Ricerche, Rome.

Benveniste, E. (1971), *Problems in General Linguistics*, trs. Meek, M. E., Coral Gables, Fla.: University of Miami Press.

Bernstein, B. (1960), Language and social class, *British Journal of Sociology*, 11, 271–276.

Bloom, Lois, (1970), *Language Development: Form and Function in Emerging Grammars*, Cambridge, Mass.: M.I.T. Press.

Bloom, Lois, (1973), *One Word at a Time: the Use of Single Word Utterances Before Syntax*, The Hague: Mouton.

Bloomfield, L. (1933), *Language*, New York: Holt; London; Allen & Unwin.

Brown, R. (1970), *Psycholinguistics*, New York: The Free Press.

Brown, R. (1973), *A First Language: the Early Stages*, Cambridge, Mass.: Harvard University Press; Longon: Allen & Unwin.

Bruner, J. S. (1972), The nature and uses of immaturity, *American Psychologist*, 27, 1–22.

Bruner, J. S. (1973), Organisation of early skilled action, *Child Development*, 44, 1–11.

Bruner, J. S. (1975), The ontogenesis of speech acts, *Journal of Child Language*, 2, 1–19.

Bruner, J. S., and Sherwood, Virginia (1976), Early rule structure: the case of peekaboo. In Bruner, J. S., Jolly, A., and Sylva, K. (eds), *Play: its Role in Evolution and Development*, Harmondsworth: Penguin Books; New York: Basic Books.

Bühler, K. (1934), *Sprachtheorie: die Darstellungsfunktion der Sprache*, Jena: Fischer.

Campbell, R., and Wales, R. (1970), The study of language acquisition. In Lyons, J. (ed.), *New Horizons in Linguistics*, Harmondsworth: Penguin Books.

Chafe, W. L. (1970), *Meaning and the Structure of Language*, Chicago: University of Chicago Press.

Chomsky, N. (1965), *Aspects of the Theory of Syntax*, Cambridge, Mass.: M.I.T. Press.

Clark, Eve (1973), What's in a word: on the child's acquisition of semantics in his first language. In Moore, T. E. (ed.), *Cognitive Development and the Acquisition of Language*, New York: Academic Press.

Cohen, J. (1974) Speech acts. In Sebeok, T. A. (ed.), *Current Trends in Linguistics*, vol. 12: Linguistics and the Adjacent Arts and Sciences, The Hague: Mouton.

Collis, G. M., and Schaffer, H. R. (1975), Synchronization of visual attention in mother–infant pairs, *Journal of Child Psychology and Psychiatry*, 16, 315–320.

Cromer, R. F. (1974), The development of language and cognition: the cognition hypothesis. In Foss, B. (ed.), *New Perspectives in Child Development*, Harmondsworth: Penguin Education Series.

DeLaguna, Grace (1927), *Speech: its Function and Development*, New Haven, Conn.: Yale University Press.

Donaldson, Margaret, and Wales, R. (1970), On the acquisition of some relational terms. In Hayes, J. R. (ed.), *Cognition and the Development of Language*, New York: Wiley.

Dore, J. (1974), Communicative intentions and the pragmatics of language development. Unpublished paper, City University of New York.

Dore, J. (1975), Holophrases, speech acts and language universals, *Journal of Child Language*, 2, 21–40.

Durkheim, E. (1933), *The Division of Labor*, Glencoe, Ill.: The Free Press.

Edwards, D. (this volume), The sources of children's early meanings.

Fillmore, C. J. (1968), The case for case. In Bach, E., and Harms, R. T. (eds), *Universals in Linguistic Theory*, New York: Holt, Rinehart & Winston.

Garfinkel, H. (1963), Trust and stable actions. In Harvey, O. J. (ed.), *Motivation and Social Interaction*, New York: Ronald Press.

Garvey, Catherine (1974), Some properties of social play, *The Merrill-Palmer Quarterly*, 20, 163–180.

Gombrich, E. (1975), Mirror and map: theories of pictorial representation, *Philosophical Transactions of the Royal Society* (Biol. Sci.), 270, 119–149.

Greenfield, Patricia M. (1972), Playing peekaboo with a four-month old: a study of the role of speech and nonspeech sounds in the formulation of a visual schema, *The Journal of Psychology*, 82, 287–298.

Greenfield, Patricia M. (1973), Who is 'Dada'? ... some aspects of the semantic and phonological development of a child's first words, *Language and Speech*, 16, 34–43.

Greenfield, Patricia M., Bruner, J. S., and May, M. (1972), *Early Words* (a film), New York: Wiley.

Greenfield, Patricia M., and Smith, J. H. (1976), *The Structure of Communication in Early Language Development*, New York: Academic Press.

Grice, H. P. (1968), Utterer's meaning, sentence-meaning and word-meaning, *Foundations of Language*, 4, 1–18.

Grice, H. P. (1975), Logic and conversation. The William James Lecturers, Harvard University, 1967–1968. In Cole, P., and Morgan, J. (eds), *Syntax and Semantics*, vol. 3, Speech Acts, London and New York: Academic Press.

Harrison, B. (1972), *Meaning and Structure*, New York and London: Harper & Row.

Hess, R. D., and Shipman, Virginia (1965), Early experience and the socialisation of cognitive modes in children, *Child Development*, 36, 869–886.

Howe, Christine (1975), The nature and origin of social class—differences in the propositions expressed by young children. Ph.D thesis, University of Cambridge.

Jakobson, R. (1960), Linguistics and poetics. In Sebeok, T. A. (ed.), *Style in Language*, Cambridge, Mass.: M.I.T. Press.

Kaplan, E., and Kaplan, G. (1971), The pre-linguistic child. In Eliot, J. (ed.), *Human Development and Cognitive Processes*, New York: Holt, Rinehart & Winston.

Kaye, K. (1976), Infant's effects upon their mothers' teaching strategies. In Glidewell, J. C. (ed.), *The Social Context of Learning and Development*, New York: Gardiner Press.

Köhler, W. (1926), *The Mentality of Apes*, New York: Harcourt, Brace.

Lock, A. (1972), From out of nowhere? *Proceedings of the International Symposium on First-Language Acquisition*, University of Ottowa Press.

Loizos, E. (1967), Play behaviour in higher primates: a review. In Morris, D. (ed.), *Primate Ethology*, London: Weidenfeld & Nicolson.

Lyons, J. (1966), General discussion to D. McNeill's paper, The creation of language. In Lyons, J., and Wales, R. (eds), *Psycholinguistic Papers*, Edinburgh: Edinburgh University Press.

Lyons, J. (1974), Deixis as the source of reference. Unpublished paper, University of Edinburgh.

Macfarlane, A. (1975), Personal communication.

Mackworth, N. H., and Bruner, J. S. (1970), How adults and children search and recognise pictures, *Human Development*, 13, 149–177.

Macnamara, J. (1972), Cognitive basis of language learning in infants, *Psychological Review*, 79, 1–13.

McNeill, D. (1970a), *The Acquisition of Language: the Study of Developmental Psycholinguistics*, New York: Harper & Row.

McNeill, D. (1970b), The development of language. In Mussen, P. H. (ed.), *Carmichael's Manual of Child Psychology*, 3rd ed., vol. 1., New York: Wiley.

McNeill, D. (1974), Semiotic extension. Paper presented at the Loyola Symposium on Cognition, 30 April 1974, Chicago, Ill.

Meltzoff, A. N. (1975), personal communication.

Moore, M. K., and Meltzoff, A. N. (1975), Neonate imitation: a test of existence and mechanism. Paper delivered at the Society for Research in Child Development meeting, Denver, Colo., April 1975.

Morris, C. W. (1938), *Foundations of the Theory of Signs*, Chicago: Chicago University Press.

Nelson, Katherine (1973), Structure and strategy in learning to talk, *Society for Research in Child Development Monographs*, 38, nos 1–2, serial no. 149.

Ogden, C. K. and Richards, I. A. (1923), *The Meaning of Meaning*, New York: Harcourt Brace; London: Paul, Trench, Trubner.

Piaget, J. (1952), *The Origins of Intelligence in Children*, New York: International Universities Press (first published 1936).

Quine, W. V. O. (1960), *Word and Object*, Cambridge, Mass.: M.I.T. Press.

Raven, J. C. (1948), The comparative assessment of intellectual ability, *The British Journal of Psychology*, 39–40, 12–19.

Rheingold, H. L., Gewirtz, J., and Ross, H. (1959), Social conditioning of vocalisations in the infant, *Journal of Comparative Physiology and Psychology*, 52, 68–73.

Ricks, D. M. (1972), The beginnings of vocal communication in infants and autistic children. Unpublished Doctorate of Medicine thesis, University of London.

Rosch, Eleanor H., Mervis, C. B., Gray, W. D., Johnson, D. M. and Boyes-Braem, P. (1976), Basic objects in natural categories, *Cognitive Psychology*, 8, 382–439.

Ryan, Joanna, (1974), Early language development. In Richards, M. P. M (ed.), *The Integration of the Child into a Social World*, Cambridge: Cambridge University Press.

Sander, L. W., Stechler, G., Burns, P., and Julia, H. (1970), Early mother–infant interaction and 24–hour patterns of activity and sleep, *Journal of the American Academy of Child Psychiatry*, 9, 103–123.

Scaife, M., and Bruner, J. S. (1975), The capacity for joint visual attention in the infant, *Nature*, 253, no. 5489, 265–266.

Schoggen, M., and Schoggen, P. (1971), Environmental forces in the home lives of three-year-old children in three population subgroups. D.A.R.C.E.E. Papers and Reports, vol. 5, no. 2, John Kennedy Center for Research on Education and Human Development, George Peabody College, Nashville, Tenn.

Searle, J. R. (1969), *Speech Acts: an Essay in the Philosophy of Language*, Cambridge: Cambridge University Press.

Searle, J. R. (1975), Speech acts and recent linguistics. Paper read at the Conference on Developmental Psycholinguistics and Communication Disorders, New York Academy of Sciences, 24–25 January 1975.

Silverstein, M. (1975), Shifters, linguistic categories, and cultural description. Unpublished manuscript, University of Chicago.

Sinclair-de-Zwart, Hermina (1969), Developmental psycholinguistics. In Elkind, D., and Flavell, J. H. (eds), *Studies in Cognitive Growth: Essays in Honor of Jean Piaget*, New York: Oxford University Press. Also in Adams, P. (ed.), *Language in Thinking*, Harmondsworth: Penguin Books (1972).

Slobin, D. (1973), Prerequisites for the development of grammar. In Ferguson, C. A., and Slobin, D. (eds), *Studies of Child Language Development*, New York: Holt, Rinehart & Winston.

Sugarman, Susan (1974), A sequence for communicative development in the pre-language child. Unpublished paper. University of California, Berkeley.

Trevarthen, C. (1974a), Conversations with a two-month old, *New Scientist*, 62 (896), 230–235.

Trevarthen, C. (1974b), Infant responses to objects and persons. Paper presented at the Spring 1974 meeting of the British Psychological Society, Bangor.

Urwin, Catherine (1973), The development of a blind baby. Unpublished manuscript presented at Edinburgh University, January 1973.

Vygotsky, L. (1962), *Thought and Language*, Cambridge, Mass.: M.I.T. Press.

Wall, Carol (1968), Linguistic interaction of children with different alters. Unpublished paper, University of California, Davis, Calif.

Wall, Carol (1974), *Predication: a Study of its Development*, The Hague: Mouton.

Wittgenstein, L. (1953), *Philosophical Investigations*, Trs. Anscombe, G. E. M., Oxford: Basil Blackwell; New York: The Macmillan Co.

Wolff, P. H. (1969), The natural history of crying and other vocalisations in early infancy. In Foss, B. M. (ed.), *Determinants of Infant Behaviour*, vol. 4, London: Methuen.

Wood, D., Bruner, J. S., and Ross, Gail (1976), The role of tutoring in problem solving, *Journal of Child Psychology and Psychiatry*, 17, 89–100.

3

SOME ORGANIZATIONAL ASPECTS OF PRE-VERBAL COMMUNICATION

Susan Sugarman-Bell

In the past few years several authors have stressed that communication develops before language and aids the child functionally in learning to talk. It has been suggested, for instance, that specific semantic-pragmatic functions found in language, for example requesting and rejecting, may be expressed earlier by particular non-verbal means (Bruner, 1975; Carter, 1974; Dore, 1974). It has also been suggested that the elaboration of idiosyncratic child-caretaker behaviours or rituals carrying specific meanings assist the child in learning a conventional code (Bruner, 1975).

Implicit in these studies is the idea that children who do not yet talk evolve particular meanings, and forms for the expression of these meanings. In addition, these children are developing ways to make themselves more clearly and completely understood by those around them. It is possible that the same gain is also achieved by systematic changes in the way children organize neutral social and pragmatic behaviours in social contexts. Looked at another way, there may be general shifts in the pre-verbal child's social interactions which make the child's pragmatic intentions, and the fact that he is communicating, increasingly clear.

This chapter explores the development of this kind of general communicative and intentional marking in the pre-verbal period. The study to be reported focused on the co-ordination between actions and vocalizations directed toward a person, on the one hand, and actions directed toward an object on the other hand. Pilot observations suggested that young children of different ages exhibit different levels of person–object co-ordination in their social interactions. The following two cases exemplify the key difference observed. Child A strained to pull an object from his mother's lap, and devoted his full attention to the object. Child B solicited his mother's attention by touching her arm and looking at her face, and then grasped at the object. Important to the communicative value of each episode is the fact that each occurred in a social context and that each pointed to the child's desire to possess something. The difference was not, then, what intentions the children had, but rather how visibly evident those intentions were. By combining explicit bids toward the mother with efforts to obtain the object, the second child was perhaps indicating his intentions to someone else, rather than simply pursuing them. It could be said that this child marked behaviourally and primitively what action or reaction was expected of whom regarding what thing.

Pilot data indicated that the more explicit co-ordinated bid would follow the less explicit singly focused approach in ontogenesis. Other developmental findings provided indirect support for this pattern of events. Investigations of instrumental co-ordination involving only physical objects, for example use of a stick to retrieve an object, had shown that before the handling of one object was subordinated to the obtaining of another object, the two objects were likely to be handled separately (Piaget, 1963; Duncker, 1945). Further, the constituent behaviour patterns involved not only manifested themselves separately prior to co-ordination, but developed separately as well. This principle of gradual hierarchization has been observed in a still broader spectrum of developmental phenomena, ranging from motor co-ordination (Bruner, 1968; Werner, 1948) to cognitive and symbolic acquisitions, including language (Piaget, 1963; Werner and Kaplan, 1963: Sinclair and Bronckart, 1972; Brown, 1973; Bowerman, 1974).

Thus, it was hypothesized in this study that the child's first transactions with persons and objects in social contexts are largely mutually exclusive. The child may then begin to exhibit increasingly differentiated behaviour within each orientation alone. Next, the child should start to combine person- and object-oriented activity in a single exchange. This was the developmental endpoint of the present enquiry. Later, however, with conventional signals, such as pointing and particularly language, which typically dominate the child's repertoire after one year (Ingram, 1971, p. 901; Werner and Kaplan, 1963, p. 77), the social orientation of exchanges can be considered implicit for both child and adult.

In the progression outlined the child is integrating persons into his manipulation of the physical environment and is using objects to manipulate the social environment. Either manoeuvre exhibits a means–ends relation in social interaction between a social object and a physical object. Analogously, elementary tool use involves a means–ends relation between two physical objects. In order to explore the possibility of a developmental connection between these two kinds of activity, subjects observed for person–object integration in social interaction were given tests for instrumental relations involving inanimate objects.

Following a presentation of the method and the trends found for person–object and object–object co-ordination, the closing discussion will touch upon (1) the present social-interactive sequence as an exemplar of sensorimotor communication, (2) the sequence as a prerequisite to language, and (3) the effect of the social environment on the sequence. A pilot investigation of institutionalized infants will serve as the working data base for the latter two objectives.

1. Method

A large body of spontaneous social-interactive behaviour data was obtained from the observation of seven first-born infants. Subjects were observed at home with their mothers at monthly intervals for 5 months. The study began with four infants 4–5 months of age, but the family of one of the subjects (male) left the area unexpectedly during the second month of the study. Observation of another four infants began at 8–9.5 months, and the 5-month observation period was completed in each case. Two younger and two older infants were female, and the remaining three infants were male. Each family was residing in Amherst, Massachusetts, at the time of the study, each was white Caucasian, and its members were native U.S. citizens. The parents of subjects were solicited through the mail on the basis of the Amherst birth records, and final arrangements were made by phone. The time of observation was arranged at the convenience of the family and according to the infant's sleeping–waking schedule. Families were informed that the infant's communicative behaviour and his play were being observed.

1.1 Procedure

Mothers were asked to follow their normal routine about the house and with the infant. Social-interactive behaviour of both infant and mother was recorded in a special notational system by the otherwise passive observer (author). When the child approached the observer, the observer responded minimally and recorded the sequence. Ongoing activity, for example nappy-changing, was also noted. Table 3.1 presents a list of notational symbols, and a representative data sheet appears in Table 3.2 (see pp. 52, 53).

The joint satisfaction of two criteria determined an instance of social interaction for recording purposes: (1) activity by two people; (2) at least one participant orients at least partially toward the other. Sequences of interaction were considered terminated when either of the two above criteria was no longer being met. However, instances in which one participant remained oriented toward the other were noted, for example mother disappears and child looks in direction of exit. Normally observation was terminated after an hour. If the infant was drowsy the observer remained present until a minimum of 45 sequences had been recorded. Prolonged observation was necessary in three out of 35 sessions.

The Uzgiris and Hunt (1966) scales for 'Means for Achieving Desired Events' and 'The Development of Causality' were administered by the author, but only after the observation session. Thus the test results did not affect the observations. Language produced during the session and maternal reports of language heard outside the session were recorded. Language output was rare during sessions.

Due to limited resources one observer recorded all sessions. In view of the lack of reliability assessment at this phase, the study must be considered exploratory. However, as will be shown later, other authors report supporting findings.

1.2 Scoring

The behaviour record was scored immediately after each observation session. The child's behaviour in each sequence of interaction was coded. The scoring categories chosen were based upon the orientation and complexity of activity.

Two orientation categories were used: *single orientation*, toward person *or* object,

TABLE 3.1   Notation symbols for social-interactive behaviour

Referent	Symbol
Participants	
participants in interaction	a, b, c, etc.
Objects	
object	ob
objects (alternative to *ob*)	bottle, car, etc.
object of action or glance unclear	x
Actions	
looks at	O
smiles	S
laughs	L
touches	T
holds	H
reaches	R
pulls	P
points	N
approaches	A
recedes	D
gives	G
takes, receives	C
frets, cries	F
vocalizes	V
pulls self up on	U
global, diffuse activity	Z
all other actions*	(written out as necessary)
Sequence	
sequential behaviours	(A)—(B)
simultaneous behaviours	(A)·(B)
Context	
ongoing behaviours, noted separately	nappy-changing, feeding, etc.

*In some cases in which subjects were becoming capable of increasingly complex behaviour, a more global notation was employed, for example *mother demonstrates act* (stacking rings on pole)—*child watches act—child reproduces act.*

TABLE 3.2   Consecutive sequences observed for subject MM at 9·5 months

Sequences	Context Notes
	m = mother
	c = child
	s = observer
1. mV·Oc—cSm—mVc—mSc	(in living room; m on
2. mOc—cOm	couch; c on floor; s in chair)
3. mA·Oc—cOm—mV·Oc—cV·0m	(m off couch)
4. cOs—sOc	
5. cOs—sOc	
6. cOs—sOc	
7. cAm—cTm—cPm—mOc—m(Lift)c—mVc—cV·S·Om	
8. m(Kiss)c—cV·Om	
9. m(Roll)ball c—cH ball—cOm—mV·Oc—cOm—	(m and c at opposite
mV·Oc—cOm—mO·Vc—c(Roll)ball	ends of room; m saying,
	'Roll the ball, (etc.)')
10. cOm—mS·Vc—cSm—cV	
11. cH ball (toward)m—mO·V·Sc—cH ball	
(toward)m—mO·Vc—cZ·O·Vm	

Note Notational symbols in Table 3·1.

and *co-ordinated person–object orientation*. In a single person-oriented exchange, the child focuses only on the person and treats her socially, for example by directing gesture, eye contact, and/or vocalization to the adult. In a single object-oriented interaction, the child directs his behaviour toward an object external to both child and adult. While a social context is present in object-oriented interactions, no obvious social bidding occurs. Thus the adult serves simply as the location or occasion of the child's activity, rather than as a social partner. In contrast, co-ordinated person–object interaction combines behaviour directed toward person and object.

The simple–complex distinction was made within the single-orientation category. This distinction was intended to reflect how visible the child's intentions were. Piaget (1963, 1971) makes the same distinction in the physical realm between unitary actions applied to an external object (secondary circular schemata) and the combination of such actions which permits the appearance of a distinguishable means–ends relation. In the second case the child demonstrates a clear means–ends relation by inserting acts (for example obstacle removal) designed to further goal-attainment, between initial action and achievement (or lack thereof) of the desired result (Piaget, 1963). In the scoring of social interactions, sequences which involved a series of similarly oriented discrete behaviours were likewise thought to be better reflections of clear goal-directed efforts than were mere unitary action schemes.

Theoretically the complex single-orientation category could include instances in which the child actually used a material intermediary, for example a stick, to obtain a result or another object. It will be recalled that one of the primary objectives of the analysis was to determine whether the child would set up an instrumental relation between two objects before he integrated a person and an object in the same manner.

A description and some examples are presented below for the social interactive scoring categories.

Simple single-orientation (a) *Simple person-oriented acts.* These sequences involve one or two types of behaviour directed to a person. Examples: (1) child looks or smiles at adult; (2) adult looks at and vocalizes to child—child smiles at adult. These exchanges can be repeated several times in succession.

(b) *Simple object-oriented acts.* The child manipulates or turns his attention to an external object. Another person is involved only incidentally. Behaviour clusters are limited to unitary, largely repetitive acts, for example beating, mouthing. Example: adult holds object over child's cot—child beats at object without making direct social contact with adult—adult continues to dangle object, etc.

Complex single-orientation (a) *Complex person-oriented acts.* These include approaches or responses to another person involving a combination of different behaviours directed to that person. Examples: (1) child looks, smiles at adult— touches, tugs at adult clothing—adult lifts child; (2) adult vocalizes to, touches child—child looks, vocalizes, and reaches out toward adult—adult touches, shakes child; (3) reciprocal imitation.

(b) *Complex object-oriented acts.* Different discrete behaviours are combined and directed exclusively toward an external object. The child does not direct his attention to the adult, nor does he clearly solicit the adult's assistance if he needs it. Examples: (1) child attempts to pull object away from adult's lap—adult holds object on lap— child continues to pull, twist object—adult removes object; (2) adult gives child box and lid—child takes objects without acknowledging adult—child puts lid on box.

Co-ordinated person–object orientation The child marks his objective regarding the object, and approaches the person involved socially. Examples: (1) child looks up, touches adult's arm—adult acknowledges child—child reaches toward object in adult's lap: (2) child holds jar toward adult—looks at adult and vocalizes—adult takes jar from child, vocalizes to child; (3) adult jangles bell in front of child—child reaches toward bell, laughs at adult, touches adult's arm—adult jangles bell; (4) child vocalizes to adult, reaches toward chair—adult places child in chair.

It should be noted that some of the surface features of the more sophisticated complex person-oriented exchanges observed overlapped with those of the co-ordinated-orientation category. Consider, for instance, the child who approached the adult, looked up, reached and tugged at the adult's arms. Some of the features are consistent with both the co-ordinated and the complex-person categories. To some extent the child marked his objective and how the other person was to help accomplish it. However, the approach and message behaviours were continuous, and the constituents of the act were less differentiated than they would have to have been if an external object were involved. Thus, sequences of this sort were considered to lack the requisite features of co-ordinated interactions, and were readily categorized as complex single (person) interactions.

In summary, observations were categorized in terms of the orientation and integration of the behaviours involved; for the single-orientation categories the variety of actions was also a factor. Length of sequence was not a variable. Further, although various forms of locomotion added approach behaviours to the child's repertoire, this had no effect on the social-interactive trends recorded. A separate analysis of non-locomotive sequences revealed the same development trends as were found in the entire pool of interactions for all subjects (the lowest number of non-locomotive sequences in any one session was 32). The results for locomotive and non-locomotive sequences are combined below.

The author and an independent rater scored seven consecutive sequences from the middle of each session for three subjects, spanning the entire age range observed. Inter-rate agreement for these 105 sequences was 98 per cent. This ensures the reliability of the scoring of the total data, although it of course does not bear on the reliability of the original recording.

1.3 Analysis of the Data

The mean frequency of interactive sequences per session was 64·1 for the entire sample (range, individual means = 52·6–74·8; range, individual sessions (N = 35) =. 45–113). The frequency of interaction did not correlate with time for any subject.

The proportion of sequences in each category was computed for each session, based on the total number of sequences of interaction for that session. The data presented below contain trends in these proportions for each subject. A combined index of mother–child and observer–child interactions was used in the analysis since similar trends were found in both sets of data.

Categorized sequences accounted for an average of 79 per cent of the sequences recorded in a session (s.d. = 10·57). For all subjects but one there was no trend with age in the proportion of categorized/uncategorized sequences. The exceptional case (JF) resulted from a gradual build-up of rituals (see below) which accounted for the consistent but small decrease in categorized sequences. A more pervasive circumstantial effect involved an inflated proportion of simple person-oriented interactions at the outset of each session. At this time subjects repeatedly studied the observer and then the mother, as if to compare them. However, since this effect appeared in all five sessions, it should not have affected the trend in any of the proportions. It merely made the proportions in the remaining categories smaller than might otherwise have been the case. No other observer or environmental effects were found.

Sequences which were noted but left unscored include those in which the orientation of the infant's activity was not clear (for example flailing arms and legs upon being tickled by adult), sequences in which the infant's activity and/or attention was directed elsewhere entirely while the mother made social contact, and those sequences in which fretting was the child's only activity. For the present it is not clear how some of the more diffuse sequences were related to the categories used, i.e. whether they involved the same behaviours unoriented or different behaviours entirely. Additional unscorable sequences include sequences in which both the person- and object-orientations were present, but in which (1) the adult clearly elicited each focus in succession (for example adult dangles object before child's face, then adult removes object and looks into child's face) or (2) the relation between the two foci was otherwise uncertain (for example child manipulates object, suddenly looks up at adult across the room, returns to manipulating object, etc.). A final unscored group of sequences comprises rituals (for example 'peekaboo'), i.e. reciprocal exchanges built up over time by adult and child in which there was a fixed set and order of actions. These sequences often involved a training element and/or a reliance on the mother's stereotyped behaviours. For a variety of reasons it was decided that these sequences would ultimately require a different kind of analysis.

2. Results and Discussion

The main finding was a three-step sequence of social-interactive behaviour during the pre-verbal period. First, the subjects' repertoire was dominated by unitary, repetitive actions directed toward a person or toward an object, with no clear attempt to manipulate the environment. Next to appear were differentiated actions directed toward a person or object. Last, integrated person–object activity emerged. With this final step the child began explicitly to focus his pragmatic pursuits on other people.

Figure 3.1 presents graphs of the proportions of the social interactive categories, plotted over the five sessions, for each infant. The data from session 4 were not plotted for AF of the older group, since this infant was recovering from illness at the time and was cranky and tired. The results of the Uzgiris–Hunt assessments of means–ends and causal activity are indicated in the graphs in Figure 3.1, in Piagetian (1963, 1971) sub-stages (see pp. 58, 59).

The combined graphs indicate that simple single-orientation sequences developed before the age at which the youngest children were studied in this investigation. The time of onset for complex single-orientation sequences ranged from 4·5 months (LF) to 7 months (CF). The first signs of co-ordinated-orientation interaction were exhibited by infants between 8 and 10 months.

The peak or marked rise in each category occurred in the same order in the present sample. In the younger group the simple single-orientation sequences reached their peak between 4·5 and 7 months. In the older group MM and JF showed slightly lower proportions at initial encounter (8·5 and 9·5 months respectively), and AF and JM appear to have been even further beyond the category peak at 9 and 9·75 months. In the entire sample the complex single-orientation sequences rose markedly between 7·75 and 10·5 months. For AF and JM (older group) the proportion of these interactions may already have reached peak level (20–26 per cent) by the first session. It should be noted that in the session not plotted for AF, the trends in simple and complex single-oriented activity were reversed. Simple single interactions increased dramatically, while complex single sequences decreased. The inflated proportion of simple single-orientation interaction was due almost entirely to an increase in simple bids directed to the mother, accounting for 60 per cent of all sequences recorded. These sequences might have indicated the presence of heightened attachment behaviour, as has been noted to occur in infants in times of illness and stress (Ainsworth, 1969).

The younger subjects showed only a negligible incidence (2–5 per cent) of co-ordinated-orientation interactions by the final observation session. However, each older subject manifested a steady increase in this behaviour across the five sessions. Again, AF showed a slight dip in this trend during the session in which she was ill. JF and MM displayed a more rapid increase in co-ordinated sequences after 12·25 and 11·75 months respectively. The two consistently more advanced infants, AF and JM, showed actual dominance of the category (*circa* 40 per cent) over the others by 13 months. All four older subjects produced their first words, sparsely, during this period.

Where comparable, the timing of the marked rise of one category with the emergence of another also appeared consistent across the sample. The emergence of complex single-orientation interactions co-occurred with or immediately followed the peak in simple single-orientation sequences (see younger group). Co-ordinated sequences emerged during or after the marked rise in complex single-orientation interactions. Since proportions are being used, these trends are not entirely independent. However, it will be recalled that (1) there were three categories into which the behaviour could be scored, and (2) these three categories were not exhaustive of the total number of sequences recorded (see above, 1.3 Analysis of the data). Therefore, variations in one category will not necessarily lead to compensatory variations in another particular category.

Finally, the trends in the three types of social interactions were confirmed by a special task administered to the subjects by the observer. The child's interest in a novel object was elicited while the child was seated. The object was then abruptly withdrawn out of the child's reach and was held back away from the tester's head, in the child's visual field. This procedure was repeated at least five times per session. Subjects' responses to the removal of the object were scored into categories slightly more differentiated than those applied to the naturalistic data. For every subject the dominant response score correlated with the peak or marked increase in the comparable category in the observational data. There were no reversals in the order of appearance of the categories in the test data.

Aspects of the present sequence are suggested elsewhere in the social-interactive literature. Independently of this investigation, Bates, Camaioni, and Volterra (1973) have identified a pre-language sequence in which the child keeps his social and non-social interactive schemes separate, before using either set in service of the other. These authors base their findings on longitudinal video-tape records of three Italian children. More recently Bates, Benigni, Bretherton, Camaioni, and Volterra (in press)

58

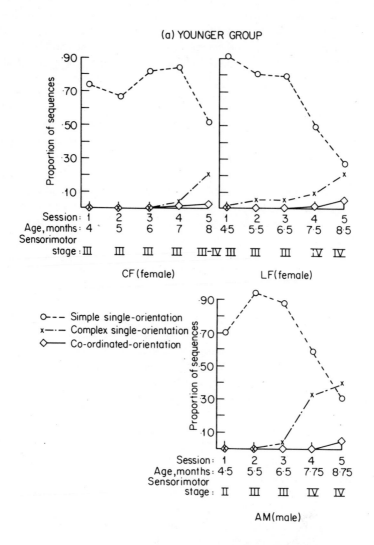

FIGURE 3.1. Proportion of sequences observed in individual social-interactive categories

(b) OLDER GROUP

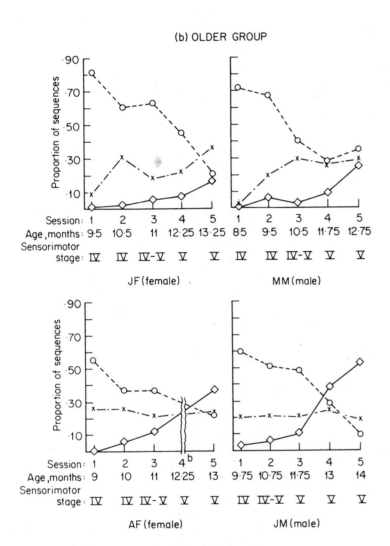

^bData from AF session 4 are omitted: see p. 56.

based on total number of sequences observed

and Snyder (1975) have replicated the sequence on a much larger sample of American and Italian children. In addition, Blount (1971, p. 44) and Sander (1969, p. 194) report data which suggest the performance of dichotomized focal exchanges in the last quarter of the first year, followed by an expressed interest in social interaction *per se*, as well as by more fully integrated social-interactive behaviour.

2.1 Object–Object Instrumentation and Person–Object Integration

In the present investigation analogous developments in social-interactive behaviour and the manipulation of physical objects occurred in the same order, and at the same time. Specification of the relations between these sequences is clearly premature at present. However, the observed regularities, particularly in ordinality, suggest that the child's cognitive development may be·important in the child's organization of communicative means, at least in the pre-verbal period.

Simple single-orientation social interactions reached their peak when the infants were engaging in simple repetitive schemes with physical objects alone (sensorimotor stage II). These 'secondary circular reactions' and 'procedures to make interesting inputs last' (Piaget, 1963) involved actions such as hitting or pulling at objects, to produce noise, regular movement, etc. As already noted, social interaction involved either simple social contact with the adult or behaviour directed exclusively toward an object on or around the adult. Thus, if the caretaker held a toy over the infant, the infant would engage himself with the object alone, for example beating it, or with the adult alone, for example back-and-forth vocalization. In either of these instances the infant repeated an effect by repeating the action associated with it. What further connection, if any, the child might have seen or intended between his action, the adult, and the object, was not clear from his behaviour.

The peak of complex single-orientation interaction occurred when the infants were demonstrating simple goal-directed behaviour with respect to physical objects (sensorimotor stage IV). In the course of reaching for an object, the child might push aside an intervening obstacle, for example a pillow. However, at this point the child probably would not attempt to use the intervening object as a tool in his efforts to reach the more distant source. The child's social interactions remained dichotomized during this period, but the approach to persons and to objects in social contexts became more differentiated. Thus, in person-oriented interaction the child would combine various behaviours, for example tugging at adult clothing, reaching up to the adult's face and shoulders, in order to obtain or maintain social contact. Although not considered in the present analysis, elaborate play rituals between mother and child appeared during this period : a specific bid became the cue for a specific response or sequence of exchanges, rather than for social contact in general. In the child's object-oriented interactions for means–ends structure was more apparent. After trying a direct approach, such as pulling an object from the adult's hand, the child's object-oriented interactions the means–ends structure was more apparent adult's hand from the object. If the child met with resistance from the adult he might persist by pulling at the object with his mouth, adjusting his grasp, etc. What was striking about these exchanges was that in spite of the child's propensity to make social entreaties, no social contact was apparent, and the child would not look at any part of the adult's body other than those parts impeding the action. This peculiar dichotomy becomes more comprehensible in the light of the subjects' contemporaneous manipulations with physical objects. In solitary object manipulations, as in object-oriented social interactions, the child himself had to act directly upon any objects he wanted. It seems that the subjects had not yet learned to set in motion either instruments or agents to help them attain their goals.

It was when subjects began to subordinate the use of one (physical) object to actually manoeuvring a second (stage V) that they showed a co-ordination of object pursuit and social focus in their interpersonal exchanges. Bates *et al.* (1973), Bates *et al.* (in press), and Synder (1975) report the same correspondence. In the present sample (extending to 14 months) beginning instrumental activity involved use of a string or support (i.e. means attached to the goal–object), and first attempts to use an adjacent stick, to retrieve an object. In an analogous fashion the child would now use an adult to obtain something, in his social interactions. The child could accomplish this by signalling the adult, for example by looking, touching, vocalizing, etc., and then by pointing out the goal–object or attempting the manoeuvre the child wanted done, for example obtaining the object, twisting off a lid. In both the social and the physical manoeuvre, the child used one means (manoeuvring a stick, signalling an adult) which produced an effect (the approach of the object, or the action of the adult), leading the child to his goal.

Hence the subjects made analogous and contemporaneous progress toward instrumental co-ordination in social and physical contexts at this stage. However the children also differentiated physical and social instrumental relations to some extent. While manoeuvres with physical objects entailed direct manipulation of the intermediary at one year, most co-ordinated-orientation interactions were not direct at this time. When subjects began to invoke adult aid in manoeuvring objects, they mostly cued the adult without materially manipulating her. Some interesting transitional interactions were noted in this regard. Just before showing a decisive increase in integrated person–object behaviour, subjects occasionally used part of the adult as an instrument, as when the child pushed the adult's hand toward an object out of the child's reach. Piaget (1971, pp. 295–296) has identified the same kind of behaviour in children approaching stage V. Additional transitional interactions lacking marked social contact approximated social bidding more closely when the child brought the object to the adult's hand, rather than bringing the adult's hand to the object (Piaget, 1971, pp. 311–312).

Generally, then, it seems that the subjects' social-interactive manoeuvres developed not only toward the elaboration of instrumental relationships, but also toward the differentiation of another person as an agent in those relationships. However, without independent assessment of the child's intentions in these situations, the degree to which the child attributed volition to the adult remains unclear (Bates *et al.*, 1973, p. 26). Nevertheless, it seems reasonable to speculate that while an instrumental basis evolves for social transactions, the child eventually distinguishes communication from manipulation, certainly by the time he begins to talk.

2.2 Pre-language Communicative Patterns and Speech Onset

Halliday (1971, p. 143) and Bruner (1975) suggest that mastery of a general social-regulatory function is an essential step in language development. The attempt to trace the development of person—object integration in this study represents an effort to find an exemplar of this basic function.

At all three levels of interaction distinguished, the infant exerted a measure of control over his caretaker(s). It is the extent to which the child marked his intentions in these interactions which changed. In the first phase, when unitary (single-orientation) actions prevailed, the caretaker made (relatively) reliable adjustments to the infant by means of mutual expectancy patterns based on these simple infant behaviours (Bruner, 1968, p. 57; Richards, 1974, p. 90; Lewis and Goldberg, 1969; Piaget, 1971, p. 286). Next, when the child had moved beyond merely repeating efficacious behaviours, he adjusted and elaborated his behaviour around a particular goal, thereby lending clarity to his intentions (Bell and Ainsworth, 1972, p. 1185; Ainsworth, 1969, p. 193). In the socially focused goal-directed activity which followed the child did not always make his wishes clear. However, the subjects had begun to specify what was expected of the social environment in which they were acting, even if that expectation was limited to having the adult attend to some display. The children might thus have been showing an intent to communicate, apart from an intent simply to accomplish something. This possibility was suggested also by the beginning divergence noted above between direct and indirect manipulation in social-instrumental and physical-instrumental activity. Perhaps in a preliminary way the children showing person—object co-ordination were demonstrating a higher-order intention in which they referred to or encoded their more pragmatic intentions, although not necessarily in words.

While one may argue on an intuitive basis that starting to talk to other people requires some form of intentional communication, one is still left with the problem of how specific sensorimotor developments are related to the onset of language. Cross-sectional pilot observations of six institutionalized infants 5—19 months (with no reported medical complications) suggest caution in drawing conclusions about sensorimotor contributions to language.

The infant—caretaker ratio in the New York institution was approximately 3:1. On a given day each child was in contact with four adults, one of whom was a full-time staff member and permanently assigned to a particular group of infants. The methods used in observing the children were identical to those employed in the home-reared study, save that the Uzgiris—Hunt (1966) scales were not administered to the institutionalized group.

The trends in the three social-interactive categories were the same as those found for the home-reared infants. The correlation between these trends and age was also the same for both samples. However, while the home-reared subjects produced a few words around the time of the marked increment in co-ordinated-orientation interaction, the institutionalized infants displayed no sign of language production until 6 months later, at 18 months. The retardation of language, particularly production, in institutionalized infants has been reported by other investigators (Provence and Lipton, 1963, p. 91; Ainsworth, 1966, p. 162).

For some reason(s) beyond the failure to develop some kind of communication, these children did not begin to talk when most children begin to talk. Unfortunately the insufficiency for language onset of some form of pre-verbal communicative capacity leaves a list of possible causes of language retardation from which it is not easy to select on the basis of existing knowledge. The possible factors include quantitatively deficient social and linguistic input; qualitative abnormalities in the interactive situation, for example lack of response to infant non-crying output, general lack of consistent and contingent response; possibly deficient cognitive-symbolic functioning (Ainsworth, 1966; Provence and Lipton, 1963, pp. 92–100). It is noteworthy, nonetheless, that other investigators studying home-reared children have emphasized that the pre-verbal child is functionally primed for language by elaborative rituals between itself and the caretaker (Bruner, 1975) or simply by repeated exchanges with at least one central interpreting figure (Blount, 1971; Main, 1974; Ryan, 1974). As these exchanges develop, a network of meanings and conventions for their expression evolve. In institutions the rotating staff, the high infant–caretaker ratio, and the consistently enforced schedule of feeding, napping, etc., all reduce the tendency to establish elaborate signal systems.

Whatever the precise set of language-retardation factors may be, these did not appear to differentially affect development of person–object integration in the pre-language social interaction of the institution and home-reared subjects. Perhaps the development of this communicative pattern requires only a minimum of input from the environment, or input somewhat different from that required for language. If there was a disturbance in other aspects of cognitive development in the institutionalized subjects, this also did not affect the developmental course of this kind of communication. Studies which have identified cognitive deficiencies among institutionalized children have pointed mostly to difficulties in representational rather than sensorimotor development (Paraskevopoulos and Hunt, 1971; Ainsworth, 1966). The correlation between the social-interactive sequence and other trends in cognitive development found among the home-reared infants in this study suggests that representational capacity is not necessary for the construction of a basic communicative framework. However, the ability to represent may be necessary for the insertion of words into the child's communicative schemes (Bates *et al.*, 1973; Sinclair, 1971). Finally, other authors have observed a social precocity among institutional infants (Bridges, 1933, p. 37; Robertson and Robertson, 1971, p. 290), despite the cognitive, linguistic, and social-input deficiencies often cited. These observations converge with the present findings in attesting to the normally timed development of some form of communicative ability in institutionalized infants.

3. Summary and Conclusion

Both home-reared and institutionalized infants developed person-oriented and object-oriented social-interactive patterns separately, before combining them into socially focused expressions about a given state of affairs. This development consisted of a three-step sequence which appears to be related to other pre-language cognitive acquisitions involving instrumental co-ordination.

Further empirical study and theoretical development must decide what form the relationship(s) between these social-interactive and physical-manipulative developments take. In particular, the present findings do not address the relationship between communication and physical cognition once these processes become materially different, i.e. once the child's communication is largely linguistic. The correspondences found in the present study do suggest that an instrumental basis of some sort evolves for pre-verbal social transactions. This basis may be such that (1) experience in one domain directly influences experience in the other or (2) performance in either domain is mediated at least in part by common underlying schemes. The first possibility would require strict temporal relationships between the two trends, although this would not provide sufficient grounds for eliminating the second alternative. The existence of a mediated connection between the two kinds of performance would require ordinal, but not temporal, correspondence, as suggested by the findings of other authors studying early parallels between social developments and physical cognition (Bell, 1970; Gouin-Decarie, 1965). Intuitively a temporal correlation does not seem likely to occur, especially in the same direction, across all cases. There may be occurrences of physical disability (for example, thalidomide children) extreme enough to make complicated manoeuvres with inanimate objects impossible or very difficult. That the object manipulations can develop without the corresponding social manoeuvres can probably be shown in the development of autistic children. The author has already observed one such child extensively in this regard.

The present study provides other, albeit partial, evidence which suggests the presence of a complex relationship between the physical and social trends. While tool use and co-ordinated person–object social manoeuvres at first converge on some basic organizational points, they ultimately diverge as well. It was suggested that the differentiation of communication and manipulation may be mediated in part by the child's evolving notion of external agency. It is possible that some of the groundwork is laid for the separation when the very young, presumably pre-instrumental, infant begins to reserve a special repertoire of individual behaviours for persons (Ainsworth, 1969; Bruner, 1968; Trevarthen, 1974). Perhaps more generalized symptoms of a differentiation could be traced from there, leading up to the structural difference established when the child attributes external agency to persons. It is thus at the intersection of person–object differentiation and instrumental co-ordination that intentional communication may rise.

The pilot study of institutionalized infants indicates that the form of sensorimotor communication studied in the present investigation was able to develop at the same rate in both home and institution, despite the variation between the two settings. However, the findings also indicated that this development was not sufficient for the onset of verbal communication. It was projected that certain kinds of pre-verbal communication identified among home-reared infants by other authors occurred very little, if at all, in the institution. The absence of these exchanges might have produced some of the difficulty the institutionalized children were having with language acquisition. Efforts to examine different facets of pre-verbal communication and cognition in different settings might further elucidate the relation between communication before language and communication with language.

Acknowledgements

The present text was completed while the author held a pre-doctoral traineeship (2T01 HD00153–06A1) in developmental psychology at the University of California, Berkeley. The research reported formed part of a bachelor's thesis completed at Hampshire College, April 1973. The author thanks the following people for advice and comments on the manuscript during its various stages of preparation: Neil Stillings and James Koplin, Hampshire College; Michael Cole and Sylvia Scribner, The Rockefeller University; Susan Goldberg, Brandeis University; Jonas Langer and Mary Main, University of California, Berkeley.

References

Ainsworth, M.D.S. (1966), Reversible and irreversible effects of maternal deprivation on intellectual development. In Harvey, O.J. (ed.), *Experience, Structure and Adaptability*, New York: Springer Publishing Co.

Ainsworth, M.D.S. (1969), Object relations, dependency, and attachment: a theoretical review of the infant–mother relationship, *Child Development*, 40, 969–1025.

Bates, E., Camaioni, L., and Volterra, V. (1973), The acquisition of performatives prior to speech. Technical Report no. 129, Consiglio Nazionale delle Ricerche, Rome.

Bates, E., Benigni, L., Bretherton, I., Camaioni, L., and Volterra, V. (in press), From gesture to first word: on cognitive and social prerequisites. In Lewis M., and Rosenblum, L.(eds), *Origins of Behavior: Communication and Language*. New York: Wiley.

Bell, Sylvia (1970), The development of the concept of object as related to infant–mother attachment, *Child Development*, 41, 292–311.

Bell, Sylvia, and Ainsworth, M.D.S. (1972), Infant crying and maternal responsiveness, *Child Development*, 43, 1171–1190.

Blount, B. (1971), Socialization and pre-linguistic development among the Luo of Kenya, *Southwestern Journal of Anthropology*, 27, 41–50.

Bowerman, M. (1974), Learning the structure of causative verbs: a study in the relationship of cognitive, semantic, and syntactic development. In Clark, E. (ed.), *Papers and Reports on Child Language Development*, no. 8., Stanford University Committee on Linguistics.

Bridges, K. (1933), A study of social development in early infancy, *Child Development*, 4, 36–49.

Brown, R. (1973), *A First Language: the Early Stages*. Cambridge, Mass.: Harvard University Press; London: Allen & Unwin.

Bruner, J. S. (1968), *Processes of Cognitive Growth: Infancy*, Worcester, Mass.: Clark University Press.

Bruner, J. S. (1975), The ontogenesis of speech acts, *Journal of Child Language*, 2, 1–19.

Carter, A.L. (1974), The development of communication in the sensorimotor period: a case study. Unpublished doctoral dissertation, University of California, Berkeley.

Dore, J. (1974), *The Development of Speech Acts*. The Hague: Mouton.

Duncker, K. (1945), On problem-solving, *Psychology Monographs*, 58.

Gouin-Decarie, T. (1965), *Intelligence and Affectivity in Early Childhood*, New York: International Universities Press.

Halliday, M.A.K. (1971), Language structure and language function. In Lyons, J. (ed.), *New Horizons in Linguistics*, Harmondsworth: Penguin Books.

Ingram, D. (1971), Transitivity in child language, *Language*, 47, 888–910.

Lewis, M., and Goldberg, S. (1969), Perceptual-cognitive development in infancy: a generalized expectancy model as a function of the mother–child interaction, *Merrill-Palmer Quarterly*, 15, 81–101.

Main, M. (1974), personal communication.

Paraskevopoulos, J., and Hunt, J. McV. (1971), Object construction and imitation under differing conditions of rearing, *Journal of Genetic Psychology*, 119, 301–321.

Piaget, J. (1963), *The Origins of Intelligence in the Child*, New York: W.W. Norton & Co.

Piaget, J. (1971), *The Construction of Reality in the Child*, New York: Ballantine Books.

Provence, S., and Lipton, R. (1963), *Infants in Institutions*, New York: International Universities Press.

Richards, M. P. M. (1974), First steps in becoming social. In Richards, M. P. M. (ed.), *The Integration of a Child into a Social World*, Cambridge: Cambridge University Press.

Robertson, J., and Robertson, J. (1971), Young children in brief separation: a fresh look. In Eissler, R. S. *et al.* (eds), *The Psychoanalytic Study of the Child*, vol. 26, London: The Hogarth Press.

Ryan, J. (1974), Early language development: towards a communicational analysis. In Richards, M. P. M. (ed.), *The Integration of a Child into a Social World*. Cambridge: Cambridge University Press.

Sander, L. W. (1969), The longitudinal course of early mother–child interaction; cross-case comparison in a sample of mother–child pairs. In Foss, B. M. (ed.), *Determinants of Infant Behaviour*, IV, London: Methuen.

Sinclair, H. (1971), Sensorimotor action patterns as a condition for the acquisition of syntax. In Huxley, R., and Ingram, E. (eds), *Language Acquisition, Models and Methods*. New York: Academic Press.

Sinclair, H., and Bronckart, J. (1972), S.V.O., a linguistic universal? A study in developmental psycholinguistics, *Journal of Experimental Child Psychology*, 14, 329–348.

Snyder, L. S. (1975), Pragmatics in language disabled children: their prelinguistic and early verbal performatives and presuppositions. Unpublished doctoral thesis, University of Colorado, Boulder.

Trevarthen, C. (1974), Infant responses to objects and persons. Paper presented at the Spring Meeting of the British Psychological Society, Bangor.

Uzgiris, I., and Hunt, J. McV. (1966), An instrument for assessing infant psychological development. Unpublished manuscript, University of Illinois.

Werner, H. (1948), *Comparative Psychology of Mental Development*, New York: International Universities Press.

Werner, H., and Kaplan, B. (1963), *Symbol Formation*, New York: Wiley.

4

THE SOURCES OF CHILDREN'S EARLY MEANINGS

Derek Edwards

Studies of meanings in early child language, especially those coming out of the recent growth of 'developmental psycholinguistics', have tended to be dominated by the linguistics of adult grammar. The impression is gained that what we are studying is a particular model of the adult linguistic system in the making. Language development is studied as the 'acquisition' of a formal linguistic system rather than as an integral part of the child's growing personal, cognitive, and social competence. Another related characteristic of such studies has been a rather casual use of situational contexts (with the possible exception of Bloom, 1973) in determining the meanings of children's utterances. Meanings have tended to be determined for each token utterance separately according to the observer's perception of its immediate situational context. The nature of the situational context of any single utterance is apparently assumed to be uncontroversial and determinate, so that the problem of deciding what particular aspects of the context, as perceived by the child, are crucial to the child's intended meaning, is ignored. What can easily happen in the analysis of child language is that the child's words are interpreted in terms of the observer's own semantic system, and this is then checked against the immediate situational context for confirmation. So if a child says *pull* when pulling a door open he is credited with the possession of a 'verb' or 'action word' with a meaning close to its adult counterpart. This chapter offers a cognitive and social-psychological perspective for the study of early meanings, and proposes that situational 'contexts', instead of being casually exploited aids in the analysis of particular utterances, should be the central focus of study as part of the total act of communication.

The meanings of a child's first one- and two-word utterances evidently derive from three sources. These are first, the child's understanding of how the physical world of objects, space, and persons is structured and operates (Edwards, 1973), second, the child's pre-linguistic and concurrent social relationships, and third, arising out of the first two, the function of reference itself—the conventionalized semiotic relation between sign and referent. Cognitive and social-relational competence overlap to the extent that the child's involvement in social relationships requires cognition—of what persons are, what they can do, of oneself as a person, and of the general world of persons, objects, space, and time within which the social relationships take place. Similarly the child's cognitions of the immediate physical world include some understanding of the social world—of who particular persons are, what kinds of actions they might be requested to perform, and so on. All three of these proposed sources of early meanings are considered to be pre-linguistic and not even uniquely human, to operate in and beyond infancy as areas of competence to which the child's comprehension and use of linguistically mediated meanings is assimilated.

All utterances derive from all three sources; it is merely a convenience for the purposes of conceptualization and exposition that the sources of meanings are divided here into a set of three. Even those utterances spoken in monologues (Piaget, 1926; Weir, 1962) are ones whose form and meaning are learned in and are derived from social interaction. This triple complexity may be illustrated by examining what is generally considered the semantically most simple and elementary form of utterance, the naming of objects. The importance of 'reference' here is obvious, but object-making also has a social-relational and cognitive stucture which underlie the nature of reference itself. Object-naming typically occurs in the context of what Brown (1956) called 'the original word game', in which child and caretaker (usually mother) supply each other with names for pointed-at objects and pictures, or point out things named by the other. Typically the 'game' is linguistically mediated by much more than mere object names; it is full of questions and answers, locative and deictic expressions life 'what's that?', 'there it is', 'that's a kangaroo', 'it's a box', 'it's over there', and so on. Moreover these expressions are integrated into a context of sequenced looks and gestures which are crucial to their function in the total communication setting. Consider the following sequences from separate data corpuses from two unrelated children we may call 'Alice' (A) and 'Mark' (Mk). 'M' is Mark's mother, 'S' (Sheila) is Alice's caretaker during daytimes when her parents are at work.

LANGUAGE		CONTEXT
Mark, 20 months		
		M and Mk sitting together looking at the pages of a picture book. M turns to picture of a bus.
(M: what's that?)		
	Mk: car	
		Mk stands up and walks away. M turns to picture of a biscuit and holds book up facing picture towards Mk.
(M: Mark. What's that?		Mk turns round and looks at picture.
	MK: [ʔəː]	
(M: biscuit)		
	Mk: [gɪ]	Mk looking up into M's face.
(M: biscuit)	⋮	

⋮ (several minutes of interaction)

Mk sitting on floor playing with toy blocks.

(M: Oh Mark, what's that?)

M pointing towards fly in window beyond and behind Mark.

Mark?)
What is it?)
What's that Mark?)

Mk looking up at M, then looking round behind him in the direction M is pointing.

(M: there it is)

Mk: [ʔə] Mk suddenly fixating and pointing towards the fly.

(M: see? right up there?)

M pointing to where the fly has now flown and landed higher up on the curtain. Mk has lost sight of it.

Mk looks round at M and then looks up towards where M is pointing.

Mk: [ʔəː] Mk seeing and pointing at fly.

Alice, 18 months, 3 weeks

A and S looking at picture book.

A: horse ↑ A pointing to picture of a goat.

horse ↑ A still pointing at goat, now looking up at S's face.

(S: no, no, that's not a horse)

A: cats ↑ A looking at the picture (goat).

cats ↑

(S: No.)

A: what's [æt]

(S: What is it?)

A: [ʔɪs æt]

(S: that's a goat. Alice say goat.)

Goat.)

S tapping goat with forefinger.

A: [ʔɪs æt] A looking and pointing at picture of
[ʔɪs æːt] cow (on the end of a row of
[s æt] pictures).

(S: oh you know the end one)

A: moo

(S: moo (Laughing). That's a cow)

⋮ (several minutes of interaction)

A and S looking at large circus picture
containing many animals.

A: monkey A pointing at monkey.
see monkey↑

(S: Yes, that's the
monkey.)
Where are the
penguins?)

(2 penguins are visible in the large
picture.)

Alice find the penguins.
Where are they?) A: [ʔIZ]·gone A looking at picture.
(S: (laughing): where's it
gone?)
Where's the penguins?)

A: see A suddenly pointing to one of the
penguins.
(S: Yes. There's one, two.) S pointing to the 2 penguins in turn.
A: [ʔəz] that A pointing to same penguin again
(S: The penguins. Two.
One two.) (S does not point.)
Where's the clown?)

A: see clown A looking (not pointing) directly
at clown.
(S: Where is the clown?)
5 seconds
Alice touch the clown.)

A: touch↑ clown↑
A looking at clown; no hand
movements.
(S: Touch the clown.)
7 seconds
Alice touch the clown.)

A: touch↑ clown.↑

(S: Where is the clown?)

A: see A brusquely prodding right forefinger
down on clown's face.

Mark clearly has some competence at the game even though in terms of word production he is virtually pre-linguistic. The naming of objects occurs in the context of a well organized pattern of social interaction in which child and mother are able to co-operate in what Bruner (1975) terms 'regulating joint activity and joint attention'. Mark is competent in the understanding and use of eye gaze, eye contact, and pointing with the forefinger, and knows what is required of him within the sequence of interaction—for example that he is to supply (or attempt to supply) a particular object label at a particular point in the interaction. Alice is able to play both roles, able also to solicit and direct S's attention and ask for object names. Moreover, the language used by M and S, and by Alice, embeds the object-labelling within an explicitly interactional ('what's that?', directed at the other person) and deictic-locative context. Alice's word *see* apparently functions not as a label for the process of visual perception, but rather as a deictic word like 'there', used in locating for the addressee the named object (cf. Gruber, 1967; Edwards, 1973).

The deictic-locative context of object-naming reflects part of the cognitive basis for the game. Objects, whether real or pictured, can be consistently labelled only if they can be perceived and recognized on different occasions as discrete entities, differentiated from and locatable within their physical environment. The game has two complementary versions. In object-naming the child supplies a name for a located object. In pointing at named objects he indicates their location (for a fuller discussion, see Edwards, 1973).

We shall now examine some aspects of early language deriving from the cognitive and social-relational sources of meanings, and look at a way of determining meanings from contexts which throws light on the meanings of so-called 'holophrases'.

1. Locatives and Action Words

Case-grammatical studies of meaning in early child language have identified a dozen or so kinds of semantic relationship that are apparently universal across a diverse variety of languages and cultures (Slobin, 1970, 1972; Brown, 1970, 1973). It has been argued elsewhere in some detail (Edwards, 1973) that these early meanings derive from particular Piagetian sensorimotor schemes which constitute cognitive constraints on the meanings acquired and expressed. The meanings of adult words are assimilated to the child's understanding of the contextual situation, event or relationship to which they refer. One important conception is of the nature of persons, who (including the child himself) are apparently perceived in two basic ways, both as physical objects, like any others having solidity, size, shape, and occupying positions in space, and also as agentive beings able to initiate their own actions (Piaget, 1954). The latter is a particularly important conceptual basis for the growth of competence in social communication. It underlies the child's knowledge that persons can be requested to do things for him, as well as engage in the whole range of social responsiveness and reciprocity.

The present discussion will concentrate on the problem of determining meanings from contexts, focusing on the distinction between words describing either actions and movements or changes in location. We shall use the concept 'verb' in a deep-structural 'notional' sense (cf. Lyons, 1966) to include words that describe actions, movements, states, and relations between objects. Thus the term includes many adult adjectives and locative prepositions as well as surface-structure verbs (cf. Chafe, 1970). It was proposed in an earlier paper (Edwards, 1973) that a study of meanings in early child language should look for a distinction between, on the one hand, verbs which describe actions or movements performed or undergone by persons and objects but specify no particular change of spatial position (for example the adult words *roll*, *walk*, *spin*), and, on the other hand, verbs which specify positions or changes in position of objects or persons but describe no particular kind of action or movement performed or undergone (for example *rise*, *enter*, (is) *inside*).

It is suggested by Greenfield and Smith (1976) in an analysis of two children's one-word speech that '*Down* said while jumping down could refer to the act of jumping or to its destination ... Action and resultant State are not differentiated'. This conclusion is supported by the fact that all of the children's early words describing 'action performed by agents' are locative words, typically adult prepositions such as *up* and *down*. But do these words confound action and positional change? Clearly if we look at each utterance of each word separately in terms of its situational context we should never be able to determine whether *down*, for example, refers to a particular change in location only, or to the whole action involved in, say, walking down stairs, or indeed for that matter any of a great many other more idiosyncratic meanings. However, it may be possible to look across the variety of contexts in which each word occurs with the assumption that the child's meaning, that is that aspect of each context which is described by the child's word, may emerge as the aspect that all of the various contexts have in common. Let us examine some contexts of *up* and *down* cited by Greenfield and Smith (1976) for the two children 'Matthew' and 'Nicky':

UTTERANCE	CONTEXT

(i) UP

	Matthew
up	reaching upwards
up...light	pointing to place on ceiling where light has been
	Nicky
up	going up step
up	reaching up to fan

(ii) DOWN

	Matthew
down	while getting down from his mother's lap
mommy...down	sitting in high chair calling mother to get him down
down	having just thrown something down
nana down	when he put the banana down on the table
(*down* also reported once to mean 'up')	

	Nicky
down	sitting down in Ring o' Roses game
down	going down steps
down	sitting down
down	when N pulled his train down

Although this cannot be an exhaustive list of uses of each word for each child, it would appear that generally the actions and movements performed are variable across contexts (sitting down, climbing down, throwing something down, etc.), but the directionality of change of spatial position is constant. Greenfield *et al.* state that 'the word *down* occur(s) thirteen times in six different situations relating to Nicky's movement up or down'. The occasionally interchangeable uses of *down* and *up* are found also in Bloom's daughter Allison (Bloom 1973, pp. 87 ff.). Nevertheless we still have for each child a constancy of direction of positional change (in the vertical plane) independent of the kind of action or movement involved. Thus for Matthew and Nicky, even in the absence of vocabulary for actual movements or actions, the cross-content data seems sufficiently coherent for us to include in the semantic description of *up* and *down* only the consistent directionality and not the actual action or movement performed, which would seem of no more direct semantic relevance than the rest of the situational context.

One problem with the cross-context abstraction of meaning used here is that the utterances cited from Nicky and Matthew occurred across a time period of several months, so that the possibility of developmental change in the children's usage of the words is obscured. Nevertheless the method does yield a coherent description of the words in terms of the child's own usage, and could be used more convincingly where appropriate data are available for single recording sessions or sessions close to each other in time. Also if there is such development it is not clearly linear. The same uses of words tend to recur both before and after other uses. However, the unlikely possibility always remains that the child may mean something different on every occasion he uses a particular word even within the same recording session. Situational contexts of single-word utterances are so ambiguous, and word meanings therefore so indeterminate, that if such a possibility were taken seriously it would render the understanding of children's one-word speech virtually impossible without making unwarranted tacit appeals to adult meanings. The method of abstracting meanings across contexts is valuable to the extent that it helps to reduce descriptions of complex situational contexts to semantic descriptions which are not only coherent but also constrained by consistencies in the child's actual usage of words, and which may therefore have some measure of psychological reality.

Indeed cross-context abstraction of meanings may yield data relevant to the determination of semantic universals in child speech. Although no claims can yet be made for universality, it is possible that the description of locative changes independently of action or movement is common across many different children. It is evident in much of my own data, as for example in the first few recorded utterances of *up* and *down* by Alice:

74

LANGUAGE	CONTEXT

Age 17 months, 3 weeks

A offering to S three Lego building bricks; one falls out of A's hand onto floor.

A: down

(S: Oh. All fall down.)

A: up Alice   A sitting in high-chair looking into S's face. A lifts feet up onto seat of chair.

A: down ↑   A still sitting in high-chair, looking into S's face, holding arms up towards S. (S fails to get A to say 'please' and lifts A out of chair.)

Age 18 months, 3 weeks
(S: What's that up there?)

S pointing to clock in picture, on wall above the cats S and A have just been talking about.

A: up
up

(S: What is it?)

A: up there   A pointing at clock.

(S: Up there. It's a clock.)
  Say clock.)

A: up there   A still pointing at clock.

⋮

A has been trying in vain to pull lid off box, holding box in left arm and pulling upwards with right hand fingers under rim.

A: up ↑   A standing in front of D (myself) holding out box. D accepts box pulls lid open. A immediately snatches box and empties out contents.

Age 19 months, 1 week
(S: Come and build your bricks up.)

A: bricks   A looking at S's face, then at bricks on the floor by S's feet.

(S: bricks)

A: up

(S: Bricks up hmm)

A: bricks up	A squatting down and picking up a brick. (A does not build them up.)
A: mummy down	A upstairs with S, looking at S's face. (A's mother not at home.)
down stairs	

down stairs
down

Although not all unimitated, Alice's uses of *up* and *down* clearly display a variety of described and requested actions and movements. The contexts of use are clearly quite different in terms not only of action but also of agents performing the action, and of objects undergoing it. The constant feature is the relative position or vertical directionality of positional change of some object (including both small physical objects and also persons). It is possible that that imitations are for Alice learning situations. What she is learning here is not the imitated word so much as its contextually appropriate uses—the word she already knows. Thus Alice learns that *up* and *down* label particular relative positions and changes of position independent of action because she is able to map various adult contextual uses onto a cognitive-perceptual ability to differentiate action and location. Such a theory would accord with Macnamara's (1972) description of a general cognitive basis for language learning.

Similar use of cross-context abstraction of meanings can be made in support of recent criticisms (Bloom, 1973; Campbell, 1975) of the 'one-word sentence' or 'holophrase' theory of early utterances. The most extreme version of this old and variously defined theory is that when a child uses, say, *apple* to express some global statement or request such as 'I want an apple' or 'that is an apple', then the whole sentence meaning should be contained within the semantic description of that one word. It is not a word with discrete reference, but rather some kind of 'undifferentiated verbal protoplasm' (Guillaume, 1927) that expresses actor, action, object, etc., in some semantically undifferentiated way. Statements of the theory are both ancient and modern, but instructive for our present purposes. For example: James Sully (1897): 'Each of these words serves in the first baby language for a variety of sentences. Thus "Puss!" means sometimes "Puss is doing something", at other times "I want Puss", and so forth.' Stern and Stern (1907): 'The child's "mama" cannot be translated into adult speech as the word "mother", but only as sentence units "mother, come here", "mother, give me something," "mother, put me on the chair", "mother, help me", etc.' Otto Jespersen (1922): ' "Up" means what we should express by a whole sentence, "I want to get up" or "lift me up".... "Father" can be either "here comes Father", or "this is Father", or "he is called father", or "I want father to come to me", or 'I want this or that from father".' David

McNeill (1966): 'In the beginning, each (lexical) entry, although it sounds like a word to adults, is a sentence for the child, which means that each entry actually has a great number of interpretations.'

Notice, however, that in all of the examples quoted by these authors the child's one-word utterance (puss, mama, father, up, etc.) occurs as a distinct word in each of the various sentence-interpretations. Clearly the child's word is understood always to have a coherent reference across all situational contexts, which surely militates against the 'holophrase' theory. How could a word refer clearly to a single entity and simultaneously express an entire, and variable, proposition? These words are indeed used in a variety of contexts and messages, but it is the contexts and non-linguistically expressed messages with which the words combine that gives them the illusion of expressing, in themselves, various whole sentences (cf. the argument by Greenfield and Smith, 1976).

Although the cross-contextual analysis of *up* and *down* and of some so-called 'holophrases' has yielded descriptions that are close to adult meanings, the next section shows that this is not always so.

2. Constraints on Actions as a Source of Meaning

Face-to-face social relationships are inherently communicational. From birth onwards an infant becomes increasingly able to engage in social exchanges with his caretakers, getting his needs met and out-of-reach objects handed to him through the co-ordination of signals such as reaching and pointing, smiling, looking, crying, and vocalizing. The infant's caretakers talk to him throughout, and it is within this context that the child's first linguistically realized messages come to be expressed.

It could also be claimed that all social relationships in which the infant engages are inherently socializing. However, a sub-set of such relationships is that in which the child's activities are being directly regulated or curtailed by a caretaker for some reason, whether to avoid physical damage to the child or to some object, or else simply to suit the caretaker's convenience or taste in persons. In this section we shall look at a set of early linguistically-expressed messages which derive from contexts of direct socialization where the child's freedom of actions is being or has previously been constrained. The significant factor for the child, as some of the data indicate, seems sometimes to be not the source of the restriction—whether imposed by the nature of the physical world or else merely by social prohibition—but simply the fact that there *is* a constraint operating on his or her freedom of intention and action.

We shall therefore be looking at meanings derived from (or assimilated to) both physically and socially imposed constraints, thus cutting across the distinction between cognitive-actional and social-relational sources of meanings. Drawing mainly on some data of my own from several children we shall examine what adult grammar would define as three very different sets of meanings: negation, possession, and a set of verbs and adjectives. Although on linguistic grounds this is a rather unlikely selection to be treated together, we shall see that from the child's own view it may be a rational selection, brought together by the notion that the meanings of adult words and expressions can be assimilated to the child's conception of physically and socially imposed constraints on his intended actions. The discussion also highlights the problem of making a formal linguistic description of early meanings in the semantically simple and adult-grammar-oriented way this has been done to date.

2.1 Negation

It was demonstrated by Bloom (1970; also Greenfield and Smith 1976) that children's use of negation in early syntax comes to serve at least three different semantic intentions, the earliest of which tends to be what Bloom calls 'rejection'. Thus the child might exclaim *no soap*, rejecting by pushing away from himself a bar of soap at bath-time. We shall propose that this kind of rejection–negation expressed by young children belongs to a larger category of meanings which include not only 'rejection' as such, but also some sense of the physical impossibility of, or a socially-imposed prohibition upon, the child's actions; that the child acquires the 'rejection' use of negation from contexts in which it is his own actions that are being constrained, and out of such contexts the child generalizes the usage into the linguistic expression of his own desired constraints and impositions upon the world. Thus the use of negation to mean 'rejection' belongs to a more general class of uses of negation which are united by their expression of constraints and impositions, meanings which derive ultimately from the child's experiences of constraints on his own behaviour.

In the first three two-hour sessions of tape-recorded data from Alice, the proportion of S's negations which encoded rejection or prohibition of Alice's actions was only one third (for example, 'No, you must leave it open', 'No, not up there, no', 'No, that's bad'). The rest of S's negations encoded denials of propositions (for example, 'They're not dirty now', 'No, it's not dirty', 'Oh no, he's not in there'). Nevertheless Alice's negations at first exclusively expressed constraints on actions. Here are some representative examples:

LANGUAGE	CONTEXT

Age 17 months, 3 weeks

1.		A enters the room, throwing the door open. It bangs loudly against the sideboard.
	A: no (loud voice)	A turning and looking at door.
	no door	A walks back to door and shuts it.
2.	A: Lego	A trying with difficulty to fit some Lego bricks together.
	no ↑	A looking at S.
(S: No? Yes you can.)		
	A: no ↑	A trying again in vain to fit bricks

together. (Eventually pushes too hard and they fall apart.)

3.   A: no   A (voice sharp, loud and frustrated) failing to force a slotted wooden cylinder onto its peg.

4.   A has recently been admonished by S for drawing on the wall: (the drawings have since been wiped off by S).

                A: no   A holding a pencil, standing looking at
                pencils   the wall. A looks at S, then buries
             no pencils   her face in a chair cushion.

              no Alice   A looking at S.
               ⋮

             no Alice
             stop Alice
             stop it

5.   A tries to stand up on seat of high-chair: kneels down facing wrong

(S: Alice. Where are you   way.
going?)
   Alice all fall down.   S getting hold of A.
Alice.)
                A: no   (A protesting.)
(S: Come on. Back
round.)   S sits A the right way round.

6. *Age 18 months, 1 week*   A has lifted up her clothes to bare her tummy.

(S: No, now put that
tummy away.)
   Go on, put it away.)

                                A pushes her clothes down again.
            A: no: do   (A's voice loud, stentorian.)
           [ʔæ · ʔou:]
(S: No do that.)
7. *Age 19 months, 1 week*   (A has refused to hand toy penguin to D (myself).)

(S: Can Sheila have it?)
   Thank you. Thank   A looking at and walking towards S,
you.)   holding penguin out. S reaching for it.

A stops short of S, clutches penguin to
her chest, looking at S.

(S: Come on then.)

A: no penguin

8. A: no touch A standing looking at D's tape-
recorder.

(S: No touch. No that's
correct.)

Alice's early negations occur on the occasion of both socially-imposed (nos 1, 4, 6, and 8) and physically-imposed (nos 2 and 3) constraints on her actions. The fact that the same word *no* begins to occur on the occasion of both types of constraint at the same point in development suggests that, whether imposed by the physical world, or in the other, quite different case, by social prohibition, the notion of constraints on the child's freedom of action is probably psychologically real in the child's own experience and semantic intentions, and not a mere descriptive convenience of my own. Further evidence for this is that the other kinds of constrained-action meanings we shall now look at occur in the same contexts as negation, and are often uttered along with negations.

2.2 Possession

When possessive relations between persons and objects are first expressed in early speech, the relation understood by the child to hold between person and object is not quite the concept of 'ownership' that adults have. Some early utterances classified as 'possessive' seem to encode, or occur in the context of, no more than a perceived consistent association between a particular person and some object—for example, an item of clothing, or a toothbrush (Greenfield and Smith, 1976). However there tends also to develop concurrently some primitive notion of ownership which is based on socially-imposed restrictions on the child's actions with certain objects, so that the notion involved is one of privileged access of particular persons to particular objects (Edwards, 1973, pp. 428–429). The contexts of some of my daughter Helen's possessives illustrate this:

LANGUAGE	CONTEXT

9. *Age 24 months, 3 weeks*

(M: Off. Leave them alone, Helen.)

H reaching for M's glasses on top of television set.

H: mummy glasses

H pulls back, pointing at glasses.

10. *Age 25 months, 1 week.*

H: daddy

H picks up one of D's books, looks at D, putting book down.

daddy book (H is generally forbidden to play with D's and M's books and has her own.)

(D: Yes, that's daddy's book.)

11. *Age 32 months, 3 weeks*

(D: Hey, come out of there.)

H creeping behind television set which is backed against corner of room.

H: [s] daddy's television

The last example (11), like all children's errors, is particularly instructive. My objection to Helen's action was not that the television set was particularly my property (in fact it was rented), but rather that the back of a television set is a dangerous place for children to play. Helen would never have heard the television set described as belonging to D. Nevertheless D's comment was interpreted by Helen in terms of her understanding of the basis of social prohibitions on her actions towards particular objects—that is, in terms of her notion of possession. The way in which such notions of possession are linked in the child's use and understanding of language to negation through this kind of prohibition is shown in the following data from Alice at 19 months. The first example (12) is of course the same event, now described further, that was listed above as the negation *no touch* (no. 8).

LANGUAGE	CONTEXT

Alice, age 19 months, 1 week

12.

A: no touch — A standing looking at D's tape-recorder.

(S: No touch. No that's correct.)

A: mummys tape — A pointing and looking at tape-recorder.

13.

A: dont ↑ mummy watch — A looking at her mother's watch on the table and out of A's reach.

(S: Mummy's. No touch.)

A: dont touch

14.

S absent.
A starts pulling a (parent's) book down off a shelf. (D is myself.)

(D: Hey. Alice.)

A: daddys daddys book — A pushing the book back.

(D: Daddy's book is it?)

A walks into centre of room, looking at
the toys on the floor.

A: doggie ↑ A pushing toy dog-on-wheels out of
her path.

my doggie

⋮

A: toys ↑   A carrying a small wooden xylophone
to D, puts it in D's lap.

my toys ↑
my: toys ↑

(D: Oh thank you.)   ⋮

S enters.
A takes xylophone off D's lap and A
A: my toy   handing xylophone to S

The first two examples (12 and 13) show the close connection in Alice's mind
between prohibitions, expressions of negation and expressions of possession. Indeed,
in the same recording session the negation *no penguin* quoted above (no. 7) occurred
in a context in which Alice could well have asserted 'Alice's penguin', clutching it to
her chest and refusing to hand it to S.

Example 12 (*mummys tape*) is yet another instructive use of possession. The tape-
recorder, as an object not to be touched, was assimilated by Alice to her general
schema of objects 'possessed' by her mother, just as Helen did with the television set.
In fact Alice's parents did not own a tape-recorder and have never been present at a
recording session, so that there was no way in which Alice could have directly
acquired the notion that the machine belonged to her mother. It is interesting in
example 14 how Alice asserts her own possession of her toys in contrast, first, to her
assertion of her father's possession of his books and, second, in the social-
interactional context of actually handing the toy to somebody else. Alice is
establishing her rights of access in two situationally appropriate contexts: first, the
establishment of others' rights and, second, the otherwise apparent relinquishing of
her own.

2.3 'Verbs' and 'Adjectives'

We turn now to a consideration of the meanings of a selection of words which in
adult grammar would be classified as 'verbs' and 'adjectives'. The cross-context
analysis of a child's early words frequently demonstrates that the child does not
share with the adult quite the same intended meaning. The child's meaning is often
either more generalized or more situation-specific. Words identical or similar in
meaning to the ones we shall examine are common in child language data.

Alice's negation *no touch* or *dont touch* quoted above seems to encode a meaning identical to her single lexical item *leave*:

| LANGUAGE | CONTEXT |

Age 19 months, 1 week
15.

(S: Leave.)   A pulling at zip on a parent's brief-case.

            A: leave   A letting go of zip.

            no: Alice ↑   A and S eye contact.

(S: hm?)

            A: no Alice↑. cant ↑

Although Alice's utterance was an imitation of S's, she clearly comprehended its force and re-encoded it immediately in her more usual form, negation. The word *leave* was reported by S to have occurred in similar contexts since 17 months, but appeared here at 19 months in my recorded data for the first time. It would be usual, even using situational contexts to determine meanings, to classify *leave* as a verb (or 'action-word'), and negation as something quite different in terms of its semantic-syntactic linguistic description. Yet a closer examination of the contexts across which both expressions are used suggests that to give such descriptions would be to be misled by the adult usage of the words, and to be seduced by the convenient anticipation of the adult linguistic system at as early a stage and in as simple a form as possible in the development of the child's language.

Ignoring for the moment children's indiosyncratic meanings and interpreting their vocabulary from the perspective of adult semantics, children's early 'adjectives' would seem to label those features of objects that are perceptually salient and which describe particularly those perceptual discriminanda which are criterial of constraints on the child's actions upon the objects concerned (Edwards, 1973). These include constraints both physical and social. Many ostensibly physical attributives seem to be acquired from parental speech in the context of prohibitions on the child's actions (hot, wet, sharp, heavy, dirty, etc.) and may indeed therefore be acquired with idiosyncratic meanings related to their appropriateness of use in such contexts. Thus *sharp*, for example, could refer not so much to the physical property 'sharpness' as to some kind of 'not to be touched' property that adults seem to attribute to kitchen knives. Similarly, *tired* and *busy* may be used in the context of a mother who is simply for any reason unavailable for play and conversation. Thus Bloom's child Kathryn said *mommy busy* when her mother was not even present (Bloom, 1970) and there are similar occurrences in my own data.

In my data on Mark there is an interesting word, *big*, which for some time occurred exclusively in the context of Mark having difficulty in pushing a variety of toy cars through narrow gaps where the car would frequently get stuck. The following three contexts show how the word was acquired and used, and link the expression with negation.

LANGUAGE	CONTEXT

Age 22 months
16.

Mk: no: Mk trying to push toy car through gap
go car go car between 2 block towers; car is stuck
and Mk lets go, leaving it in the gap.

(M: It's too big that one.)
  Try another one.)

Age 23 months
17.
(M: It's going in there is
it?)
(M: 's too big)

Mk: [ʔ ə : b ə:]
car: Mk looking up into the air and
shouting.

Mk pushes toy car into a narrow gap
between 2 bricks. The car pushes
one brick aside: Mk moans loudly.

Age 24 months
18.

Mk: [bɪ:ʔ b ʌ: ʔ]
(= 'big bus')Mk pushing toy bus through tight gap
between two blocks. (The bus is the
smallest of Mk's three toy buses.)

Example 16 shows Mark encoding this particular kind of physical constraint on his actions with a negation. His mother describes the car (though significantly omitting the word 'car') as 'too big', and does so again at 23 months, at which age, for the first time in my data, Mark attempts the word *big*. Thereafter the word becomes productive in a variety of similar contexts (not always involving toy blocks) for objects large and small. Mark's use of the word *big* is probably a common early usage of words which in adult grammar are dimensional adjectives. The word does not for Mark label a dimensional property of a particular object, but rather a baulked-action relation between one object and another, involving a physical constraint upon the child's intended action. Another child, James (aged 2¹/₂ years), used the expression *too big* when one object would not go inside another (a foot into a shoe, a toy elephant into a car, etc.). If we suppose that for James, *big* was a descriptive dimensional adjective, then his usage of *too big* was somewhat bizarre; he used it inappropriately to 'describe' the container as well as the contained—a shoe was described as *too big* if his foot would not go into it. Clearly *too big* was not so much descriptive of object dimensions as expressive of a particular kind of baulked action. It was not for James the size or even the relative size of the objects that was important, so much as this special kind of physical constraint on the insertion of one into the other. Similarly Helen's word *heavy* was not used as a value on a perceptual scale on which all objects can be ordered. Rather, objects were simply *heavy* or they were not, and the criterion was whether Helen had any difficulty in lifting them. Very heavy objects like real cars, buses, tables, and cows were not described as *heavy* any more than James described them as *big*. These words were apparently acquired from parental speech in the context of the child's experience of difficulty in lifting or moving objects in the home, and it was to such experiences that Helen assimilated the adults' meaning.

Finally we may examine Alice's words *pull* and *stuck*. For some time Alice's use of the word *pull* was limited to contexts in which the object pulled at was always stuck fast and would not move: a closed door, a toy hammer caught inside a string bag, a toy purse with a difficult catch. When Alice was pulling an object that moved freely—if the door was open, if she was pulling a wheeled toy along the floor, or pulling lengths of string out of a box—the word *pull* was not spoken. Alice's word *pull* thus had a similar usage to her own and other children's word *stuck*, a prerequisite criterion for its use being this physical constraint on Alice's intended action (opening the door, etc.). Indeed the word *stuck* was itself used even when an object was not strictly stuck at all but free to move, except that Alice could not, try as she might, fit it over some peg or into some container. Despite their apparently appropriate use in any particular context, to categorize *pull* as a semantic verb and *stuck* as an attributive adjective would clearly be to impose adult semantic categories onto the child. At a certain point in Alice's linguistic development we can say only that these words were used in the context of some physical constraint on particular intended actions (in the case of *pull* the action was always pulling).

3. Conclusion

Modern child language studies were given impetus by the application of the principles of distributional analysis to children's early sentences, out of which emerged the well-known 'pivot grammars'. The child's language was formally described for the first time as a system in itself rather than as an inchoate approximation to adult grammar. The use of situational contexts of utterances for the determination of meanings has considerably enriched our understanding of early child language (Brown, 1973). Yet it is possible that, now at the conceptual-semantic level, we have been misled in the description of 'structural meanings' by the child's use of recognized words which have obvious meanings in adult language. The child says the words *open door* when opening a door, so we interpret the word 'open' as a semantic or deep verb with a meaning similar to its adult counterpart. Yet Alice was pulling when she said *pull*, and the object was stuck most times when she said *stuck*. It is clear that the context of use of a single utterance can be misleading. With a full description of the child's ongoing contextualized behaviour at the moment of utterance we can examine the *variety* of contexts across which any particular word is uttered in the expectation that the common features of such contexts will help us narrow down our description of the word's usage or meaning out of the many meanings possible in any single context, towards an understanding of what kind of meaning the word has for the child. The 'contexts' then become less contextual and more the central object of study, and it becomes increasingly clear that we should begin the study of children's first utterances not only with the adult language end-product (or some currently popular theory of it) constantly in mind, but also with the understanding that early utterances are parts of contextualized interpersonal messages, whose meanings are the product of the assimilation of language addressed to the child to the child's own cognitive and interpersonal competence.

References

Bloom, L. (1970), *Language Development*, Cambridge, Mass.: M.I.T. Press.

Bloom, L. (1973), *One Word at a Time*, The Hague: Mouton.

Brown, R. (1956), Language and categories. In Bruner, J.S., Goodnow, J.J., and Austin, G.A. (eds), *A Study of Thinking*, New York: Science Editions Inc.

Brown, R. (1970), The First sentences of child and chimpanzee. In Brown, R., *Psycholinguistics: Selected Readings*, New York: The Free Press.

Brown, R. (1973), *A First Language: The Early Stages*, London: Allen and Unwin; Cambridge, Mass.: Harvard University Press.

Bruner, J.S. (1975), The ontogenesis of speech acts, *J. of Child Language*, 2, 1–19.

Campbell, R. (1975), Three problems in the description of child language. Paper presented at the Conference on Language and the Social Context at the University of Stirling.

Chafe, W. (1970), *Meaning and the Structure of Language*, Chicago: University of Chicago Press.

Edwards, D. (1973), Sensory-motor intelligence and semantic relations in early child grammar, *Cognition*, 2, 395–434.

Greenfield, P.M., and Smith, J.H., (1976), *The Structure of Communication in Early Language Development*, New York: Academic Press.

Gruber, J.S. (1967), Correlations between the syntactic constructions of the child and of the adult. Paper presented at biennial meeting of the Society for Research in Child Development.

Guillaume, P. (1927), Les Débuts de la phrase dans la langage de l'enfant, *Journal de Psychologie*, 24, 1–25.

Jespersen, O. (1922), *Language: Its Nature, Development and Origin. Book 2: The Child*, London: Allen and Unwin; New York: Holt.

Lyons, J. (1966), Towards a 'notional' definition of the 'parts of speech', *J. Linguistics*, 2, 209–236.

Macnamara, J. (1972), Cognitive basis of language learning in infants, *Psychol. Review*, 79, 1–13.

McNeill, D. (1966), Developmental psycholinguistics. In Smith, F., and Miller, G.A. (eds), *The Genesis of Language*, Cambridge, Mass.: M.I.T. Press.

Piaget, J. (1926), *The Language and Thought of the Child*, New York: Harcourt, Brace.

Piaget, J. (1954), *The Child's Construction of Reality*, New York: Basic Books.

Slobin, D. (1970), Universals of grammatical development in children. In Flores d'Arcais, G.B., and Levelt, W.M. (eds), *Advances in Psycholinguistics*, Amsterdam; North-Holland.

Slobin, D. (1972), Seven questions about language development. In Dodwell, P.C. (Ed), *New Horizons in Psychology*, 2, Harmondsworth: Penguin.

Stern, C., and Stern, W. (1907), *Die Kindersprache*, Leipzig: Barth.

Sully, J. (1897), *Children's Ways*, New York: Appleton-Century-Crofts.

Weir, R. (1962), *Language in the Crib*, The Hague: Mouton.

5

CONDITIONS FOR THE ACQUISITION OF SPEECH ACTS

John Dore

Even the most cursory observation of language behaviour reveals that it requires some knowledge about the world, about other people, and about the structure of language itself. That is, in speaking, it is obvious (1) that we talk about objects and events and how they are related in our environment; (2) that we get others to do things and to tell us about their internal states, and we presume they know what we mean; and (3) that we speak according to grammatical rules for putting sounds together in such a way that they convey certain meanings. Yet theories of how language develops in children have tended either to overlook one or another of these kinds of knowledge or to make them more fundamental than the others. Regarding the relationship between grammar and communication, for example, some nativist theories have maintained that grammatical structures emerge independently of communicative skills and that they are primarily dependent upon maturational factors (Lenneberg, 1967) and/or innate constraints on linguistic knowledge (Chomsky, 1965); functionalist theories, on the other hand, have typically maintained that the functions of linguistic communication essentially determine the structures of grammar (DeLaguna, 1927; Halliday, 1975). Theoretical positions intermediate between such extremes have rarely had the chance to become prominent. This chapter is an attempt to assess or, more properly, to reassess the contributions of genetic endowment and communicative experience to the child's early language.

Most of the research on child language during the 1960s focused on the child's acquisition of grammar. This research was heavily influenced by Chomsky's (1965) syntactically based theory of transformational-generative grammar and by various semantically based versions of that theory (Lakoff, 1969). Essentially, the transformational approach defines grammar as knowledge of the phonological, syntactic, and semantic elements and rules which underlie the production and comprehension of sentences. Applications to child language have been revealing: McNeill (1970), for instance, has indicated how the speech of children as young as 2 years could be described in terms of formal syntactic relations like the subject and predicate of a sentence; and Bloom (1970) has demonstrated how early grammars express underlying semantic relations. Much of this kind of research assumed, if only implicitly, some sort of constraints on the kind of linguistic structures children could acquire.

More recently interest has shifted to the pragmatics, as opposed to the grammar, of child language. For present purposes pragmatics can be taken as a cover term to represent the social aspects of language use, especially the interpersonal value of communicative acts. Bruner (this volume) points out the danger of overlooking such factors and he argues in general that 'one can establish continuities between pre-speech communication and language' (p. 17). He specifically claims that

> the early language for which a grammar is written is the end result of psychological processes leading to its acquisition, and to write a grammar of that language at any point in its development is in no sense to explicate the nature of its acquisition [pp. 17–18] ... to master a language a child must acquire a complex set of broadly transferable or generative skills—perceptual, motor, conceptual, social, *and* linguistic—which when appropriately co-ordinated yield linguistic performances that can be described (though only in a limited sense) by the linguists' rules of grammar. (p. 18)

Bruner makes it quite clear that language acquisition involves more than grammar. However, he refers to grammar as only a description, and not as an explanation of what is acquired. Yet if the 'linguistic' skill referred to depends upon innate constraints on possible grammatical structures (as proposed in the theory of universal grammar articulated by Chomsky, 1975, and Fodor, 1976), then this notion of grammar explains in part what is acquired. The central question to which this chapter is addressed is then: how do constituent skills *and* grammatical knowledge interact to determine speech?

The particular position I will try to defend views these skills as partly systems for realizing grammatical knowledge in speech, and this position requires the following initial assumptions. There are three kinds of necessary conditions for the acquisition of language; for convenience, I will call them the conceptual, the communicative, and the grammatical. In an effort to adapt to the physical world of objects, events, properties, and relations the child constructs mental representations of these, perhaps in the manner described by Piaget (1952) as the infant's sensorimotor acquisitions. In an effort to adapt to the 'inner worlds' of other people and to communicate with them, the child constructs representations of their knowledge, intentions, beliefs, and affective states (representations of such phenomena are described in detail by the authors of the papers in Richards, 1974). And in an effort to adapt to the world of linguistic communication, the child cognitively reorganizes these conceptual and communicative inputs into a grammar, with the aid of a purely linguistic input, perhaps of the sort referred to by McNeill (1970) as a 'strong linguistic universal'. Language development can then be comprehensively viewed as the integration of these distinct inputs within some pragmatic-grammatical unit of language behaviour. The hypothesis here is that the conceptual, communicative, and grammatical inputs are each necessary for and jointly sufficient to cause the emergence of language.

The initial problem for such a position is to decide on the appropriate pragmatic-grammatical unit. The problem is crucial for any theory of language development because the decision entails a claim about what exactly is acquired. Prior to the advent of transformational theories of grammar, child language investigators had to rely on such traditional notions as parts of speech or on phrase structure rules for types of surface sentences or on intuitive notions about what constituted an utterance. Transformational theories have of course provided explicit formulations of the rules which underlie the production of utterances. However, these have been sentential theories only, not theories about communicative acts. They explain little about how sentences are psychologically processed and actually used in communication. A sentential grammar, for example, cannot tell us much about what non-linguistic assumptions are shared by participants with respect to the contexts of utterance, or about how speakers structure their conversations. Hence the dissatisfaction with purely grammatical theories.

A unit which appears to be able to incorporate some of these supra-sentential phenomena is the *speech act*. The notion was introduced by Austin (1962) partly because of the failure on the part of philosophers of language to deal with the capacity of utterances to perform communicative acts and to accomplish goals for speakers. The fullest treatment of speech acts appears in Searle (1969). Here it suffices to say that Searle describes the speech act as consisting of a proposition and an illocutionary force: the proposition is the conceptual content of the utterance, organized in terms of a predicate taking one or more arguments; the illocutionary force conveys how the speaker intends his utterance to be taken. In the utterance 'Is John eating an apple?', for example, the proposition is 'John eat apple' while the illocutionary force is a question. The same proposition can be conveyed as a description ('John is eating an apple') or as a command ('Eat an apple, John!'); or 'John' himself may say 'I promise to eat an apple' which has the force of a promise. Searle views speech act theory as compatible with standard transformational theories in so far as the latter describe sentences which he takes to be devices for expressing propositions and forces. But he claims that speech acts 'are the basic or minimal units of linguistic communication' (p. 16). For purposes which will soon become clear, it is convenient to distinguish the 'semantic meanings' of propositional content from the 'intentional meanings' of illocutionary forces, especially since the intention motivating the choice of a given sentence is often not manifested in any surface structure signal.

Several investigators have adopted the speech act as the unit of analysis in child language. In Dore (1973) I proposed an outline of the development of speech acts in children from the time just prior to their acquisition of words to the end of their 'one-word stage' which was described in terms of the repertoire of 'primitive speech acts' they control. Bruner (1975) elucidated some of the pre-linguistic processes that foster the acquisition of speech acts. These processes concern the development of shared attention and mutual action patterns with caretakers, and of the 'awareness' of others and the order of items in action sequences. And Garvey (1975) described the kinds of 'interpersonal meaning factors' which are understood by pre-school children as operating in the 'domain' of the speech act called 'action request'. Thus the speech act seems to be one appropriate unit for the analysis of the child's developing communicative competence. But its application to child language is not without problems and requires considerable revision. The terminology of speech act theory can be applied to pre-linguistic behaviour only in a metaphorical sense; moreover, the description of child language in terms of speech acts does not eliminate the need to explain the emergency of grammar.

I will try to evaluate recent research on communicative development in terms of this work's contribution to a speech act framework. In doing so, I will also try to integrate the findings about the early social and conceptual development with the fundamental insights of the 'grammatical model'. For example, although Bruner (this volume) has provided an unprecedented documentation of the communicative determinants of early speech, I will suggest ways in which his pragmatic approach does not effectively allow for the contribution of grammar; I will also suggest ways in which Nelson's (1974) theory of conceptual development needs to be extended in order to account more fully for language acquisition. The format of the discussion will be first to review the findings which contribute to a pragmatic-conceptual view of acquisition and then to extend and/or reinterpret these findings in the light of the particular version of the speech act approach I recommend.

1. Pre-linguistic Communication

Several proposals have recently appeared which share the assumption that the social process of communication largely determines the acquisition of language, that grammar is secondary. In this section I will treat what I take to be the more revealing aspects of these proposals while pointing out their limitations, at least from the perspective I recommend. For example, Bruner reminds us that most studies have overlooked the basic fact that 'speech is meaningful social behaviour' (this volume, p. 21), and his paper documents the necessity of social-communicative experience for language emergence. He provides convincing arguments for the general position that before speech begins the child constructs representations of 'communicative requirements established over a long period of interaction between infant and caretaker'. And he suggests that these representations 'help the child crack the linguistic code' (p. 23). To the extent that 'help' here means that communicative experience is a prerequisite for some aspects of language behaviour, there is no problem. But a problem does arise when Bruner suggests that 'it is not extravagant to say that initial language at least has a pragmatic base structure' (p. 22) because the suggestion implies that *this* pragmatic base structure might replace, or in some sense be the foundation for, grammatical base structure. (Bruner's sense of pragmatic structure concerns initial communication but not 'initial *language*'.) The term 'base structure' has been used to refer to the abstract configurations which specify the propositional relations among grammatical constituents. Language behaviour presumably also has some pragmatic *basis*, but pragmatic skills cannot be construed as base structures in anything like the grammatical sense. Below I will suggest various ways in which the two kinds of phenomena might be not mutually exclusive, but complementary co-requisites for language acquisition.

1.1 Pre-speech Communicative Intentions and Communicative Acts

Many investigators have observed that an intention to communicate precedes the production of speech. In Dore (1973) I outlined the development of pre-linguistic 'orectic attitudes'—these are intentions that underlie the infant's attempts to communicate to adults that he wants or is striving for something—and I argued that these attitudes were the precursors of the illocutionary forces of speech acts and that they develop independently of the sensorimotor schemas which are the conceptual inputs to words. Initial communicative intentions can be construed as new means for accomplishing familiar goals which were previously accomplished by the child himself. Sugarman-Bell (1973) in fact suggested that 'the intention to accomplish something and the intention to communicate' could both be accounted for by the 'general cognitive apparatus' proposed by Piaget. She described the development of pre-speech communication as the social adjunct to the child's object-and-event-oriented sensorimotor acquisitions. But one of her conclusions was that 'since language acquisition and use require the intervention of higher modes of cognitive activity, new conceptual dimensions will have to be added to an account of communicative development that includes the development of language' (p. 15). I would add that these 'new conceptual dimensions' must be determined by the grammatical input to language acquisition, but that nothing in Piaget's 'general cognitive apparatus' can account for the appearance of grammar.

In a study by Bates, Camaioni, and Volterra (1975) the notion of a speech act is employed to describe pre-speech behaviour. They propose a stage-theory of communicative development directly paralleling Austin's (1962) aspects of the speech act:

> (1) a *perlocutionary* stage, in which the child has a systematic effect on his listener without having an intentional, aware control over that effect; (2) an *illocutionary* stage, in which the child intentionally uses non-verbal signals to convey requests and to direct adult attention to objects and events; (3) a *locutionary* stage, in which the child constructs propositions and utters speech sounds within the same performative sequences that he previously expressed non-verbally. (p. 4)

It seems indisputable that this sequence is accurate. But the value of phrasing it in speech act terminology is questionable; the metaphor, though intriguing, may be misleading. It implies that at stage two the communicative acts children perform non-verbally are essentially illocutionary acts, like 'requesting', and that the later use of propositions is merely a verbal substitute for the prior behaviour. Yet, when one considers the various accounts of the nature of genuine requests—namely, that the communicative intention is an inducement in a listener of the recognition of a complex set of the speaker's internal states (Grice, 1975; Dore, 1976), that the proposition contains specifications of the agent, future act, etc., and that its use involves assumptions about the listener's willingness and ability to perform the future act (Searle, 1969)—the analogy breaks down. What Bates *et al.* describe is the pre-speech development of communicative intentions only, not of speech acts; the description over looks the grammatical contribution to speech acts. Thus, although a speech act approach to acquisition seems promising, nothing is gained by describing pre-linguistic behaviour in terms of linguistic functions.

There is in fact a general tendency by many current pragmatic theorists to identify linguistic acquisitions with behaviour before speech. To take an example from Bates *et al.* again, they contend that 'the eventual commerce of propositions is first carried out with an exchange of concrete objects or an indication of visible events' (p. 18). Such a statement seems to beg the crucial questions regarding language development. Acting on objects may require some pictorial representation or a Piagetian-like schema guiding the action pattern, but propositional representation is more remotely related to particular contents and contexts: propositions are grammatically organized predicate-argument constructions which (1) involve the computation of entities more abstract than action pattern constituents, (2) accommodate the representation of processes and states as well as actions, and (3) are evaluated in terms of truth values and not as practical accomplishments. Thus, although experiences with exchanging objects and their required conceptual representations may constrain the possible propositional content of early utterances, they cannot account for the more abstract level of propositional representation itself. The true value of the work by Bates *et al.*, as I see it, is to show that there are some pragmatic inputs to the acquisition of elements of propositions; using a term to refer, for example, involves the assumption that the meaning of the word one chooses is shared by the listener. However, knowledge of propositional structures cannot be explained by any pragmatic inputs thus far proposed. The most critical problem with some pragmatic approaches is that they lead to a theoretically untenable conflation of grammar with communication: Bates (1976), for example, claims that '*all* of semantics is *essentially* pragmatic in nature' (p. 20). (Bates takes semantics, in part, to be the lexical component of a transformational grammar, as I do in this chapter; also, see Kempson (1975) for a detailed delimitation of semantics and pragmatics.)

The 'meanings' that are attributed to infant vocalizations are 'intentional (pragmatic) meanings' as distinct from 'lexical' or 'propositional meanings'. That is, from early on it is fairly easy to infer *that* the child intends something, though *what* exactly he intends awaits later elaboration. Ryan (1974) has characterized this distinction with exceptional clarity in her study of adult interpretations of infant vocal behaviour. She found that

> much of the child's speech and other vocalizations take place within a context of interaction with adults who are motivated to understand the child's utterances ... many young children experience extensive verbal interchanges with their mothers. During these the mother actively picks up, interprets, comments on, extends, repeats and sometimes misinterprets what the child has said. (p. 199)

Ryan describes in detail the difficulties that adults have in interpreting children's meanings at various periods. Initially, when the child is 'making unrecognizable noises with no familiar intonation or gesture, and with no apparent relation to the context or preceding speech of others', she claims that 'no interpretation is possible'

(p. 200). Nevertheless, other investigators (Wolff, 1969; Ricks, 1971) have shown that, rightly or wrongly, mothers typically try to interpret infant vocalizations as somehow meaningful from the earliest months.

A second kind of difficulty in interpretation arises later, when 'the child may be making noises that are unrecognizable because they are not part of the standard adult vocabulary, but she may be making them in such a way that adults think she may be trying to say something' (Ryan, 1974, p. 201). In interpreting these vocalizations and the child's first conventional words, Ryan claims that adults rely not only on *aspects* of the utterance itself but also on the child's gestural *accompaniments* and the *circumstances* of the utterance. She emphasizes the importance of the fact that adults act 'as though' the child were trying to say something; and she suggests that from such adult behaviour the child learns about the communicative functions of sound sequences.

A third difficulty occurs 'when a child utters a recognizable word but it is unclear what she means by uttering it or why she has said it' because, Ryan points out, 'the child is using the same word to make several different utterances, on different occasions' (p. 202). In other words, following Grice (1975), she makes the distinction between 'what words and sentences mean and what people mean by uttering words, etc.' (p. 209). This amounts to the same distinction between lexical and intentional meaning mentioned above.

These interpretive difficulties described by Ryan serve to underscore two points: any 'meaning', apart from the intentional, attributed to the infant before the end of the first year is based on the adult's interpretation and not on the child' contribution; and the adult's interpretation itself is based on pragmatic knowledge of the particular child and the particular context. Moreover, Ryan poses the central question about the pragmatics of acquisition:

> How, for instance, do we decide whether or not a child is using words to name, to comment on, to desribe, to assert the existence of something, to request, to refuse, to point out related features for which the appropriate words are not known, to greet—plus all the other plausible functions that a child's utterances can be interpreted as having? It is crucial for any full account of language development that we should know what kinds of acts young children can perform with words, and particularly what developmental changes occur in this respect. (Ryan, 1974, p. 204)

Concerning the linguistic acts that children perform, in Dore (1974) I offered a decision procedure for classifying one-word utterances into a contrastive set of 'primitive speech acts', a set which is strikingly similar to the utterance types listed in Ryan's question. As evidence I used not only the three sources used by Ryan, but also the mothers' responses to children's utterances because at this stage mothers *sometimes* do know what the child's intention is in using a word, when it is obscure to the investigator. (And often a child's response to his mother's response clarifies his original intent.) And in Dore (1975) I suggested how primitive speech acts undergo changes, especially how the child's intentions and propositions become grammaticalized as full speech acts. Here I wish to suggest that whereas pragmatic approaches tend to reduce semantics to pragmatics, grammatical approaches tend to reduce pragmatics to semantics. Both extremes are theoretically unsound; the two kinds of phenomena are incompatible, so that neither can be reduced to the other; hence they cannot be dealt with by the same theoretical apparatus. Why this is so will become clear in the subsequent discussions.

With respect to the roles that infants learn to play in communicative situations, Bruner (this volume) has spelled our precisely the stages of development. He demonstrates how 'A close analysis of the first year of an infant's life provides not only a catalogue of the joint "formats" in which communicator and recipient habitually find each other, but also provides a vivid record of how roles developed in such formats become conventionalized' (p. 22). These formats arise through a succession of 'modes of interaction' with caretakers. The infant comes equipped with a 'demand mode', with a tendency to express discomfort, for instance. Such expressions are 'usually responded to, with the effect of establishing an expectancy of response' in the infant. The 'request mode' then emerges in which the infant's cries are less intense and after which there is a pause 'in anticipation of response'. Next is the 'exchange mode' characterized by the infant's involvement in repeated give-and-take situations in which 'he reverses roles with himself first as recipient of action, then as agent' (p. 38). The succession culminates in the 'reciprocal mode': 'Interactions are now organized around a *task* that possesses *exteriority*, *constraint*, and *division of labour*'. This progression from demand to reciprocity, Bruner believes, is 'of central importance to the development of speech acts (or, more properly, communicative acts) and, as well, to the establishment of a ground work for the later grasping of case in language' (p. 38). The distinction between 'speech act' and 'communicative act' will prove to be crucial, as will the notion of 'ground work' for 'case' (see below).

The description of this communicative development is straightforward and convincing, and it is easy to see how such skills might be necessary for language behaviour to emerge. Such experience is surely required 'ground work' for the elaboration of communicative intentions in so far as these are partly defined by the kind of 'expectancy' which Bruner has found so early on in ontogenesis. But whether the emergence of grammar itself requires such experience is questionable. It can be argued that the child's practical experience in communicative roles has the same cognitive status as his actions on objects—they both lead to sensorimotor schemas of some sort, though much work needs to be done on the characterization of schemas for social roles. At any rate, schemas are inputs to the grammar to the extent that they are reconstituted on an independent linguistic plane, but it is not clear how experience with communication itself is required for the grammar. It may even be that role experience provides a pragmatic input to the acquisition of concepts like ACTOR-UPON (as more 'ground work'), but such concepts, too, are cognitively distinct from grammatical categories. More fundamentally, it is perfectly conceivable that the human infant, like other species, could continue using a communicative system of signals without ever creating a grammar whose purpose is to mediate between sound and meaning and whose structure is independent of communicative and other cognitive systems. Thus, the experience described by Bruner seems to be 'of central importance to the development' of the infant's social relationships and it perhaps prefigures aspects of illocutionary intent, but it in no way relates to the grammatical structure and propositional content of speech acts. Now let us consider some differences between behavioural-communicative acts in general and illocutionary acts in particular.

For an act to be considered communicative, it should involve: (1) some intention to communicate; (2) some cognitive representation of what is communicated; and (3) some behaviour which functions to signal both (1) and (2). Not many would deny that these elements appear before speech. An illocutionary act, on the other hand, requires: (1) an illocutionary force determined largely by a 'communicative intention' defined as the inducement of recognition of certain expectations (Grice, 1968; Dore, 1977); (2) a sentence (or in some cases merely a circumscribed formula) representing what is communicated (Katz, 1972); and (3) a linguistic marking device (including position of utterance in context and conversation) to convey both (1) and (2) (Searle, 1969). Clearly there are strong similarities, suggesting continuities from pre-speech communicative acts to illocutionary acts—and the research findings cited above offer evidence that there is in fact a communicative continuity. But nothing in the child's pre-linguistic experience is a sufficient cause for the emergence of grammar. This is quite apart from the fact that there may be conceptual and pragmatic prerequisites for acquiring particular contents of the basic constituents of propositions. To these constituents we now turn.

1.2 Propositional Content: Reference and Predication

In the philosophical literature there are two principal traditions for characterizing the notion of 'proposition in natural language'. The dominant tradition sees the proposition as a predicate-argument construction in which a predicating expression is conjoined with one or more referring expressions. It is argued that speakers know which kinds of predicating expressions can take which kinds of referring expressions; and that this knowledge is testable by criteria of truth and well-formedness; that is, a speaker knows when a proposition is true or anomalous. Transformational-generative linguistics is in this tradition. The second tradition concerns not what is known but what is done. Here a propositional act consists of the acts of referring and predicating, and the propositional act itself is part of a superordinate act like the speech act. In its extremist form (perhaps in Wittgenstein, 1953) this position views meaning as essentially the rules for using words and sentences in linguistic and non-linguistic contexts, as the rules of the 'games' in which words are used. Recent pragmatic approaches to language are in this tradition. Although these traditions have clashed over most matters of meaning, I will try to show that, as applied to language acquisition at least, they are not contradictory but rather concern two different parts of linguistic acts.

Bruner has emphasized the pragmatic aspects of acquiring reference: 'The objective of early reference ... is to indicate to another by some reliable means which among an alternative set of things or states or actions is relevant to the child's line of endeavour. Exactitude is initially a minor issue. "Efficacy of singling out" is the crucial objective' (this volume, p. 29). This accomplishment involves three aspects: (1) the child's early *indicating* procedures, that is the 'gestural, postural, and idiosyncratic vocal procedures for bringing a partner's attention to an object or action or state'; (2) behavioural *deixis*, the 'use of spatial, temporal, and interpersonal contextual features of situations as aids in the management of joint reference'; and (3) *naming*, 'the development of standard lexical items that "stand for" extra-linguistic events' (p. 29). And Bruner adds that 'these phenomena point to the early existence of means for managing joint reference. Yet none of them moves very far along the line toward discource-sensitive, deictically dependent reference' (p. 36).

These three accomplishments do seem to constitute pragmatic inputs to the process of reference. Yet the idea of a word, that it 'stands for' a concept, requires a level of representation beyond the pragmatic and conceptual. The child must be able to project a specific 'designation hypothesis' regarding reference; he must come to know that a linguistic category signalled by a sound-sequence represents a concept independently (1) of the concept's own representation of objects, events, etc. (a sensorimotor schema perhaps); (2) of the defining characteristics of the concept; and (3) of its active involvement with instances of the concept. Each of these last three notions is discussed separately in the section on conceptual prerequisites for language acquisition. Here I will consider evidence for this theory. When we look at pre-linguistic vocal behaviour in a different way, there are three aspects of that behaviour which can be interpreted as evidence that the child does indeed make the designation hypothesis: the uses of vocalizations before word acquisition, the existence of 'non-standard words' during acquisition, and the non-communicative uses of words.

1.3 Evidence for the Designation Hypothesis Theory

Dore, Franklin, Miller, and Ramer (1975) reported the results of a videotaped study of four children's vocalizations just prior to their production of genuine words. We found 'phonetically consistent forms' (abbreviated PCF) which are transitional between babbling and words. In terms of form, these vocalizations (1) are readily isolable units, bounded by pauses; (2) occur repeatedly as items in a repertoire; (3) are more phonetically stable than babbling though less so than words; and (4) can be loosely correlated with features of the environment and/or the infant's behaviour—that is, they are neither as random as babbling nor as rule-governed as words. An analysis of the functions of PCFs revealed four distinct types: (1) *affect expressions* convey moods and attitudes, stabilize around specific affects such as joy or anger, and do not appear to be addressed to anyone; (2) *instrumental expressions* accompany acts of striving and involve a directed gaze toward an object or adult, with the apparent intention of obtaining the object or engaging the adult in interaction; (3) *indicating expressions* are communicative but not directive, and most often involve pointing but not dissatisfaction when action fails to ensue; and (4) *grouping expressions* reflect an interaction between subjective state and attention to objective properties—sometimes varying forms are associated with similar objects which apparently have the same affective import for the infant, while at other times the same form is used with different objects having the same affective import.

Notice that most PCFs exhibit the characteristics of prelinguistic communicative acts. PCFs are not, however, genuinely referential because they lack the linguistic components of words. Neither the phonetic features of PCFs nor their uses conform to conventions of the linguistic community. The indicate only ambiguously, as pointing does; for example, they do not distinguish between the object and its properties, location, etc. (This is evidenced by frequent mismatches in the caretaker's understanding of the child's content and by the children's frustrations at such mismatches.) PCFs do not have a systematic relation to each other: that is, a term A referring to members of the set (X, Y, Z) and a term B referring to members of set (Q, R, S) where the terms are in complementary distribution. PCFs are not detachable from their uses. A word, on the contrary, may be used for different purposes. The word 'no', for instance, can be used as the *answer* to a question or as a protest to another's action; and a different word, like 'stop', can be used to perform the same act of protest. Thus children, who perform these primitive speech acts soon after they begin producing words, can detach the lexical meanings of words from the communicative purposes (intentional meanings) for which words are used. It seems, therefore, that unambiguous indication, complementary distribution, and detachability of use are some of the specifically linguistic criteria for 'grammatical' reference. The point here is that although the infant can 'pragmatically' indicate earlier, grammatical reference requires the projection of the designation hypothesis.

The second source of evidence for the designation hypothesis theory is the existence of 'non-standard words'. Numerous investigators who have kept diaries of children's development have reported that, at about the time children begin producing words conventionally, they also produce 'non-standard' vocalizations. About these, Ryan has claimed 'the child has learnt something general about speech, independent of specific forms learnt from adult speech. She appears to have learnt something general about the notion of a word, as regards its circumstance and manner of usage, that is not tied to any particular actual instance' (1974, p. 202). This 'something general', I would suggest, is the awareness that sound-sequences can represent meanings independently of adult usage, that is, apart from established conventional symbols for specific socially shared meanings.

The third kind of behaviour recommending the theory is the non-communicative uses of language. Most investigators of early speech have observed that children sometimes look at an object and label it, without apparent intention to communicate anything to another (there is no eye-contact, no pause for response, etc.). Dore (1973) reported that one child often engaged in lengthy 'naming routines', successively labelling items in a given domain, like toys on a shelf or utensils on a table. In fact, about 75 per cent of her utterances over a 3-month period were non-communicative; these were coded in terms of the functions of labelling, practising words out of context and imitating the words of another without addressing that person. These were contrasted with the communicative functions of requesting, calling, greeting, protesting, and answering, each of which involves an interlocutor. The majority (63 per cent) of the utterances of another child in the study functioned communicatively. Thus I suggested there were at least two styles of early language function, the 'symbol-oriented' (characterized by symbolic organizations of conceptual and emotional experiences) and the 'message-oriented' (characterized by attempts to communicate); these are strikingly similar to the two styles Nelson (1973) identified as the 'referential' and 'expressive' respectively.

The existence of non-communicative functions (and especially of a non-communicative style of acquisition) clearly indicates that, from the very onset of speech, language fulfils more than the purpose of communication. Rees (1973) has reviewed four principal kinds of non-communicative functions for the child: (1) the *concept-formation* function (citing Werner and Kaplan's (1963) view of language as 'a tool for knowing'); (2) the *directive* function (citing Luria's (1961) work on how language directs the infant's other behaviour); (3) the *magical* function (words-as-objects themselves and words-as-actions in the Malinowski tradition); and (4) the function of establishing the *self-image* (how language serves the development of personality). Rees concluded that

The expression and communication of ideas and feelings should be viewed as only one of the functions of language in the child. The non-communicative functions ... are of crucial importance in an understanding of the role of language for the child. The sources of the child's motivations for learning language are more satisfactorily found in these non-communicative functions than in the traditional function of communicating ideas and feelings. (Rees, 1973, 18–19)

At the very least, this theoretical distinction in function indicates a fundamental dichotomy of communication and language, the latter emerging separately from the former.

In sum, the referential inadequacy of infant vocalizations prior to word acquisition, the infant's general knowledge as manifested by the occurrence of non-standard words, and the non-communicative functions of early speech all contribute to the view that the postulation of something like the designation hypothesis is a necessary condition for the emergency of genuine reference. In other words, whereas the experience of intentionally 'indicating something to another' is a pragmatic co-requisite for reference, the notion that a sound-sequence represents a concept independently of communicative experiences with instances of the concept, and which shares in a specifically linguistic system of categories, is the grammatical co-requisite.

One final way of stating this issue is as follows: although certain conceptual developments, say object constancy, may be required in order for a child to acquire any particular name, a more abstract category specifying what can count as a 'nameable thing' must also be available to the child; and while there may be specific conceptual constraints on what names are actually acquired, these constraints cannot account for the more abstract linguistic category of 'nameable thing'.

1.4 The Predication Hypothesis Theory

Concerning the precursors of predication, Bruner has argued that 'mutual-action formats ... constitute the implicit ... topics on which comments can be made' (this volume, p. 41). The first and simplest form of comment, he claims, is 'giving indication that a topic is being shared in joint action, and it is principally revealed in the child's management of gaze direction' (pp. 41–42); when a child makes eye-contact with his mother during an interaction, 'the topic is the joint activity, the comment is the establishment of "intersubjective" sharing in connection with that activity' (p. 42). To me, the practical behaviour of eye-contact during interaction (where the looking and the doing are inseparable) seems irretrievably remote from the linguistic operation of predicating a property of an object (where the two elements must by definition be conceived separately). Nevertheless, the infant's intersubjective awareness is undeniable and crucial: some intersubjectivity, like other communicational factors, must have its roots in the pre-linguistic formats described by Bruner; and such pragmatic factors may very well contribute to the acquisition of predication.

We have already maintained that the child must make a designation hypothesis. For grammatical predication, however, the child must make another linguistic hypothesis, namely, that words can be combined and recombined to express states of affairs independently of his immediate experience and of his communicative intentions—quite early on in the production of multiple-word utterances children say things they could never have heard and say things representing states of affairs they could not have experienced. Moreover, grammatical predicates, like other grammatical relations, are what Chomsky (1971) calls 'structure-dependent'. An example of a structure-dependent rule is: in order to convert the assertion 'The dog that is in the corner is hungry' to a question, 'we first identify the subject noun phrase of the sentence, and then we move the occurrence of "is" following this noun phrase to the beginning of the sentence' (p. 26). Thus, 'the operation considers not merely the sequence of elements that constitute the sentence but also their structure' (pp. 26–27). An example of a 'structure-independent' rule would be: 'take the left-most occurrence of "is" and move it to the front of the sentence', which would yield the ungrammatical '*Is the dog that in the corner is hungry?'. The structure-independent rule fails to account for the fact that the phrase 'the dog that is in the corner' is the subject. Chomsky (1971, pp. 27–28) argues that

the structure-dependent operation has no advantage from the point of view of communicative efficiency or 'simplicity' ... we have very little evidence, in our normal experience, that the structure-dependent operation is the correct one ... It is however, safe to predict that a child who has had no such experience would unerringly apply the structure-dependent operation the first time he attempts to form the question ... Furthermore, all known formal operations in the grammar of English, or of any other language, are structure-dependent.

For the most part, the transformational rules proposed for the languages thus far studied have not been shown to be explainable in terms of the pressures of communication nor by any principle of conceptual efficiency. While grammar is structure-dependent in this sense, the pragmatic aspects of language use can be construed as context-dependent.

In addition, the arguments listed earlier in support of the designation hypothesis also hold for predication. In order to acquire syntax the child must articulate structural relations among lexical items within prosodically complex envelopes such that the meanings of individual items are constrained by their collocation, yielding the superordinate compositional meaning of the phrase or sentence. But prior to syntax children produce multiple-item utterances containing 'non-standard words'. Bloom (1973) noticed this phenomenon: her daughter produced / widə / with genuine words in single intonational envelopes, but these combinations had no apparent meaning. Because of this phenomenon and because of the occurrence of 'successive-single-word utterances' (each word having a falling intonation contour and a pause after it), Bloom suggested that children *learn* syntax by coding their conceptual representations of experience in terms of the linguistic categories they induce from the speech they hear (pp. 130–132). Dore *et al.* (1975) also found several kinds of vocalizations (called presyntactic devices) transitional between single words and genuine syntax. We concluded merely that

> successive-single-word utterances express two separate referring items in two separate intonation patterns; presyntactic devices express one referential item and a non-referential item within a single intonation pattern. These are two failures to produce integrated syntagmas, the first lacking prosodic integration and the second lacking referential integration. Both of course lack a relational component. (pp. 25–26)

Although the data are the same in both studies, there is a difference in interpretation. Bloom claims that syntax is learned, yet she provides no explanation of how the 'linguistic coding' of 'conceptual representations' is made possible. Her assumption here is, I believe, that conceptual *content* (plus some unspecified general-purpose cognitive processes) is a sufficient basis for acquiring the grammatical code. This assumption, I have been arguing, is unwarranted. Although the issue was not broached in Dore *et al.* (1975), the present argument is that the acquisition of the syntactic code requires the presence of the specifically linguistic predication hypothesis. The hypothesis theory is also recommended by the facts that (1) children produce 'non-standard predications', indicating some general knowledge about predication which is not restricted to knowledge of particular predicates, and (2) they use syntax for non-communicative purposes.

On the basis of a different set of arguments, Fodor (1976) reaches a similar conclusion as to how grammar could be acquired:

> Learning a language involves learning what the predicates of the language mean. Learning what the predicates of a language mean involves a determination of the extension of these predicates [which] involves learning that

they fall under certain rules (i.e., truth rules). But one cannot learn that P falls under R unless one has a language in which P and R can be represented. So ... one cannot learn a first language unless one already has a system capable of representing the predicates in that language *and their extensions*. (pp. 63–4)

Thus Fodor's position is that if grammatical properties are acquired by the process of hypothesis-testing (a position which is apparently accepted by the majority of developmental psycholinguists in America) then the child must already possess a language-like representational system from which to project and conform hypotheses: in particular, in order to figure out the truth of a given predicate, the child must have available a propositional (and computational) system in terms of which he can do his figuring out. Of course, the notion of 'predication hypothesis' I have been advocating is closer to Peirce's notion (1957) of an 'admissible hypothesis' which the mind is predetermined to entertain, but this, too, presupposes something like Fodor's representational system.

2. Conceptual Conditions for Language Acquisition

In the discussion thus far little has been said about the purely conceptual inputs to language. A conceptual basis must of course be assumed for most of the communicative and linguistic aspects of development already mentioned, but some investigators would argue further that a complete account of concept development would be sufficient to explain the emergence of grammar. The arguments in the present section suggest why this cannot be the case; specifically, I will try to supplement some recent proposals about development in order to account more fully for language. For example, Nelson (1974) offers a view of concept formation which is compatible with many of the known facts about language acquisition; her 'functional core' notion of a concept, if it is correct, settles some of the problems in developmental psycholinguistics. Yet it falls short, I think, of accounting for grammar.

Nelson argues that none of four theories—the Abstraction, the Semantic Feature, the Piagetian, and the Relational Concept theories—alone can adequately explain concept development. For example, in contrast to the Abstraction and Semantic Feature theories, Nelson offers the following characterization of the infant's forming of concepts on the basis of instances of objects (instances being what she calls 'perceptual whole elements'):

Whole elements ... take on definitions as concepts in terms of the synthesis of their functional or dynamic *relations*. Subsequently, other whole elements that enter into the same set of relations can be granted concept status within this previously defined concept. Analysis of parts of the whole is unnecessary to this initial concept formation process. At the outset, analysis is also unnecessary to identification of new instances of the concept, which takes place on the basis of the similarity of relations into which the concept instance enters .. . . Thus synthesis of the functional relationships of an individual whole is the essence of the concept formation process. (Nelson, 1974, p. 276)

After the infant conceptualizes instances of an object by synthesizing certain functional relations, he can proceed to analyse the invariant properties of different instances of the same concept, and then to name it. 'Naming may begin', Nelson claims, 'when the child recognizes that a word used by others is used consistently in the context of instances of one of his concepts'. But she speculates that 'it could be that he is specifically tuned to look for such relationships' (1974, p. 279).

Nelson describes the relation between concepts and first words:

when instances of these first concepts came to be named, it would be expected that they would be named only in the context of one of the definitionally specified actions or relationships. The word, the object, the action, and the relations to other objects would all be used in a totality that included the child as definer and integral member. (1974, p. 280)

Thus, she suggests that initially the word, for object-concepts at least, is simply another peripheral 'non-core' relation. The full representation of the concept BALL, for example, is as follows: its 'functional core' relationships are 'rolls' and 'bounces'; its 'non-core implicit' relationships include 'actor', 'action', and 'location'; 'optional' relationships include 'possessor'; 'descriptive features' are 'shape', 'rigidity', 'texture', 'size', 'colour'; and its 'names' include 'ball', 'baseball', etc.

Notice that all the defining relationships of BALL, except 'names', are based on conceptualizations of perceivable characteristics. Although 'names' do possess perceivable phonetic shapes, they also involve another relation, one between sound and meaning, which amounts to a separate level of representation: the concept BALL is a cognitive representation of the relationships into which objects can actively enter; the word 'ball', however, represents the concept BALL on a linguistic level. This very obvious fact, that words *refer* to concepts, requires some distinction between lexical representation and conceptual representation. And, since nothing in the defining relations of the concept itself necessitates the existence of naming, one is forced to consider other explanations for the ontogenesis of naming. In other words, the phenomenon cannot be explained on the basis of the 'logical act' of conceiving a single instance (as Nelson, following Cassirer (1953), puts it) any more than it can be explained by induction across instances. Rather, as Nelson has speculated, the child seems to be 'tuned to look' for the relation between the word and the concept. Other relationships, including those in the 'core', do not require this 'tuning' to look for meaning; they require only direct mappings of functional and perceptual features onto conceptual structures.

But word acquisition requires the making of what is described above as the designation hypothesis. And the substance of this hypothesis can be viewed as the 'tuning' which accounts for the child's realization of the relation between concept and name. This must be the case. Otherwise, we cannot explain how or why 'the child recognizes that a word used by others is used consistently in the context of instances of one of his concepts', as Nelson puts it. Therefore, despite the putative 'totality' of word-object-action, a name, for example the name 'ball', has a cognitive status *as a name* independent of the 'defining relationships' of the concept (in this case, BALL) from the very beginning of speech. This position does not conflict with, so much as complement Nelson's account; the inclusion of the designation hypothesis is in fact partly adumbrated by her formulations and by her claim that 'naming' is temporally the last relationship of the concept to be acquired.

More importantly, her account provides a coherent view of the conceptual contributions to the child's language development. Grammatically oriented theories have maintained that the child's production of first single words are 'holophrastic', meaning that they embody sentential relations. Nelson's account offers a strong argument against this position: 'the word refers to the object in one of a set of relations that defines the concept. The concept contains all the known relational information; the word that is attached to it then may refer to the whole concept while naming the concept in one of its defining relations as an instance of that concept' (1974, p. 280). Thus, what grammatical theorists have attributed to the child as syntactic (McNeill, 1970) or semantic (Ingram, 1971) knowledge, Nelson has demonstrated to be actually a conceptual relation. That is, the single word is not an elliptical subject or predicate, nor a case relation like agent or recipient. The only knowledge that can legitimately be attributed to the child at this stage is lexical-conceptual: the single word refers to a single concept. Naturally, naming the concept involves naming it in a context where at least one of its defining relations is apparent to the listener. Grammatical theorists and mothers (both of whom do organize their utterances grammatically) mistake this conceptual relation *inherent* in the concept for a syntactic or semantic relation (which by definition goes beyond the individual concept). They fail to appreciate that the transfer from percepts to semantic features is initially mediated by concepts. As Nelson (1974, p. 272) points out. Clark's (1973) semantic feature analysis, which assumes that perceptual attributes map directly onto meanings, 'cannot account for conceptual meaning independent of lexical items'.

Regarding the conceptual inputs to syntax, Nelson argues that

> When the differentiation of the functional core from other relational specifications has taken place, the child becomes able to both name the concept independently of its involvement in a defining relationship (for example, as represented in a picture or in a new location) and to express the concept and the relations independently, thereby making it possible to form relational statements. (1974, p. 280)

But she adds that 'labeling objects *independently* of their functional relationships (e.g., "X is a ball") is a significant advance over naming them in the context of their actions and relationships . . . . This new ability to recombine known concepts with previously unrelated concepts implies a significant cognitive reorganization and accompanying increase in cognitive flexibility' (p. 282). Nelson does not explain how this 'cognitive reorganization' takes place. But she suggests a way in which 'general abstract categories' might emerge: first, the child probably comes to recognize redundancies in relations across concepts; second, the use of words 'for concepts may lead to recognition of their independence of *specific* relationships and therefore to reorganization and recombination in language' (p. 283). Again, however, it seems highly plausible that the 'reorganization and recombination in language' requires something like the predication hypothesis.

2.1 Concept Formation and Grammatical Categories

On the basis of Nelson's account, three interrelated arguments can be made: that the 'reorganization and recombination in language' requires the predication hypothesis; but that case grammars cannot adequately describe predication and other grammatical relations; and that the communicative, conceptual, and grammatical requirements for language emergence are best viewed as developing components of speech acts. To the latter two arguments we now turn.

Consider some of the major discoveries about early multiple-word utterances from the past decade of intense research. McNeill (1970), for example, in analysing the initial multiple-word utterances of a child from an earlier study by Brown and his colleagues, found that almost all the utterances could be construed in terms of grammatical relations of the sort postulated by Chomsky: these are formal syntactic relations defined as abstract configurations of categories in hierarchical organization. McNeill could identify subject of a sentence, main verb of a predicate, object of a predicate, modifier of a noun phrase and head noun of a noun phrase. The analysis is most revealing in the light of the enormous number of possible combinations that were *not* realized in the child's speech. Similarly, Bloom (1970) found that word order in the early speech of her subjects was highly constrained which, she argued, was partly due to certain semantic relations underlying the surface syntax. And a great deal of other research during this period makes it abundantly clear that early patterned speech is to some extent organized grammatically. However, whether the grammar is syntactically based or semantically based and whether the child at this time possesses linguistic competence in Chomsky's sense are issues still to be decided.

Brown (1973), taking as given the grammaticality of child speech, evaluated the most prominent theories proposed to account for this grammaticality. Apart from examining the work of McNeill, Bloom and others, Brown also evaluated the aptness of case grammar (as conceived by Fillmore, 1968) for describing Stage I speech. He then judged the adequacy of competing theories according to three criteria: completeness, in terms of how much of the collected corpora could be analysed in terms of the grammar; the simplicity of the generalizations used in characterizing speech as Stage I; and the ability of the grammar to account for errors, surprising absence of errors, and pecularities of distribution.

2.2 The Case Against Case Grammar

Before discussing the inadequacy of case grammar as a description of early speech, let us first consider the theory in relation to adult linguistic competence. Fillmore

(1968) introduced his version of case grammar into linguistic theory when criticizing Chomskyan grammar for not fully explicating semantic roles such as agent, instrument, dative, and so on. Essentially, Fillmore suggested replacing underlying phrase markers (where the basic sentence constituents are noun phrase and predicate phrase) with case rules (where the sentence consists of a modality and a proposition, the latter having a verb which takes noun phrases specified with regard to role). But case grammar has been severely critized: there are no constraints on the postulation of new cases; some of those put forth by Fillmore are ill-defined; and cases provide no major advantage (without accompanying complication) over phrase markers in transformationally deriving surface structures from deep structures. But perhaps the most serious problem is that cases are simply unnecessary. Katz (1972) has shown how in a Chomskyan grammar 'the semantic roles expressed by a sentence are represented at the semantic level by its reading ... the grammar's account of semantic roles is determined in part by the syntactic information contained in definitions of grammatical relations, but also in part by the inherent meaning of the lexical items of the sentence' (p. 112). Thus a grammatical relation, say the subject of a sentence, is indeed distinct from the semantic role of agent, as Fillmore rightly emphasized; but for any given verb–noun phrase pair, the amalgamation of their semantic markers in the specified syntactic relation will predict whether or not the noun phrase is to be interpreted as agent. That is, semantically interpreted deep structure phrase markers provide sufficient information about propositional role and, since propositional, lexical, and transformational information are needed anyway, cases are therefore redundant. So the initial motivation for Fillmore's grammar is lost. It is of course possible that revised versions of case grammar may become more adequate as formal theories (Stockwell, Schachter, and Partee (1973) have made some interesting proposals along these lines), but at present there is no compelling reason to include a case component in a transformational grammar.

In child language, too, cases seem to be unnecessary. Brown (1973) found case grammar inadequate on several grounds. One of its shortcomings in analysing what Brown calls Stage I speech (when the child's mean length of utterance in morphemes is about 1·75) is 'the lack of any account of the imperative, negative and interrogative operations' (p. 139). For example, it explains nothing about the acquisition of Wh-questions. For speech after Stage I, he points out, there are 'many other shortcomings: no account of verbal auxiliaries or of inflection for number or of determiners and almost nothing on embedding and conjoining' (p. 139). Nothing in case grammar suggests why there are no case markings, no determiners, and no occurrences of the verbs 'have' and 'be' at Stage I (pp. 139–40). Also, there are several kinds of errors—such as pronouns of objective form in the subject position, as in 'her crashed'—which go unexplained. Finally, Brown interprets McNeill as claiming that 'formal relations like subject and object serve to mark particular semantic roles associated with verbs as their various logical arguments' (p. 146); he then speculates that this 'may be the level at which psychological reality exists' for the child, and suggests that 'Intermediate semantic abstractions like agent, patient, beneficiary, and so on, may only be an imposed taxonomy. What the child may know is that for each particular transitive verb, like hit, call, see, the formal subject and object mark persons and objects in the respective quite specific semantic roles' (p. 146). And there are other quite different reasons for suggesting that cases are indeed 'an imposed taxonomy'.

Nelson's account of development focuses on object concepts, but she also discusses action concepts. First, object concepts themselves are partly defined in terms of implicit relations like 'actor upon', 'actions upon', 'location', 'possession'. And she hypothesizes that these relations

> are in general not object specific, their presence in many different object concepts will lead to the cognitive organization of their recurring functional relationships. That is, the actor category will take on the values of all possible actors in available concepts .. .. What emerges then must be a kind of network of concepts defining the possible relations among actor, action and object concepts. (Nelson, 1974, pp. 281–282)

These claims suggest the following picture of language acquisition. First, concepts like BALL and MOTHER are specified as to relations like 'acted upon' or 'actor upon'; the former cannot be an actor, the latter most often is. When these concepts become represented lexically their defining relations are converted to semantic features like animacy; the word 'ball' is inanimate, 'mother' animate. (As mentioned earlier, Nelson's theory does not explain the conversion itself so much as what exactly gets converted.) Finally, when the child begins to acquire syntax, nouns like 'ball' and 'mother' will take on syntactic markers as well which, together with the verbs they combine with, will determine the noun's semantic role in the sentence. Again, since there is some independent evidence that the child acquires semantic features (at the very least in Clark's sense of percepts marked for semantic distinguishers) and syntactic markers (McNeill, 1970) anyway, cases seem superfluous.

A point about which most grammatical and conceptual approaches agree, but which I think especially recommends the predication hypothesis theory, is that verbs are central to the sentence formation process. Nelson assumes that this is so because verbs 'entail the fewest specific *conceptual* implications' (1974, p. 282). But she does not attempt to explain how action concepts give rise to verbs, she just assumes their isomorphic correspondence. Yet not all possible action concepts are encoded as verbs and not all verbs express actions (for example, 'be' and 'have' and stative verbs like 'know'). Still, the verb is the archetype of a grammatical category, at least in the sense that it contributes the most to the sentence formation process. Similarly, the notion 'main verb of a predicate phrase' seems to be an archetypical grammatical relation ('subject noun phrase of a sentence' being another). Again, if we ask what is required for only certain action and non-action concepts to give rise to verbs, a likely candidate for an answer is the predication hypothesis. And, as mentioned earlier, the verbs that are acquired contain syntactic and semantic markers specifying the kinds of arguments they can take, for instance, which noun phrases can be subjects.

In concluding this section, it seems appropriate to try to place my speculations about the grammatical contribution to language acquisition within the larger perspective of studying *the whole language of the whole child*. Grammar, though necessary for language acquisition, may have a quite limited role in determining the whole character of language behaviour. Among the things a sentence-grammar, for example, cannot explain are: (1) how sentences are actually produced in speech performance; (2) what is talked about; (3) the intentions motivating the choice of sentences; (4) the uses to which sentences can be put; and (5) the shared assumptions speakers bring to their conversations.

Two examples of research (on (1) and (4) above) which can be construed as supplementing rather than replacing the role of grammar in ontogenesis are the work of McNeill (1975) on speech production and of Halliday (1975) on speech functions. McNeill argues that knowledge of language structure, knowledge of the appropriate word order for instance, does not explain how speakers, in their utterances, actually organize their words into that order. He proposes that in the child's earliest patterned speech the schema for producing words in a given order is often guided by a separate schema, one which represents the action sequence which is the content of the utterance to be produced. And Halliday, in characterizing the multiple functions of a given utterance, proposes that the utterance is best viewed as the realization of certain semantic choices from among a large network of potential choices. These theoretical orientations require versions of a 'grammar' differing both from each other and from the standard 'grammar' of the 1960s, but neither attempts to replace the grammar in the way that the radical pragmatic approaches do.

3. Conclusion: the Case for Speech Acts

The central question still remains: how does the child come to recognize abstract grammatical relations such as subject and main verb of a sentence? Chomsky's (by now infamous) proposal that the child is innately prepared to recognize them has been much criticized. And, indeed, caution is warranted; ongoing work repeatedly demonstrates the importance of the social and conceptual determinants of language. Yet, as I have tried to show, these are not sufficient to account for grammar; nothing thus far discovered about the infant's pre-linguistic experience necessarily leads to grammar. Thus, while innate constraints on grammatical knowledge in the form of something like the 'linguistic hypotheses' may not in itself constitute a satisfactory explanation, it still seems to be an unavoidable option given the present state of the science. The characterization by Chomsky (1971) of the primary problem still remains: 'A system of knowledge and belief results from the interplay of innate mechanisms, genetically determined maturational processes, and interaction with the social and physical environment. The problem is to account for the system constructed by the mind in the course of this interaction' (p. 21). But in the case of language the problem of accounting 'for the system constructed by the mind' has proven to be greater than the problem of accounting for knowledge about formal relations among sentences. However elegant the theory of linguistic competence is, it does not account for speakers' knowledge of how to use sentences for purposes of communication (nor was it ever meant to). What is needed is a theory of communicative acts which will have as a component a sub-theory of grammar.

The theory of speech acts is a relatively well-defined theory of communicative acts. At the most fundamental level, speech acts are units which simultaneously manifest the structure, content, and function of language. The structure of the speech act is its grammar. The content consists of the conceptual substance of the proposition and it constitutes what is talked about. Its function is its illocutionary force which consists of the speaker's intentions and expectations. Moreover, much of the structure of conversations can be viewed in terms of speech acts. The speaker's choice of one speech act over another, for example, typically constrains the listener's choice of response. In fact, Garvey has shown that children as young as 3 years understand the 'domain' of a speech act type such that certain utterance types characteristically precede the speech act and others follow as consequences of it.

Consider as an example of a primitive speech act the utterance 'I first', produced by a child of 26 months in the context of beginning to play a game with other children. The content involves the concept of self and the concept of a turn in a game. The grammatical structure can be viewed as a predication of a certain sort about the self; also, the grammar requires that the personal pronoun for self in the subject position be of a certain form, and that the predicate phrase occur last. (At that time the child did not control the copula in English, but this child some months later began to use 'I'm first' in the same situation.) The function of the utterance can be viewed as a primitive illocutionary force which we can call a 'claim'. Claims establish facts by merely being stated; by saying 'I first' the child *is* first at taking turns, unless some other procedure for turn-taking is in force. Further, the utterance reflects the child's understanding of this social rule. And she must assume that her interlocutors know of the same rule and that they will accept her claim, unless they have some reason to challenge it. In other words the utterance makes manifest a right of the speaker and creates a fact relevant to the interaction with others. A similar analysis could be provided for children during their one-word stage who say 'me' to perform a claim, or 'no' to perform a protest or to answer a question, and so on.

If we fail to characterize the function of utterances for children on this level, then we fail to capture what they know about using language at this age. Clearly, such a characterization goes beyond the grammar. Theories of child grammar have in fact not even attempted to treat utterance types such as greetings, leave-takings, protests, getting someone's attention, and so on. Yet the character of such communicative acts is made manifest by the grammar. The speech act seems to be the most comprehensive unit of analysis because it accommodates not only the grammaticalization of conceptual content and social understanding, but also the intentions motivating the utterance and the speaker's expectations regarding the consequences of it. Regarding the ontogenesis of speech acts, the child's pre-linguistic communicative experience and conceptual development, along with the grammatical inputs described above as the 'linguistic hypotheses', can be viewed as conditions for the acquisition of speech acts.

The process by which speech acts are acquired can be characterized roughly as follows: it proceeds, on the one hand, from sensorimotor schema to concept to word to propositional constituent; and, on the other, from intersubjective awareness to communicative intent to illocutionary force to sentence mood or modality. The current work on pragmatics by Bruner, Bates, Ryan, and others demonstrates that non-linguistic communicative frames develop first, sentences being inserted into them later; but it does not explain how communicative and conceptual content become grammaticalized in sentences. In some of this work there is a tendency to assume that communicative acts and sentences are mutually exclusive or to assume that the former somehow account for the latter. I would advocate, in our analyses of child language, that we adopt Searle's position that speech acts and sentences are different units of descriptions for different purposes of somewhat overlapping phenomena. Speech act theory explicates the 'constitutive rules underlying linguistic acts' and sentence grammars explain the 'conventional realization' of these rules.

To conclude, I do not wish to perpetuate useless dichotomies. But I would suggest that some of our confusion and polemics (both of which limit our understanding of children) are due to our failure to keep in mind two 'real' dichotomies. The first is the (grammatical) code versus the (communicative) message; the second is (mental) representation versus (social) communication. Enough has been said above to flesh out these distinctions. If we bear them in mind I think our enterprise will be more fruitful.

Acknowledgements

I would like to thank Margery Franklin, Maryl Gearhart, William Hall, Ivana Marková, Denis Newman, and Marylin Shatz for very helpful comments on drafts of this paper.

References

Austin, J., (1962), *How to Do Things with Words*, Oxford: Oxford University Press.

Bates, E., (1976), Pragmatics and sociolinguistics in child language. In Morehead, D. and Morehead, A. (eds), *Language Deficiency in Children: Selected Readings*, Philadelphia: University Park Press.

Bates, E., Camaioni, L., and Volterra, V., (1975), The acquisition of performatives prior to speech, *Merrill-Palmer Quarterly*, 21, (3).

Bloom, L., (1970), *Language Development: Form and Function in Emerging Grammars*, Cambridge, Mass.: M.I.T. Press.

Bloom, L., (1973), *One Word at a Time: the Use of Single Word Utterances Before Syntax*, The Hague: Mouton.

Brown, R., (1973), *A First Language: The Early Stages*, Cambridge, Mass.: Harvard University Press; London: Allen & Unwin.

Bruner, J., (1975), The ontogenesis of speech acts, *Journal of Child Language*, 2, 1–19.

Bruner, J. (this volume), From communication to language: a psychological perspective.

Cassirer, E., (1953), *Structure and Function and Einstein's Theory of Relativity*, trs. Swaby, W.C., and Swaby, M.C. New York: Dover Publications.

Chomsky, N. (1965), *Aspects of the Theory of Syntax*, Cambridge, Mass.: M.I.T. Press.

Chomsky, N., (1971), *Problems of Knowledge and Freedom*, New York: Random House.

Chomsky, N., (1975), *Reflections on Language*, New York: Pantheon.

Clark, E., (1973), What's in a word: on the child's acquisition of semantics in his first language. In Moore, T. (ed.), *Cognitive Development and the Acquisition of Language*, New York: Academic Press.

DeLaguna, G., (1927), *Speech: Its Function and Development*, New Haven, Conn.: Yale University Press.

Dore, J., (1973), The development of speech acts. Doctoral dissertation, City University of New York.

Dore, J., (1974), A pragmatic description of early language development, *Journal of Psycholinguistic Research*, 4, 343–350.

Dore, J., (1975), Holophrases, speech acts and language universals, *Journal of Child Language*, 2, 21–40.

Dore, J., (1977), Children's illocutionary acts. In Freedle, R. (ed.), *Discource Comprehension and Production*, New York: Lawrence. Erlbaum Associates.

Dore, J., Franklin, M.B., Miller, R.T., and Ramer A.L.H. (1975), Transitional phenomena in early language acquisition, *Journal of Child Language*, 3, 13–28.

Fillmore, C., (1968), The case for case. In Bach, E. and Harms, R.(eds), *Universals in Linguistic Theory*, New York: Holt, Rinehart, & Winston.

Fodor, J., (1976), *The Language of Thought*, New York: Crowell.

Garvey, C., (1975), Requests and responses in children's speech, *Journal of Child Language*, 2, 41–59.

Grice, H., (1968), Utterer's meaning, sentence-meaning and word-meaning, *Foundations of Language*, 4, 225–242.

Grice, H., (1975), Logic and conversation. In Cole, P., and Morgan J. (eds), *Syntax and Semantics*, vol. 3, Speech acts, New York: Academic Press.

Halliday, M. (1975), *Learning How to Mean*, London: Edward Arnold.

Ingram, D. (1971), Transitivity in child language, *Language*, 47, 888–910.

Katz, J., (1972), *Semantic Theory*, New York: Harper & Row.

Kempson, R., (1975), *Presupposition and the Delimitation of Semantics*, Cambridge: Cambridge University Press.

Lakoff, G., (1969), Generative semantics. In *Papers from the Fifth Regional Meeting of the Chicago Linguistic Society*, University of Chicago.

Lenneberg, E., (1967), *Biological Foundations of Language*, New York: Wiley.

Luria, A., (1961), *The Role of Speech in the Regulation of Normal and Abnormal Behavior*, New York: Liveright Publishing Corp.

McNeill, D., (1970), *The Acquisition of Language*, New York: Harper & Row.

McNeill, D., (1975), Semiotic extension. In Solso, R. (ed.) *Information Processing and Cognition*, Hillsdale, N.J.: Lawrence Erlbaum Associates.

Nelson, K., (1973), Structure and strategy in learning to talk, *Society for Research in Child Development Monographs*, vol. 38.

Nelson, K., (1974), Concept, word, and sentence: interrelations in acquisition and development, *Psychological Review*, 81, 267–285.

Peirce, C., (1957), The logic of abduction. In Thomas, V. (ed.), *Peirce's Essays in the Philosophy of Science*, New York: Liberal Arts Press.

Piaget, J., (1952), *The Origins of Intelligence in Children*, New York: International Universities Press.

Rees, N., (1973), Noncommunicative functions of language in children, *Journal of Speech and Hearing Research*, 38, 98–110.

Richards, M., (1974), *The Integration of the Child into a Social World*, Cambridge: Cambridge University Press.

Ricks, D., (1971), The beginnings of vocal communication in infants and autistic children. Unpublished Doctorate of Medicine thesis, University of London.

Ryan, J., (1974), Early language development. In Richards, M. (ed.), *The Integration of the Child into a Social World*, Cambridge: Cambridge University Press.

Searle, J., (1969), *Speech Acts*, Cambridge: Cambridge University Press.

Stockwell, R., Schachter, P., and Partee, B. (1973), *The Major Syntactic Structures of English*, New York: Holt, Rinehart & Winston.

Sugarman-Bell, S., (1973), A description of communicative development in the pre-language child. Unpublished Honors paper, Hampshire College.

Werner, H., and Kaplan, B. (1963), *Symbol Formation*, New York: Wiley.

Wittgenstein, L., (1953), *Philosophical Investigations*, trs. Anscombe, G.E.M., Oxford: Basil Blackwell; New York: The Macmillan Company.

Wolff, P., (1969), The natural history of crying and other vocalizations in early infancy. In Foss, B. (ed.), *Determinants of Infant Behaviour*, vol. 4, London: Methuen.

6

ON PIAGETIAN COGNITIVE OPERATIONS, SEMANTIC COMPETENCE, AND MESSAGE STRUCTURE IN ADULT–CHILD COMMUNICATION

Ragnar Rommetveit

1. Introduction

Current research on cognitive development is largely dominated by issues initially raised by the Genevan school and defined in terms of Piaget's general conceptual framework. The Genevan contribution appears to be so monumental and self-sufficient that researchers tend to buy it wholesalé or not at all. Recent literature is replete with replications and modifications of earlier studies, yet—despite numerous declarations of discontent—nearly devoid of significant reorientations and genuine innovations. Proponents and critics have gone into their trenches, and attempts at transcending tradition-bound premises for enquiries into language and thought are hampered by an undue transfer of respect from Piaget's impressive work on thinking to his far more sporadic comments upon the nature and role of language.

This chapter aims at a synthesis of some main features of Piaget's model of operative intelligence and an equally dynamic psychology of language. My own general approach to language has been outlined in two more comprehensive works (Rommetveit, 1972, 1974), and I shall in what follows try to show how it differs from that of the Genevan school. A critique of some of Piaget's views on language, however, may hopefully pave the way for an alliance of forces along novel research frontiers.

2. Critical Comments on Piaget's Approach

2.1 On 'Negative Rationalism' in Studies of Language and Thought

Acquisition of knowledge often entails systematic comparison: we get to know something initially unknown by examining how it resembles and in which respects it differs from something we know already or assume to be known. Thus, children's thinking may be studied and made known to us in terms of, for example, deviance from adult thought. The latter may in turn be explicated in terms of resemblance to and deviations from some fully formalized system such as, for instance, some particular logical calculus. And we may also try to assess the child's conceptual development within some field as an approximation to a given, systematically elaborated, scientific conceptual framework.

These are perfectly legitimate and useful strategies, of immediate diagnostic relevance in educational settings aiming precisely and explicitly at mastery of such calculi and scientific frameworks. The resultant knowledge is bound to be of a negative nature, though, in the sense that our initial ignorance is being replaced by knowledge of shortcomings. And our interpretation of data from experimental investigations is to a large extent contingent upon how we conceive of those formal models of language and thought against which the child's performance is being gauged.

Piaget's explication of the relationship between logic and psychology is replete with insights into extremely complex epistemological issues, yet based upon a fairly simple 'épistemologie génétique'. His meta-logic is clearly of a pragmatic nature, inspired by Bridgman's operationalism. Piaget (1957, p. 7) maintains: 'operationalism provides real ground on which logic and psychology can meet. Operations ... play an indispensable role in logic .... On the other hand, operations are actual psychological activities'. Recourse to formal logic is hence considered legitimate on the child's own premises, since the child's initial repertoire of sensorimotor operations is conceived of as the embryo out of which mastery of formal logical operations develop in a stagewise fashion.

Early thought is thus investigated by the Genevan school as the precursor of perfect mastery of abstract logical calculi such as the propositional calculus. The assumed 'psychological reality' of operations may even pave the way for a programme for comparative analysis of initial 'outline structures' and 'logical structures characteristic of the higher stages of development'. A trace of a reductionist component in Piaget's epistemology, moreover, is revealed in his comment upon the feasibility of such a systematic comparison (Piaget, 1957, p. 48): 'The use of the logical calculus in the description of neural networks on the one hand, and in cybernetic models on the other, shows that such a programme is not out of the question'.

Piaget's outlook on the relationship between formal logic and operative intelligence is hence such that it allows him to describe the latter in terms of the former. He maintains, for instance, that 'the implications, disjunctions, incompatabilities, etc. which characterize propositional logic ... appear at about eleven to twelve years', and that 'the structures that characterize thought have their roots in action and sensorimotor mechanisms that are deeper than linguistics'. Language, on the other hand, is conceived of as 'necessarily interpersonal and ... composed of a system of *signs* ("arbitrary" or conventional signifiers)'. It is, according to Piaget, 'a ready-made system that is elaborated by society and that contains ... a wealth of cognitive instruments ... at the service of thought' (see Piaget, 1972; Piaget and Inhelder, 1966, p. 69).

A formal logical system such as the propositional calculus, however, is also a ready-made system of signs. It is indeed, by virtue of its closure and artificial construction, even more 'ready-made' than any natural language. Natural language in use, on the other hand, is after all an integral part of the matrix of social interaction out of which the infant develops into a human being. We may argue, therefore, that the assumed superior psychological reality (and primacy) of logical operations in Piaget's *épistemologie génétique* is achieved by a persistent foregrounding of the dynamic or operative aspects of formal logic in combination with an equally persistent foregrounding of the ready-made, 'tool-like', and static aspects of natural language. This is particularly transparent in his early analysis of children's notions of causality (Piaget, 1951, p. 9): 'Between the years of 6 and 9, when the relation indicated by "because" is incorrect, one can always assume that reasoning is at fault; the word "because" (parce que) is used spontaneously by the child from the age of 3 to 4 onwards'. Mastery of the expression PARCE QUE is thus dealt with as an all-or-none affair, i.e. as if full adult mastery can be safely inferred from frequency of spontaneous use. And, as Furth (1970, p. 251) puts it: 'The question about language and thinking can now be seen to have sense only if the stress in the word "thinking" is on the operative component and in the word "language" on the material, figurative component through which one language differs from another, or one symbolic medium is different from another symbolic medium.' The child's semantic competence is thus in Piaget's programme for analysis of language and thought by definition nearly devoid of operative aspects.

Formal systems such as the propositional calculus, however, were created on the basis of fragments of natural language with the explicit aim of attaining perfection and closure where everyday discourse leaves us with imperfection and openness. Genevan psycholinguists may hence—even in research on language acquisition— have recourse to formal logic. Sinclair-de-Zwart (1972a, p. 267) thus talks about 'a partial isomorphism between language and logic'. She argues, moreover (p. 275):

A distinction must be made between lexical acquisition and the acquisition of syntactical structures, the latter being far more closely linked to operational level than the former. The operator-like words (e.g., more, less, as much as, none) form a class apart whose correct use is also very closely linked to operational progress. The other lexical items (e.g., long, short, thin, thick, high, low) are far less closely linked to operativity.

Progress with respect to Piagetian thought operations is thus, according to Sinclair-de-Zwart, primarily revealed in *syntactic competence* and *mastery of 'operator-like' words*.

I shall later, and on empirical grounds, question Sinclair-de-Zwart's conclusion concerning words such as SHORT/LONG and 'operativity'. My present concern, however, has to do with her (and Piaget's) very notion of 'operativity' in connection with semantic competence. Is it possible that such a notion—because of its ultimate anchorage in formal logic and inbuilt bias in the direction of the operators of artificially created systems of signs—may serve to conceal operative aspects of natural language other than those that have been incorporated—and 'purified'—in symbolic logic?

I have elsewhere questioned the rationale for applying criteria from formal logic in semantic analysis of ordinary language (Rommetveit, 1974, pp. 6–7). The calculus of propositions, for instance, was developed for particular purposes and with carefully considered gains and costs: an algorithm for assessing truth values of composite expressions was gained at the cost of the semantic flexibility inherent in natural language. A recourse to criteria from formal propositional logic in an analysis of segments of everyday discourse may hence, of course, serve to reveal those very shortcomings of natural language which motivated the creators of the propositional calculus. We may for instance, as Katz and Fodor (1963, p. 200) have done, argue that a sentence such as 'My spinster aunt is an infant' is contradictory or even 'ungrammatical'. Such a relegation of perfectly comprehensible segments of everyday discourse from the domain of semantically appropriate language, however, testifies to *negative rationalism*: it is achieved by imposing upon a given utterance an alien straightjacket of 'propositional content' contrary to the intersubjectively established premises of the dialogue in which such an utterance is embedded.

Similar, though more subtle, symptoms of negative rationalism appear in Chomsky's and Piaget's semantic enquiries, and in particular when they deal with what may be labelled 'semantics of social realities' such as words and concepts for kinship. Chomsky's commitment to the truth functions of the propositional calculus is thus revealed in a peculiarly Procrustean 'reading' of the word UNCLE. He compares the following three expressions:

John's uncle.

The person who is the brother of John's
mother or father or the husband of the sister of John's
mother or father.

The person who is the son of one of John's
grandparents or the husband of a daughter of one of John's
grandparents, but is not his father.

And he maintains 'If the concept of "semantic representation" ("reading") is to play any role at all in linguistic theory, then these three expressions must have the same semantic representation' (Chomsky, 1972, p. 85). I have elsewhere (Rommetveit, 1974, pp. 18–19) explored some rather puzzling implications of such a claim. What is of particular interest in the present context, however, is Chomsky's sin of omission: *synonymy salva veritate* is achieved at the cost of that very significant aspect of UNCLE-ness that is subject to modification in expressions such as 'a good uncle'.

A similar sin of omission appears in Piaget's early account of children's definitions of FAMILY. Piaget (1951, pp. 115–119) distinguishes between three stages of conceptual development. What is understood by the word FAMILY at the first stage is simply all people living with the child. At the next stage, reference is restricted to people connected by blood-relationship living in the immediate vicinity. The third (and final) stage, however, is characterized by a concept of FAMILY covering people connected by blood-relationship, irrespective of where they are living.

What is disregarded in such an analysis is again brought to our attention by pondering aspects of the word FAMILY of particular significance when we talk about, for example, 'good families'. And neither Chomsky's UNCLE nor Piaget's third stage of definition of FAMILY leave us with any clues whatsoever to significant and immediately comprehensible 'metaphorical' use of the words. I may, for instance, make known an important characteristic of some particular group of people who are not connected by blood relationships by referring to that group as 'a family'. And I may convey significant aspects of my relationship to some particular older male person who is not my relative by saying: 'He is an uncle to me.'

Such use testifies to abstract mastery of the words, and it is by no means contingent upon veridical knowledge of biological descent, degrees of consanguinity, and marital law. Abstract mastery presupposes categorization of UNCLE-ness and FAMILY-ness as encountered in social interaction since, as Lévi-Strauss has put it, 'A kinship system does *not* consist of objective ties of descent or of given degrees of consanguinity among individuals ...' (my italics). The sin of omission in Chomsky's and Piaget's analysis is accordingly not restricted to esoteric, peripheral or surplus semantic potentialities of UNCLE and FAMILY. What has been omitted is simply kinship as a social reality: *synonymy salva veritate* and conformity to scientific taxonomy are achieved by disregarding those attributions of roles and categorizations of interpersonal relationships by virtue of which kinship 'exists only in the consciousness of men' (Lévi-Strauss, 1964, p. 50).

Such relational aspects of kinship, however, are in fact also dealt with by Piaget in his early analysis of decentration. His point of departure is the 'three brothers problem' from the Binet-Simon test. The child is told about a family consisting of three brothers, and he is requested to place himself at the point of view of one of them so as to count the latter's brothers. Incapacity to cope with brotherhood as a relation is then revealed in conclusions such as: 'I have three brothers, Paul, Ernest, and myself.' Piaget (1951, p. 88) maintains, therefore, that 'judgments of relations are constantly transformed into judgments of inherence (inclusion or membership)'. He is fully aware that lack of decentration in such a case mirrors deficient semantic competence as well, though, and argues (1951, p. 104): 'If the difficulties are really caused by an inability to handle the logic of relations, this same absence of relativity will have to be found in the definition of the word "brother".'

What is left unexplored by Piaget, however, is the precise relationship between the definition of BROTHER he himself takes for granted as a basis for counting and BROTHERHOOD as a relational concept. Consider, therefore, a family consisting of four brothers, Paul, Ernest, Jean, and Noam. The BROTHERHOODS involved in that case are simply the set of all possible ordered pairs: (1) Paul, Ernest; (2) Ernest, Paul; (3) Paul, Jean; (4) Jean, Paul; (5) Paul, Noam; (6) Noam, Paul; (7) Ernest, Jean; (8) Jean, Ernest; (9) Ernest, Noam; (10) Noam, Ernest; (11) Jean, Noam; and (12) Noam, Jean. Each such ordered pair represents in principle one discrete and autonomous relation in the sense that, for example, Jean may be a good brother to Noam whereas in fact Noam may be a bad brother to Jean. And such a complete enumeration of BROTHERHOODS is, of course, as 'objective' and 'referential' as— and no more 'connotative' than—the counting of heads.

What is implied by our initial description of the family as existing of four brothers, however, is precisely a counting of heads rather than of relations. It does not matter, therefore, if we, for instance, add one sister to the family above: our count of BROTHERS yields exactly the same number, even though the number of BROTHERHOODS in that case is increased by four. A response such as: 'I *have* four brothers, Ernest, Jean, Noam, and myself' may accordingly be interpreted as an attempt to comply with the 'counting-of heads' definition of BROTHER implicit in the adult's initial statement of the problem. What is achieved by that definition, moreover, is precisely a transformation of judgments of relations into judgments of membership in a class defined by a given degree of consanguinity. And the same holds true for Chomsky's 'reading' of UNCLE and Piaget's third and final stage of development of the concept of FAMILY as well: mastery of words for kinship is gauged against 'objective' knowledge of criteria for class membership only, whereas abstract and metaphorical mastery of the words in everyday discourse is clearly contingent upon experience of BROTHERHOOD, FAMILYNESS, and UNCLENESS in a matrix of social interaction characterized by distinctive kinship roles and relations.

The issue of negative rationalism in assessment of semantic competence may hence be formulated as a choice of point of departure: we may gauge mastery of words against criteria for usage borrowed from some scientific domain of discourse, or we may explore semantic competence as verbal manifestations of attributions and categorizations intuitively mastered by unlearned people in a shared 'Lebenswelt'. And this issue is by no means restricted to the semantics of kinship. The question whether 'scientific' versus 'naive' notions should serve as an anchorage for assessment of word meaning has thus been raised by Deese (1962, p. 174) who maintains that 'contrary to Zoology, associative BUTTERFLIES are as closely related to the birds as to the moths'. It is also a central theme in Vygotsky's discussion of 'scientific' versus 'natural' concepts (Vygotsky, 1962).

I have elsewhere (Rommetveit, 1974, pp. 7–11) tried to show how a recourse to scientifically defined 'conceptual realities' in generative and interpretative semantics at times may lead to a choice between alternative scientific representations, each of which may be considered an elaboration of only one particular aspect of some more multi-faceted and contextually monitored 'naive' categorization. Genuine polysemy may thereby be eliminated: we may for instance—in the case of the word BROTHER—decide to discard the *social-relational* in favour of the *biological* aspect.

What follows from such a decision, though, is a commitment to rigid premises for semantic analysis at variance with premises for intersubjectivity encountered in real life dialogues. Consider, for instance, a situation in which Noam wants to make known that his relationship to Jean is devoid of all interpersonal aspects of brotherhood. He may in fact succeed in doing so by saying:

It is true that Jean and I have the same parents, but he has never been a BROTHER to me.

What can be captured by a semantic net of negative rationalism in such a case is merely a contradiction.

Similar, though more subtle, cases of discrepancy between analytically postulated and naively assumed premises for intersubjectivity have been brought to our attention by Marková (this volume) in her critique of research on verbal reasoning. 'Operator-like' expressions such as IF–THEN, for instance, are obviously used in adult discourse most of the time for perfectly rational purposes other than those selectively adopted and purified in the propositional calculus. Thus, Quine (1972, p. 451) maintains: 'No one wants to say that the binomials of Linnaeus or the fourth dimension of Einstein or the binary code of the computer were somehow implicit in ordinary language, and I have seen no more reason to so regard the quantifiers and the truth functions.'

The assumed partial isomorphy between language and formal logic may hence easily lead us astray: We may end up assessing deficiencies of language and reasoning in terms of deviance from alien and superimposed standards instead of assessing human communication and thought on premises adopted by the speaker and thinker himself. And the danger of such a negative rationalism is—despite Piaget's own truly great contributions to our insight into the unique and intrinsic nature of children's thought—particularly salient in a synthesis of Piagetian cognitive psychology and Chomskyan linguistics of the kind attempted by Sinclair-de-Zwart (1972a, 1972b).

2.2 On Communication and Intersubjectivity

To Piaget (1951, pp. 93, 213), language is 'the index of what has become conscious'; and 'to become conscious of an operation is to make it pass over from the plane of action to that of language'. What gives rise to the child's need for verification and makes an operation pass over from the plane of action to that of language, moreover, is (Piaget, 1951, p. 204) 'the shock of our thought coming into contact with that of others'. *Verbal thought*, on the other hand, is conceived of (Piaget, 1951, p. 115) as 'the child's faculty for adapting himself, not to actual reality, but to words and expressions heard in the mouths of adults'.

My purpose with this sample of Piaget's scattered remarks on language and thought is not to do full justice to his multi-faceted views, but rather to bring into focus potential ambiguities and sins of omission. Logical operations, we are told, are 'actual psychological activities' inherent in the child's adaptation to 'actual reality', whereas verbal thought represents adaptation to 'words and expressions heard in the mouths of adults'. Language, however, is at the same time 'the index of what has become conscious' and a prerequisite for 'the shock of our thought coming into contact with that of others'. But how is such contact established? How can we decide whether some particular verbal response on the part of a child in some particular situation represents an adaptation to 'actual reality' or merely to 'words and expressions heard in the mouths of adults'?

In order to pursue this issue, let us now turn to tasks aiming at diagnosis of more specific Piagetian operations. Consider, for instance, the capacity to attend to membership in subordinate and superordinate class simultaneously, i.e. mastery of class inclusion. A variety of types of tasks may be designed for the purpose of assessing that capacity, and four different paper-and-pencil variants of such tasks were included in a large battery of Piaget-inspired problems. The latter were administered during school hours in four separate sessions to small groups of $8^1/_2$-year-old children from an upper-middle-class district close to Oslo. Instructions had been carefully elaborated in advance and standardized, and each child completed every single task without any assistance or disruption.

Their performances on these presumedly related problems, however, did not at all reveal any very consistent pattern. A child might do very well on some, but poorly on other tasks; and neither cross-tabulation of their performances nor systematic analysis of individual patterns yielded any approximation to an image of mastery of class inclusion as a unitary and scalable cognitive capacity. Success was thus to a large extent contingent upon variant task-specific features, so let us now try to explore some such significant sources of variance by examining only two sets of tasks in some more detail. The first set consists of two sub-sets, each of which contains four sentences to be completed by the child. Four sentences are of the type

It is absolutely true that there are more ANIMALS than ....

The remaining four are of the type

It is absolutely true that there is less ... than THINGS TO DRINK.

The child is in each case asked to insert a word that makes the sentence necessarily true.

The second set consists of four paper-and-pencil variants of traditional Piagetian class inclusion tasks. The child is given a drawing of, for example, five cups and two glasses and asked what there are more of in the drawing, CUPS or THINGS TO DRINK FROM. He responds by putting a check mark on one or other of the two written alternatives below the drawing of the objects.

TABLE 6·1   Performances by $8^1/_2$-year-old children on four traditional and eight sentence completion tasks of class inclusion

		No. of correct sentence completions					
		4	5	6	7	8	N
No. of correct	4	1			4	14	19
answers to	3			2		1	3
'more of'	2			2		2	4
questions	1		1	1	2	7	11
	0			1		1	2
	N	1	1	6	6	25	39

There were altogether 39 children who completed both sets of tasks, and the distribution of their performances is presented in Table 6.1. A majority of the children, we notice, mastered all eight sentence completion tasks. This is quite an impressive achievement. The tasks cover eight different referential domains of objects, and each single success implies that the child filled in some word or expression referring to a proper subordinate or superordinate class. Many of them failed on the—apparently far less difficult—traditional tasks, though. Thus, quite a few children answered that it is absolutely true there is less MILK (or TEA, JUICE, etc.) than THINGS TO DRINK, yet maintained that there were more CUPS than THINGS TO DRINK FROM in the drawing of five cups and two glasses.

What, then, can we infer about logical operations as 'actual psychological activities'? Is the child's response to the purely verbally mediated problem perhaps merely an adaptation to 'words and expressions heard in the mouths of adults', whereas his incorrect response in the traditional task reveals failure of adaptation to 'actual reality'? How, more precisely, does a request for the name of some subordinate or superordinate class which makes the incomplete statement necessarily true differ from a question concerning what there are more of, A_1's or B's, in a drawing of some A_1's and some A_2's all of which are B's?

In a preliminary attempt to find out about this, the set of traditional tasks was presented once more. The retest was a strict replication in all respects except for temporal order. This time, the question concerning what there were more of in the drawing was asked immediately *before* the drawing of objects was shown.

This version turned out to be significantly easier than the original one. There were in all 36 children who completed both versions as well as the sentence completion problems, and their performances on one sentence completion and the two versions of a comparable traditional task are presented in Table 6.2.

TABLE 6.2   Success (+) and failure (−) on three specific tasks. T_1: question asked *before*, T_2: question asked *after* drawing is shown

Task	−	+	N
Less ... than THINGS TO DRINK	6	30	36
More CUPS or THINGS TO DRINK FROM, T_1	5	31	36
More CUPS or THINGS TO DRINK FROM, T_2	17	19	36

The data yields unequivocal evidence of the impact of order of presentation: version T_1 (instruction *before*) is significantly easier to solve than T_2 (instruction *after*) and, indeed, as easy as the comparable sentence completion task. And how shall we explain this? Why do twelve children maintain there are more CUPS than THINGS TO DRINK FROM when asked while they are looking at the five cups and two glasses, but conclude there are more THINGS TO DRINK FROM than CUPS when they hear the question before starting inspecting the drawing?

Piaget's notion of thought as operations on 'actual reality' and language as 'the index of what has become conscious' leave us with hardly any clue to the solution of this riddle. What is required is rather an analysis of the subtle interplay of 'words and expressions' and 'actual reality', i.e. of operative semantic competence, and such an analysis will be attempted in subsequent explorations of specific identifying reference tasks (p. 131). But even performances on the class inclusion tasks are, in fact, embedded in acts of communication. The traditional tasks, for instance, are made known to the child by our drawings and verbal instructions jointly, and his response is in each case contingent upon his interpretation of the task. Different responses to the two versions may hence be traced to differences with respect to what the child thinks we want him to do in the two cases.

Consider, therefore, version T_2 from the perspective of adult-to-child communication. The tacitly and reciprocally endorsed 'contract' concerning interaction in that situation is such that it is taken for granted that the teacher will present problems and the child will attempt to solve them. The drawing as such serves to indicate what kind of problem is being posed: the adult is going to ask some question concerning the cups and glasses. The latter are visibly present as a taken-for-granted topic at the centre of an intersubjectively established HERE and NOW, and the two kinds of objects appear in different quantities. This, in itself, most likely makes for anticipatory comprehension: the problem to be posed has to do with those particular visible cups and glasses and will hence probably involve comparison or counting. The expression THINGS TO DRINK FROM in T_2 is accordingly immediately understood by quite a few children as OTHER THINGS TO DRINK FROM, i.e. as referring to the GLASSES. And this interpretation is prohibited when the very same question is asked in version T_1.

Hence what is made known by the very same 'words and expressions' may be different things depending upon what is taken for granted at the moment those words and expressions are uttered. Our question as to what there are more of in the drawing, CUPS or THINGS TO DRINK FROM, may hence in T_1 be understood as a problem of proper reasoning, similar to those encountered in the sentence completion task, and the child may accordingly stick to this notion and be on his guard against particular traps when he immediately afterwards turns to the drawing. Success in T_1 and failure in T_2 may therefore most plausibly be interpreted as due to deficient intersubjectivity in the latter case. What is involved, it appears, is a certain ambiguity with respect to what Ducrot (1972) has labelled the WHY of communication: the child responds on presuppositions different from those of the adult investigator.

These are issues of very little concern in Piaget's more recent work on children's language and thought. His aim is diagnosis of the child's individual cognitive capacities, but the experimental situations by which we try to assess those capacities are social situations. Cognitive operations can accordingly never be assessed *in vacuo*. Nor can we assess 'actual reality' as such, totally detached from what is said about it and from the intersubjectively established HERE and NOW of each particular experimental situation. Glasses may thus immediately—and rationally—be experienced as either ADDITIONAL or OTHER THINGS TO DRINK FROM, depending upon what else is taken for granted by the child at the moment he is watching them.

The tacitly assumed WHY of communication appears to be of crucial significance in studies of children's verbal reasoning as well, even though largely evaded by Piaget. His evidence bearing on egocentric thought is in part children's responses to why-questions. Piaget's 'why' is then often apparently a request for explanation of some physical event or state of affairs. He thus asks Vern, 6 years old, why a boat floats on the water while a little stone, which is lighter, sinks immediately. And he comments upon the boy's reaction as follows (Piaget, 1973, p. 253):

Vern reflected and then said: *'The boat is more intelligent than the stone'*. What does 'to be intelligent' mean? *'It does not do things it ought not to do'* (Note the confusion between the moral and the physical).

Piaget's conclusion about 'confusion between the moral and the physical' seems very plausible, provided we believe that Vern actually understood the question as a request for an explanation of 'physical' states of affairs. But how could he? What, in the first place, would to him be strange about big things keeping afloat which small, light things are sinking?

These are questions which, if followed up by additional enquiries, very likely would reveal a discrepancy between the adult's question and the WHY of communication as experienced by the child: we may interpret Vern as engaged in solving an Archimedian problem, whereas he is in fact trying to justify or offer reasons for success and failure. The 'physical' is in that case something superimposed upon Vern's reasoning and Vern's egocentricity becomes, in a way, a mirror image of Piaget's own centration in an 'actual reality' of natural scientific knowledge beyond the 6-year-old child's capacity for conceptualization.

Piaget's approach to children's language and thought may thus be said to entail a paradox. Hardly any psychologist has contributed more to our understanding of the unique nature of children's thought. This very uniqueness, however, seems often to be ignored or 'bracketed' in his interpretation of specific cases of adult–child interaction: it is as if intersubjectivity then must be taken for granted in order to find out *how* the child's conception of the world differs from that of the adult. And such a bracketing of problems of communication seems indeed legitimate if we comply with his outlook on language as 'the index of what has become conscious', consisting of 'conventional signifiers'.

Verbal communication, however, has its roots in pre-linguistic social interaction. The child's constitution of reality is, as shown by Bruner (this volume), monitored by the adult and is from the very beginning a genuinely social affair. His capacity to attend to some topic of discourse as introduced by the adult has its prelude in convergence of gaze onto entities of immediate significance in a shared HERE and NOW. What can be made known by verbal means is contingent upon what in that particular situation is already taken for granted by both participants in the act of communication, and intersubjectivity presupposes therefore reciprocal taking-the-role-of-the-other.

This has indeed cogently been brought to our attention by Piaget himself in his pioneering studies of egocentric speech (Piaget, 1926): lack of decentration is revealed in the pre-operational child's reference to some 'she' or 'he' *as if* the person he is talking about were already identified (or identifiable) by the listener when in fact no such presupposition is warranted at all. Piaget was thus in his very early studies of egocentrism concerned with lack of intersubjectivity in acts of communication. His analysis of egocentric use of deictic words is convincing, and lack of intersubjectivity is in such cases simply experienced by the listener as an incapacity to decide *who* or *what* is being referred to by the child.

However, transformation from 'actual' to 'social reality' is on other occasions achieved by selective categorization and attribution. I may say about a particular person I know, for instance, that he CAN GAIN PLEASURE FROM SMALL THINGS or that he IS EASY TO PLEASE (see Rommetveit, 1974, p. 113). Both utterances may be true, yet neither of them can be said to depict 'actual reality' as such. And similar options of verbal encoding apply in principle to every state of affairs, whether mental, interpersonal, or 'physical', however simple the communication situation appears to be.

Consider, for instance, the general option of active versus passive voice in English. This allows for a choice with respect to which component of some composite event, the *actor* or the *acted-upon*, is to be foregrounded and serve as the sustained topic in a dialogue about that event. A foregrounding of the acted-upon component, however, requires on many occasions an emancipation from the immediately perceived causal–temporal structure of 'actual reality' in the sense that, for example, what happened last is mentioned first. When, for instance, we say, 'The egg was laid by the hen' a reversal of order is thus built into out linguistic conversion of an 'actual' into a 'social' (i.e. talked-about) reality.

The pre-operational child's difficulties in coping with such reversals have been systematically explored by Turner and Rommetveit (1967), Sinclair-de-Zwart (1972b), and others. Centration in the immediately perceived temporal–causal structure is revealed in systematic misinterpretations of passive sentences about so-called 'reversible acts'. The child thus simply listens to a sentence such as 'The boy is chased by the girl'. When asked to point to the picture of that event, he then points out the picture of a boy chasing a girl instead of the equally available appropriate picture.

What in such a case appears as a reversal of an act is, in fact, merely a semantic confusion due to the child's incapacity of reversal of order from *talked-about* to *depicted or perceived events*. The act itself (as 'actual reality') is clearly irreversible. An observer who tells about a girl chasing a boy cannot via any sensorimotor operations analogous to, for example, adding and subtracting substance to a piece of clay reverse that particular event. It is, once observed, definitely beyond the scope of the observer's active manipulation and hence as irreversible as the event of a hen laying an egg. The option provided by sentence voice is therefore exclusively an option with respect to how that particular event may be made known to others. Once the observer tells about it, he is in control of the intersubjectively established social reality of a dialogue. What is achieved by a passive construction, moreover, is that the, apparently in some sense 'secondary', acted-upon component of an 'actual reality' becomes of primary concern when that 'actual reality' is made the topic of discourse. And this requires an emancipation from immediately perceived temporal–causal structures of events beyond the capacity of the pre-operational child.

Mastery of the passive voice is hence—like mastery of anaphorical deixis (Piaget, 1926)—contingent upon decentration, and even older children may have difficulties when a passive construction is encountered in a description of somewhat more complex states of affairs. This was clearly demonstrated in a study of children from 6 to 9 years old. Forty-four of these children were our previously mentioned $8^1/_2$-year-olds (see p. 120). In addition, there were 27 younger children from the same district. The age range of this latter group was from slightly above 6 to nearly 8 years, with an average of approximately 7 years.

Some of our tasks were simple tasks of verbal comprehension of the following forms:

A. The flower in front of the boy.
B. The boy who is chased by the girl.
C. The flower in front of the boy who is chased by the girl.

Each such description was read aloud once, and the child was on each occasion requested to identify the object described in a drawing of the referent together with the relevant set of inappropriate alternatives.

All except one of our 27 children in the 7-year-old group mastered all tasks of types A and B, but ten of them failed on task C. And so also did in fact nine of our children in the $8^1/_2$-years group, even though all of them succeeded on every task of types A and B. What happened in task C was thus that a considerable number of children interpreted the expression as referring to the flower in front of *the boy chasing the girl*, i.e. the passive construction was understood as representing an event structure corresponding to its word order. There were thus altogether 18 children who managed the 'spatial decentration' inherent in task A and the passive construction in B, yet failed when task B was nested onto task A as shown in task C.

What is required in order to attain intersubjectivity in case C is in view of these data *not* a simple concatenation or additive combination of operations involved in comprehension of A and B in isolation. An analysis of patterns of dependency and temporal order among operations must accordingly be attempted. Let us, therefore, conceive of expression C as an equation whose solution leads to correct identification of an initially unknown entity (one particular flower in the drawing). What is required for its solution as far as semantic competence is concerned is, at a minimum, simple referential mastery of the words and expressions GIRL (G), CHASE (ch), BOY (B), IN FRONT OF (fr), and FLOWER (F). The necessary and sufficient premises for correct identification may then be formulated as follows:

(1) G ch B (The girl chases the boy)
(2) F fr B (The flower is in front of that boy)

These premises may be converted into two nested questions, namely

(1) Which of the boys does the girl chase? and
(2) Which of the flowers is in front of that boy?

There is thus, we may argue, a definite pattern of dependence among premises in the sense that the second question cannot be raised until the first one has been answered.

Expression C, however, presents these premises in a form something like

F fr (B, B ch b G)

in which B ch b G is the passive transformation of premise 1. The order in which the premises (and, hence, the task as such) are made known to the child in this case, therefore, actually represents a reversal of the pattern of dependency among them. And we may ask: Are not such characteristic patterns of dependency and embeddedness crucial features of different variants of class inclusion tasks as well and—possibly—the rule rather than the exception in human thought and communication? If so, moreover, how can such patterns be revealed and systematically described? What, more precisely, are the patterns of dependency among presuppositions concerning intersubjectivity, semantic competence, and Piagetian cognitive operations in specific cases of adult–child interaction aiming at diagnosis of children's thought?

Such questions are rarely raised and hardly ever seriously explored by Piaget in his more recent studies of children's thought. They are admittedly very general and vaguely formulated questions, yet—and precisely for that reason—they are true symptoms of the state of ignorance and curiosity out of which our enquiries into message structure and operative semantic competence developed.

3. On Operative Semantic Competence

We shall start these explorations with the assumption that language is not only—nor even primarily—'the index of what has become conscious', but a genuinely and thoroughly social phenomenon. Its dynamic or 'operative' properties can accordingly only be fully revealed in human communication. A distinctive feature of an act of communication, moreover, is its inbuilt complementarity: we speak on the premises of the listener and listen on the premises of the speaker, and the resultant state of intersubjectivity represents a transcendence of the 'private worlds' of the two participants engaged in the act.

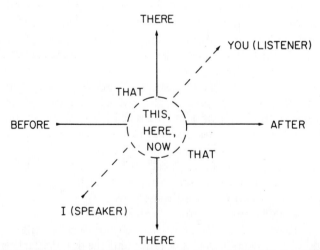

FIGURE 6.1. The spatial–temporal–interpersonal co-ordinates of intersubjectivity.

A skeleton of prerequisites for intersubjectivity is suggested in Figure 6.1. The three co-ordinates may be defined in terms of *the point in real time* at which the act of communication takes place, its *location*, and (in the case of spoken language) the *identification of listener by speaker and vice versa*. The I and YOU constitute the two poles of potential states of intersubjectivity, and a shared HERE and NOW is established by the very fact that they engage in communication. Control of that HERE and NOW, moreover, is under normal conditions unequivocally linked to the direction of communication. Which entities—and also which particular aspects of some composite entity—are going to enter the slots of THIS, HERE, NOW in Figure 6.1 are in principle—unless he is responding to some question or request—determined by the speaker. This holds true whether aspects of an experientially shared situation, remote states of affairs, or past events are made the topic of discourse.

Successful control, however, is contingent upon the speaker's capacity to 'take the role of' the listener, and Piaget's early observations of egocentric speech are thus cogent demonstrations of unsuccessful control of the HERE and NOW of a dialogue. But so also, in view of the data presented in Tables 6.1 and 6.2, are some of the Piagetian experiments on class inclusion: the child's notion of what is requested of him may in fact be at variance with the experimenter's presuppositions. It seems reasonable, therefore, to start our search for patterns of dependencies by pondering on the WHY of communication. What is tacitly taken for granted concerning the purpose and nature of their interaction the moment the two participants engage in it? Which premises for intersubjectivity are being presupposed?

These are admittedly extremely complex and as yet largely unexplored issues. Their significance, however, is clearly revealed in 'transplantations' of utterances or texts across different institutionally defined and intuitively mastered communication settings (Rommetveit, 1974, p. 29). What is said about DEMOCRACY in a patriotic speech on National Independence Day, for instance, may sound absurd in an academic lecture on forms of government. What is conveyed by particular newspaper headlines when encountered in the context of a collage poem, moreover, may bear very little resemblance to what was made known by the very same texts on the front page of the newspaper from which they were collected. What is going to happen between the I and YOU engaged in an act of communication is thus, as a rule, subject to tacitly and reciprocally taken-for-granted constraints. And some of the constraints inherent in the traditional Piagetian type of experiments with children appear to be as follows:

The adult interrogator is assumed to be in control of the HERE and NOW of the social interaction at every stage. He has the privilege of defining the problem and deciding which objects and attributes of objects are going to be in focus for convergent attention. It is tacitly taken for granted, moreover, that he also knows the answer to the problem. His question is hence unequivocally understood as a 'schoolmaster's question', i.e. as checking the child's achievement rather than requesting information out of ignorance and curiosity with respect to the topic. What the child achieves is, moreover, contingent upon what he thinks is requested of him. And this, as a rule, is made known to him by the objects and verbal instructions jointly.

Piagetian operations of thought are conceived of as interiorizations and symbolic elaborations of the child's sensorimotor operations upon 'actual reality'. Symbolic elaboration is to a considerable extent a matter of intergration of previously isolated and stimulus-bound operations into more comprehensive schemata of interrelated modes of attribution and categorization. Semantic competence may hence be conceived of as mastery of drafts of contracts concerning attribution and categorization inherent in ordinary language, and operative semantic competence is revealed in conversion of privately experienced 'actual' realities into shared social realities. Mastery of *word meaning* may accordingly be defined in terms of semantic potentials, i.e. as mastery of contextually appropriate elaborations of general drafts of contracts of categorization across variant presuppositions and premises for intersubjectivity.

Level of semantic competence is therefore—as is level of thought within Piaget's conceptual framework—to a significant degree a matter of abstraction and decentration. A pair of polar adjectives such as OLD/YOUNG, for instance, may be conceived of as essentially a general draft of a contract concerning categorization of age, and denotatively very different elaborations of that draft are required depending upon whether, for example, some PERSON or some CULTURE is being talked about. The very same 60-year-old person, moreover, may be referred to as the OLD man or intersubjectively identified as the YOUNG man, depending upon what else is taken for granted by both participants in a dialogue about him. He may, for instance, in the first case be talked about as the newcomer in a neighbourhood among only young and recently married couples, in the other case as the newly arrived resident in a home for elderly people.

Intersubjectivity implies in the latter case, though, a relativity far beyond the capacity for decentration of the pre-operational child. And circumstantial evidence from word association studies testifies, indeed, to a progressive emancipation of words from the particular experiential contingencies within which they were first encountered. Such experiential contingencies are mirrored in associative responses such as OLD–GRANNY and OLD–WRINKLED, associations we know will be replaced at some later stage by the—apparently nearly compulsory—response OLD–YOUNG. Increased abstraction and 'operativity' is thus revealed in an integration of initially loosely related antonyms into a unitary and bipolar conceptual schema.

This seems, in fact, to hold true for LONG/SHORT, THIN/THICK, and HIGH/ LOW as well, i.e. for all those particular lexical items which Sinclair-de-Zwart mentions as instances of 'items … far less closely linked to operativity' (see p. 115). And the resultant unity of the bipolar schema is even brought to our attention in studies of word perception under conditions of binocular rivalry of letters (Rommetveit and Blakar, 1973). A particular graphic rivalry pattern such as LONG presented to the right and LUNG to the left eye simultaneously may thus under given conditions be seen as either LONG or LUNG. This is no longer the case, however, if the word SHORT is read immediately before the rivalry pattern. The subject will then as a rule see LONG and nothing else, even under conditions when he is warned about the trap and explicitly asked to try to identify the contextually irrelevant member of the rivalry pair. The very process of comprehending SHORT appears thus at the stage of abstract operative semantic competence to involve activation of its antonym as well.

'Operativity' and capacity for decentration at this adult stage of semantic competence are also demonstrated in immediate comprehension of expressions such as (1) A SHORT PERSON, (2) A SHORT WAY TO GO, (3) A SHORT TIME, and (in Norwegian) even (4) A SHORT DISTANCE BETWEEN TWO POLITICAL IDEOLOGIES. The *invariance* across these different elaborations of the general draft of contract concerning categorization inherent in SHORT, moreover, can obviously not be captured merely in terms of 'sensorimotor' or 'experiential–referential' overlap: in Norwegian, A SHORT WAY TO GO is probably nearly always LONGER than A LONG PERSON, and what is made known by SHORT in A SHORT TIME is something very different from that conveyed by SHORT when DISTANCES BETWEEN POLITICAL IDEOLOGIES are being talked about. The reason why such expressions within proper contextual frameworks of adult discourse nevertheless yield intersubjectivity must hence necessarily be sought in abstract, operative, and contractual aspects of word meaning: SHORT (in Norwegian) is in every case intended and understood as the opposite of LONG. Convergence onto the same particular entities within a shared HERE and NOW, and even denotative convergence onto remote 'actual realities', are achieved by elaborations of abstract and general *drafts* into specific and contextually appropriate *actual contracts* concerning categorization.

Such convergence testifies to the existence of semantic operations upon 'actual reality' far beyond the scope of our sensorimotor operations, and so does our 60-year-old man who is intersubjectively identified as the OLD man in one case and the YOUNG man in the other, depending upon which referential domain of age constitutes part of the premises for intersubjectivity in each case. And semantic operations are thus—whatever their ontogenetic anchorage in sensorimotor operations may be—by definition transformations of 'actual' into 'social', 'talked-about', and 'intersubjectively-attended-to' realities. The hen's laying of an egg is *qua* 'actual reality' an irreversible event, yet via the option of passive voice can be intersubjectively attended to from a perspective at variance with its 'immanent' or experientially given causal–temporal structure. And people's age is also—unlike the volume or pieces of clay—clearly beyond the scope of our active, manipulatory, reversible operations, yet can be intersubjectively attended to via a bipolar semantic schema with a built-in reversibility hardly inferior to that of BIG–SMALL.

Some very important roots of operative semantic competence must therefore, despite the latter's dependency upon 'sensorimotor mechanisms that are deeper than linguistics'—be traced to the child's dependency upon intersubjectivity in social interaction with adults on premises for intersubjectivity inherent in adult language. These premises include drafts of contracts concerning categorization and attribution which, if appropriately elaborated and endorsed in specific acts of verbal communication, provide for experiences analogous to those labelled 'logical-mathematical experiences' by Piaget. The option of active versus passive sentence voice may thus be considered as roughly analogous to the option of counting a given array of objects either from left to right or from right to left. Both options make for the discovery of invariance and the emancipation of thought from perceptual and sensorimotor operations. Only one of them—reversal of order in counting—concerns individual operations upon 'actual reality', however. The other has to do with transformation of 'actual' into intersubjectively-attended-to realities. And the same may be said about the different variants of length as we move from conversations about body height to topics such as distances between political ideologies. Mastery of such variant categorizations of length, moreover, is clearly beyond the capacity of the pre-operational child. It can only develop out of 'logical-mathematical experience' in acts of verbal communication in which very different aspects of 'actual reality' are introduced into an intersubjectively established HERE and NOW by means of the same 'conventional signifier'.

What is *made known* in acts of verbal communication is thus in part determined by *meaning potentials* inherent in words and expressions. The latter are, once we focus upon intersubjectivity and language in use, drafts of contracts concerning symbolic representation (attribution and categorization) and hence potentialities of shared 'operations of thought'. Options with respect to linguistic encoding of aspects of 'actual' reality are therefore as a rule contingent upon mastery of more inclusive schemata. We may thus try to make known to others what we feel we know about a particular person by saying either

HE CAN GAIN PLEASURE FROM SMALL THINGS, or
HE IS EASY TO PLEASE.

The particular person we want to describe is in each case brought into an intersubjectively established HERE and NOW, yet in one case attended to as a potential source of action and in the other as a potential manipulandum. Intersubjectivity thus rests upon general cognitive capacities such as attributing easiness to tasks and talents to persons and—in the latter case—even a capacity for decentred shifts of perspectives on persons such that on some occasions they can be considered sources of action and on others (aspects of) tasks (Heider, 1958).

Operative semantic competence may thus be conceived of as contractually monitored 'operations of thought' aiming at intersubjectivity. Full mastery of words such as CAN, EASY, OLD, and SHORT presupposes, first of all, mastery of abstract cognitive operations upon 'actual reality' in accordance with general drafts of contracts concerning categorization. Which of all the potential elaborations of such a general draft is intended and contextually appropriate in any particular situation is, moreover, contingent upon which premises for intersubjectivity have been tacitly agreed upon, and what at that moment can be taken for granted as part of an already established shared social reality, etc. A word is thus, by virtue of its inherent contractual aspect, a 'conventional signifier', yet *in vacuo* merely a set of meaning potentials.

The intersubjectively established HERE and NOW in many Piagetian experiments on children's thinking is apparently to a large extent controlled by particular arrangements of concrete objects to be attended to and manipulated and/or talked about. Which attributes of concrete objects will be focused upon and talked about—and even which manipulations of objects are to be performed—may thus apparently be conveyed to the child via selection and systematic variation of features of an immediately experienced 'actual reality'. The task itself, moreover, may be designed in such a way that mastery of abstractly defined cognitive operations such as, for example, *cross-classification*, *ordering*, or *class inclusion* are required in order to arrive at the solution.

The adult experimenter may in such a situation conceive of his verbal communication with the child as a necessary, though rather insignificant and unobtrusive, component of the interaction between them. Intersubjectivity is taken for granted on the assumption (Olson, 1970, p. 264) that 'words specify an intended referent relative to the set of alternatives from which it must be differentiated'. We may accordingly be led to believe that Piagetian cognitive operations are 'externalized' and directly revealed in the child's sensorimotor operations upon an 'actual reality' as defined and controlled by the adult experimenter. And in view of such considerations, Piaget's evasion of the problems of intersubjectivity implicit in his interpretation of results thus appears legitimate.

Shared attendance to one and the same particular verbally described entity can only be achieved via convergent acts of 'identifying reference' (Strawson, 1969), and identifying reference, in discourse about a particular referential domain of objects attended to HERE and NOW is certainly, as Olson has shown, a matter of selective attention and perceptual differentiation. Even under such conditions, however, it is embedded in acts of communication and hence, we shall argue, it is also a matter of operative semantic competence.

4. Operative Semantic Competence and Identifying Reference in Adult–Child Communication

4.1 Identifying Reference across Different Arrangements of the Same Domain of Objects

In order to explore some of the possible relationships between semantic competence and mastery of Piagetian cognitive operations, let us now turn to specific cases of identifying reference in adult–child communication. The child is simply asked to single out one particular object from some set, and in every case appropriate identification presupposes cross-classification. One attribute (I) is always dichotomous, the second attribute (II) may be either graded or dichotomous. By combining six different conditions of object arrangements with three different types of cross-classification we then arrive at a systematic variation of tasks as indicated in Table 6.3 The object to be singled out in every cell is indicated by a cross.

Consider, first, cells 1 and 4. The sets of objects are identical in the two cells, and the particular object to be singled out is in each case the BLACK, BIG candle. The two attributes (colour and size) are *orthogonal* in the sense that the sensorimotor operations involved in identification of one of them are totally unrelated to those

TABLE 6.3. Different tasks of identifying reference

Nature and distribution of		Type of cross-classification (I × II)		
Attribute I	Attribute II	A × B	(A₁+B) × A₂	A₁ × A₂
Dichotomous, separate classes	Dichotomous	1	7	13
	Ordered (Graded)	2	8	14
	Random (Graded)	3	9	15
Dichotomous, mixed classes	Dichotomous	4	10	16
	Ordered (Graded)	5	11	17
	Random (Graded)	6	12	18

involved in the identification of the other. Cross-classification is thus of type A × B. The sub-sets of BLACK and WHITE candles, however, are spatially separated in cell 1 and mixed in cell 4. Appropriate identification in the first case may hence in principle be achieved by a temporal sequence of discriminations instead of simultaneous attendance to both attributes. An arrangement of objects such as the one in cell 1 may be displayed in front of the child, and the adult may for instance ask: 'Give me the one of the BLACK candles that is BIG.' The child may then immediately attend selectively to the sub-set of BLACK candles, and identification of BIG may be achieved at a stage when WHITE candles are already ignored or even out of sight. Such a strategy of quasi-cross-classification is of course prohibited when the objects are arranged as shown in cell 4.

Cells 2, 3, 5, and 6 portray different spatial arrangements of the same set of objects, and the object to be identified is in every case 'the one of the BLACK candles that is SECOND BIGGEST.'[1] Appropriate identification therefore presupposes ordering of the BLACK candles with respect to size. In the case of cells 2 and 3 this can be done without perceptual interference due to simultaneous attendance to WHITE candles. Correct identification in the case of cells 5 and 6, on the other hand, seems to require mastery of *class inclusion*: the ordering operation has to be confined to only one sub-set of the objects while the entire set is being attended to. Moreover, such an ordering is already provided by the purely spatial arrangement of objects in cells 2 and 5, but in the latter case is embedded in a spatial ordering of the entire set with respect to size.

The task of singling out the one of the BLACK candles that is SECOND BIGGEST thus clearly involves somewhat different combinations of operations in the four cases. For cells 2 and 3 it can be performed sequentially, i.e. as 'quasi-cross-classification'. The comparison of objects with respect to size, moreover, is more difficult for cells 3 and 6 than for cells 2 and 5. And a switch (or rather: diffusion) of attention from sub-class to superordinate class seems particularly likely to occur when the candles are arranged as shown in cell 5. In that particular case the domain of the ordering operations may hence become the entire set, and the child may consequently single out the SECOND BIGGEST one of ALL rather than of the BLACK candles.

Let us now turn to cells 13 and 16 and assume that each cell portrays persons located at different distances from a house. The task is in both cases to point out 'the one of the SHORT persons who has a LONG way to the house',[2] and cell 13 may thus be said to resemble cell 1 with respect to spatial arrangement of classes and distribution of attributes.[3] The two attributes, however, are this time SHORT as applied to height of human bodies and LONG as applied to horizontal distance between objects. They are accordingly, when compared to BLACK and BIG in cell 1, related attributes, and the task requires cross-classification of type $A_1 \times A_2$. Appropriate identification thus presupposes mastery of two different variants of the same basic set of cognitive operations, and the same holds true for cells 14, 15, 16, 17, and 18 as well. The arrangement of objects in cell 13, however, is such that the task may be solved sequentially by two different categorizations of length. This is not possible in the case of cell 16.

The target in cells 14 and 17 is 'the one of the SHORT persons who has the SECOND LONGEST way to the house'. The combinations of operations in the two cases are thus similar to those required for cells 2 and 5, and ordering of length of distances is required in both cases. The domain of the ordering operation, however, is restricted to the sub-set of SHORT persons only. Diffusion of that domain seems practically prohibited, given the spatial separation of sub-sets in cell 14. An arrangement such as the one in cell 17, however, requires simultaneous attendance to two variants of length: the child must attend to length (as height of human bodies) while ordering length (as horizontal distance) in order to select the appropriate sub-set of distances to be ordered.

Cells 7–12 differ from 13–18 only with respect to redundancy of attributes: all SHORT objects also differ from all LONG objects with respect to one additional attribute. When the objects are persons, this additional attribute (indicated by a short horizontal line) may be colour of clothes, colour of skin, sex, or some other distinctive feature. It is always orthogonal to length, however, and the resultant type of cross-classification will hence be $(A_1 + B) \times A_2$. The redundancy, moreover, allows for options with respect to categorization. And such options are revealed in selection among alternative verbal labels for one and the same target object.

4.2 Options with Respect to Verbal Description of the Target Object, Linguistically Mediated Contracts Concerning Categorization, and Cognitive Operations

It is only at this stage—after a systematic examination of the possible referential domains of objects—that we are fully prepared to proceed to an equally systematic analysis of purely linguistic components of the task. How, precisely, does the adult describe the target object in each of the cells in Table 6.3 to the child? Which contracts concerning categorization are proposed in each particular case, and which cognitive operations must be mastered in order to fulfil contracts embedded in alternative, but denotatively equivalent, descriptions of the very same target object? How, more precisely, is the object made known to the child by alternative verbal constructions?

Before attempting a systematic exploration of these very complex issues, let us first examine two very simple alternative ways of identifying the size of the target object in cell 5. We may, as already indicated, ask for

... the one of the BLACK candles that is SECOND BIGGEST.

However, we may instead ask for

... the one of the BLACK candles that is SECOND SMALLEST.

How may these *denotatively equivalent* identifying descriptions affect ease of identification?

We have already maintained that the spatial ordering of ALL candles in cell 5 with respect to size makes for diffusion of the domain of the ordering operation. This, we assume, will be the case whether the target object is described as the SECOND BIGGEST or the SECOND SMALLEST of the BLACK candles. The alternative verbal constructions, however, convey different proposals concerning starting point and direction of ordering: identifying the SECOND BIGGEST implies starting from the BIGGEST and proceeding from left to right, whereas singling out the SECOND SMALLEST implies starting from the SMALLEST and proceeding from right to left.

The SECOND SMALLEST of ALL the candles is WHITE, however. The child may hence—even though initially engaged in the ordering of ALL the candles— immediately discover the error with respect to colour and proceed one step further to the left. The construction SECOND SMALLEST thus provides a unique opportunity for self-correction of an error due to diffusion of the domain of ordering. And such a condition for self-correction is not provided when ordering proceeds from the BIGGEST of ALL candles toward the right in cell 5. The task of identifying the target object in cell 5 is hence more difficult when the candle is referred to as 'the one of the BLACK candles that is SECOND BIGGEST' than when it is made known to the child as 'the one of the BLACK candles that is SECOND SMALLEST'. And a similar effect is obtained with the alternative identifying descriptions of the target objects in cells 11 and 17: the task of identification is in both cases facilitated when 'the SECOND SHORTEST way' is substituted for 'the SECOND LONGEST way'.

Let us now, however, consider options with respect to verbal labelling of *attributes*. Imagine, for instance, that cells 7–18 contain drawings of persons located at different distances from a house, and that A_1 is simply the height of the body. The latter attribute can in Norwegian be encoded by means of two equally appropriate adjective pairs, namely *kort/lang* (SHORT/LONG) and *låg/hög* (LOW/HIGH). Only the former pair, SHORT/LONG, is applicable to horizontal distance as well. Let us also assume that all persons depicted are male, but age can only be determined by body height. The SHORT persons may then be referred to as BOYS. Hence, for $A_1 \times A_2$ in cell 17 of Table 6.3, we have the following options of identifying descriptions.

the one of (a) /the SHORT men/(b)/the LOW men/(c)/the BOYS/ who has (d) / the SECOND LONGEST / (e) / the SECOND SHORTEST / way to the house.

A_1 may thus be linguistically introduced as a *sub-class* of ALL the men, i.e. as SHORT or LOW men. One word (LOW) may be said to accentuate the difference between length *qua* vertical height (A_1) as opposed to horizontal distance (A_2), whereas the other (SHORT) serves to accentuate the resemblance between the two variants of categorization of length. But A_1 may also be referred to as a separate and in some sense autonomous category, BOYS. And such direct identification (rather than identification of a sub-class) should serve to counteract diffusion of the domain of the ordering operation.

The difference between autonomous categorization and identification via sub-class construction may perhaps be even more cogently demonstrated by an additional variant of cell 5 of Table 6.3 The six circle areas in the upper row of Figure 6.2 are arranged in the same way as the candles in cell 5. They may in one case be introduced as BLACK and WHITE circles (in Norwegian: *rundinger*) of different sizes, and the child may be asked to point out

the one of the WHITE circles that is SECOND LARGEST.

However, Figure 6.2 may also be interpreted as depicting some rubber balls and some SNOWBALLS. The target object may then be referred to as

the one of the SNOWBALLS that is SECOND LARGEST.

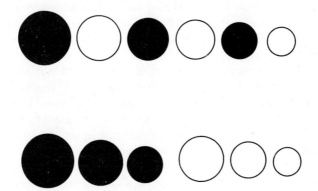

FIGURE 6.2.   Two different spatial arrangements of the referential domain for 'The one of the WHITE CIRCLES/SNOWBALLS that is SECOND LARGEST' (cells 5 and 2 in Table 6.3).

An immediate identification of the white circle areas as SNOWBALLS may serve to set them apart as unique and different from all the remaining (black) circle areas. Diffusion of the domain of the ordering operation, which is prohibited under conditions of spatial separation of classes (lower row in Figure 6.2) may hence under conditions of spatial mixture of classes be prevented by linguistically induced autonomous categorization. Returning to all six possible combinations of the options of verbalizations we have so far listed for the target object in cell 17, we may thus maximize the probability of diffusion by asking for the one of the SHORT men who has the SECOND LONGEST way to the house.

The likelihood of diffusion is reduced to a minimum, however, if we ask the child to point out

the one of the BOYS who has the SECOND SHORTEST way to the house.

Let us not proceed to column $(A_1 + B) \times A_2$ in Table 6.3. Imagine first, that the additional attribute B is colour of clothes. The redundantly generated dichotomy may then be SHORT BLACK-clothed versus LONG WHITE-clothed persons,[4] and the target object may be referred to as 'the one of the BLACK-clothed persons who ...'. Suppose, next, that attribute B is colour of skin. The dichotomy may hence be SHORT BLACK-skinned versus LONG WHITE-skinned persons. BLACK-skinned persons may also be referred to as NEGROES, however, and the target object may therefore be made known to the child as 'the one of the NEGROES who ...'. If, finally, B is sex (and pictorially portrayed by, for instance, skirt versus trousers), the dichotomy may be SHORT FEMALE versus LONG MALE persons. The target object may accordingly be described as 'the one of the LADIES who ...'.

We thus have, for every task of type $(A_1 + B) \times A_2$, first of all the option of labelling either the related (A_1) or the orthogonal (B) attribute. If A_1 is chosen, moreover, the very same verbal construction can be used across different variants of B. This means, more specifically and in the case of the three different variants of each cell in column $(A_1 + B) \times A_2$, that both SHORT BLACK-clothed, SHORT BLACK-skinned and SHORT FEMALE persons are unequivocally referred to by the construction 'SHORT persons'. But we may also simply omit the related attribute in our identifying description and label the orthogonal attribute instead.

If we want to label only the orthogonal attribute, however, we encounter an additional option: the attribute may be linguistically introduced by means of some sub-class construction (BLACK-clothed persons) or as an autonomous category (NEGROES, LADIES). Let us now proceed one step further and examine which issues emerge when we attempt to combine certain referential domains of objects with some options with respect to verbalization. Consider, for instance, the following variants of task $(A_1 + B) \times A_2$ in cell 11 of Table 6.3.:

(1) Attribute B is colour of clothes, and the target object is made known to the child as either

    (a) 'the one of the SHORT persons who has SECOND LONGEST way to the house',

or

    (b) 'the one of the BLACK-clothed persons who has the SECOND LONGEST way to the house'.

(2) Attribute B is colour of skin. The target object is referred to as either

    (a) 'the one of the SHORT persons who has the SECOND LONGEST way to the house',

or

(b) 'the one of the NEGROES who has the SECOND LONGEST way to the house'.

(3) Attribute B is sex (skirt versus trousers), and the target person is described as either

(a) 'the one of the SHORT persons who has the SECOND LONGEST way to the house',

or

(b) 'the one of the LADIES who has the SECOND LONGEST way to the house'.

These eight variants within cell 11, however, may also be compared to tasks of type $A_1 \times A_2$. We may hence add to our list of combinations:

(4) No additional pictorially portrayed attribute (cell 17), but the target object is made known as either

(a) 'the one of the SHORT persons who has the SECOND LONGEST way to the house',

or

(b) 'the one of the BOYS who has the SECOND LONGEST way to the house'.

Each of the eight tasks of identifying reference listed above represents one possible combination of a particular referential domain of objects and a specific identifying description of the target object. A thorough analysis of the relationship between semantic competence and Piagetian cognitive operations should hence make it possible to specify which combinations of operations must be mastered in order to solve each particular task. Such a specification, however, will remain incomplete until we take into consideration additional aspects of the actual adult-to-child communication. What is made known by a particular word such as 'SHORT' for instance, may vary depending upon what kind of referential domain is taken for granted by the child at the moment that word is heard. In order to analyse which combinations of operations are involved in tasks (1a) through (4b) above, we must therefore know whether the target object is described to the child before or after he has been shown the referential domain.

Before proceeding to such (and other) temporal aspects of the entire adult–child interaction, however, let us now ponder what can be maintained on purely conceptual, analytic grounds about what is often vaguely referred to as 'comprehension of words' and about Piagetian cognitive operations. Notice, first of all, that all eight tasks are of the form: 'Point out the one of I that ... II ...'. Notice, furthermore, that versions (a) and (b) for each of the four pictorial variants are identical as far as purely perceptual features are concerned. Failure in one and success in the other version must hence clearly be attributed to linguistic structuring, i.e. to operative semantic competence.

What is implied by operative semantic competence, moreover, may be further illuminated by comparing tasks (1a) and (4b). These two tasks are both of a form which makes for diffusion of the domain of the ordering operation: the ordering of objects leading up to identification of 'the SECOND LONGEST way ...' is to be performed on sub-set I only, but tends to be performed on ALL objects. In task (1a), however, we encounter in the referential domain one clearly portrayed additional attribute (BLACK) by which sub-set I can be distinguished from sub-set not-I. Task (1a) is thus easier than (4b) as far as purely pre-linguistic, perceptual features are concerned. If children at a certain age nevertheless master (4b) while failing to master (1a), they do so because different contracts concerning categorization are proposed by the adult (and more or less perfectly fulfilled by the child) on the two occasions.

4.3 Message Structure: an Analysis of Patterns of Dependencies and Temporal Order in What is Made Known Jointly by Objects and Identifying Descriptions

The extent to which such contracts concerning categorization are fulfilled by the child, however, depends in part upon what is tacitly taken for granted as the referential domain in each particular act of communication. Consider, for instance, a request to single out

the one of the SHORT persons who has a LONG way to the house

uttered immediately before the child is shown the objects in cell 16 of Table 6.3. Fulfilment of the contracts concerning categorization proposed by the adult presupposes in this case that the child—in the absence of any perceptual support— can cope with two distinctively different variants of length. In other words, subsequent correct identification of the target object is possible only if the child, while listening to 'SHORT persons ...' and 'LONG way ...', prepares for two different sensorimotor elaborations of the same abstract, interiorized cognitive operation.

Consider, next, the situation in which the child is inspecting the SHORT and LONG persons at different distances from the house while listening to the request. The topic of the discourse has then been firmly established by the visible referential domain, there is already an intersubjectively taken-for-granted domain of objects within a shared HERE-and-NOW, and the expressions 'SHORT persons ...' and 'LONG way ...' are immediately 'disambiguated' in terms of particular perceptual features of that domain. The visually displayed arrangement of objects thus serves as free information to which whatever is made known by 'SHORT persons' and 'LONG way' is bound (Rommetveit, 1974, pp. 90–93).

We may hence expect that children at a pre-operational or early concrete operational stage of development may fail on the task when the verbal request is made immediately before the objects are shown and succeed when listening to the identifying description while having the objects in front of them. Moreover, older children who succeed on both these tasks may fail on task (4a) (see p. 137). And we may ask: How do performances on such tasks relate to operative semantic competence and, more specifically, to comprehension of the words SHORT and LONG? Is it possible that a developmental pattern of performances as suggested above testify to stages of linguistic mastery of SHORT/LONG? And, if so, how shall we interpret Piaget and his associates when they maintain that a child 'comprehends' a given word used in some instruction, but fails in performing the operations of thought presumably triggered off or induced by that very word? Which criteria have in such cases been used to assess 'comprehension of the word'?

How what is seen affects and is affected by what is said about it is a very complex issue, however, and it has been explored in a series of experiments on recall of combined pictorially and verbally mediated information (Rommetveit *et al.*, 1971; Blakar and Rommetveit, 1975). Let us therefore return to the option of showing the referential domain before or after describing the target object and examine how choice of one or the other of the two alternatives affects some of the eight tasks listed on pp. 136–137. Consider, first, task (4b). The objects are in this case male persons differing with respect to no other pictorially portrayed attribute than height. The child may hence very likely immediately identify them as SHORT and LONG male persons. Such an identification is 'pre-linguistic' in the sense that it is performed before the target object has been verbally described, and it may persist while—and after—the child is listening to '...the BOYS ...'. A linguistically mediated contract to identify the SHORT objects as BOYS may hence be hard to fulfil when the child has already had the opportunity to inspect and interpret the picture on his own premises.

The adult's proposal to identify all SHORT objects as members of the familiar and in some sense autonomous category BOYS may accordingly be more readily accepted by the child if that proposal is made before he sees the picture. What has been said about the picture will then provide free information and serve as a basis for making sense of what is seen, i.e. the child will simply take it for granted that the picture contains BOYS the moment he starts inspecting it. Hence, otherwise salient perceptual features (such as LONG/SHORT) may come to play a subordinate role: they may simply be attended to as means of identifying the BOYS and—once that identification has been performed—of secondary concern.

The significance of such linguistically mediated 'pre-identification' of objects has been clearly demonstrated by Hundeide (1975) in experiments on children's discrimination learning. He found that the effect of verbal labelling upon learning performance was markedly greater when verbal labels were proposed immediately before the child was shown the objects. And similar observations have been reported by Luria, by Martsinovskaya and Abramyan, and by other Soviet psychologists (see Luria, 1961).

Whether the child will categorize what he sees in accordance with the adult's verbal 'pre-identification', however, will depend upon whether he comprehends what is said in the absence of perceptual anchorage, and *if* he comprehends it, whether certain particularly significant perceptual features provide for some competing and more dominant categorization the moment he gets to see what he has heard about. The skirts and trousers in task (3a), p. 137, for instance, may so strongly and unequivocally indicate sex that the child spontaneously identifies as LADY what has vaguely been 'pre-identified' by means of the expression 'SHORT person'.

Whatever is made known to the child is thus made known jointly by the pictorially presented referential domain and the adult's description of the target object. And nothing can be said about the impact of the temporal sequence as such. Whether verbal pre- or post-identification is the optimal condition for singling out the target object depends upon each particular combination of referential domain and identifying description. The significance of temporal order can hence only be brought out in an analysis of message structure, by examining *whether* and *how* something made known at one stage of the act of communication is taken for granted as a prerequisite for making full sense of something made known at some other stage.

This also holds true for purely intra-linguistic order as has been clearly demonstrated in a series of experiments on word order and recall by Heen Wold (in press). She examined the effect of pre- versus post-position of adjectives in orally presented descriptions such as, for example,

(A) 'A secretary who is severe, cool, extraordinary, beautiful, pleasant'

versus

(B) 'A severe, cool, extraordinary, beautiful, pleasant secretary'

Nearly twice as much was recalled when all descriptions were presented in order (A), with nouns preceding adjectives, as in order (B). And this may be attributed to isomorphy between temporal order and message structure: what is made known by 'severe' in (A) can be decided immediately since at that moment it is taken for granted that SEVERITY is being attributed to some SECRETARY. Such an immediate decision is not possible, however, when 'severe' is heard in version (B): the listener does not at that stage really know whether, for example, a WINTER, some STYLE OF ART, or some PERSON is being talked about and must accordingly postpone his decision concerning which more specific categorization is implied by the word until he is informed that a SECRETARY is being described.

We also, of course, have options of word order when describing the target object in Table 6.3. The target object in cells 2, 3, 5, and 6 may, for instance, be described as either

(A) 'the one of the BLACK candles that is SECOND BIGGEST'

or

(B)'the SECOND BIGGEST one of the BLACK candles'.

And message structure in this case may even be assessed in terms of a particular nesting of those cognitive operations by which correct identification is to be achieved. The task is solved first by identifying sub-set I (BLACK candles) and, once that subset is taken for granted as the proper domain of an ordering operation, by ordering objects with respect to size (attribute II) from BIGGEST to SECOND BIGGEST. Version (A) may hence be said to represent a word order corresponding to the pattern of dependency among operations involved in the actual identification of the object. Version B, on the other hand, appears to portray a word order contrary to the pattern of dependency, since ordering with respect to size (attribute II) is announced at a stage of the act of communication when the domain of that ordering operation (I) has not yet been made known.[5] We may be tempted to predict, therefore, that identification in general will be easier when the target object is described by means of version (A).

Before yielding to such a temptation, however, let us now examine how the issue of *word order* constitutes part of the issue of *message structure* in verbal pre- versus post-identification of the same target object across differently arranged referential domains. Consider, first, version (A) as a verbal post-identification of the target objects in cells 2, 3, 5, and 6 in Table 6.3 The referential domains in cells 2 and 3 will under those conditions allow for quasi-cross-classification. This means, more specifically, that the child may turn towards the BLACK candles the moment he comprehends the expression 'BLACK candles' and—in principle—engage in the ordering operation at a subsequent stage when the WHITE candles can be entirely ignored, both visually and mentally. He may be encouraged to do so by a pause after 'candles ...', and a trained teacher of pre-school or mentally retarded children may even monitor her instructions in such a case on the basis of the child's intermediary response: she may not even continue saying '... that is SECOND BIGGEST' until she feels safe that the child is attending selectively to the BLACK sub-set only.

Such a simple and strictly temporal concatenation of operations is, as earlier indicated, prohibited when the objects are arranged as shown in cells 5 and 6. It is also, of course, impossible with the object arrangements as shown in cells 2 and 3 if ordering with respect to size is made known prior to colour of candles (version (B)). And correct identification via quasi-cross-classification is prohibited for both versions (A) and (B) under all conditions of verbal pre-identification. The child must then, regardless of which word order is chosen and which particular referential domain is selected, keep in storage simultaneously whatever is made known to him by the expressions the 'BLACK candles' and 'SECOND biggest' until he is shown the referential domain.

4.4 Illustrations from an Empirical Study

Several identifying reference tasks were included in our initial battery of Piaget-inspired problems and presented to both the 7- and $8^1/_2$-year groups. Some of the tasks were simple cross-classifications of type A × B, cells 1 and 4 in Table 6.3, and the objects to be identified were such as 'the one of the BLACK dogs that is BIG', 'the one of the THIN pencils that is LONG', etc. These were mastered by all children, even by the youngest ones.

Four of our initial tasks, however, proved more difficult. These were in ascending order of difficulty:
(1) To point out 'the one of the BLACK dogs that is SECOND BIGGEST' in a drawing of white and black dogs randomly mixed and varying with respect to size (cell 6 in Table 6.3).
(2) To identify 'the HEAVY man who has LIGHT work' in a drawing of four men representing all combinations of heavy versus light build *and* putting stamps on envelopes versus carrying big sacks.
(3) To point out 'the SECOND BIGGEST number[6] in the SMALL circle' in a drawing of a big circle containing the typewritten numbers 7, 5, 4, 2 and a small circle containing the numbers 9, 6, 1, 7, and 5.

(4) To single out 'the one of the LONG men who has the SECOND SHORTEST way to the house' in a drawing representing a naturalistic elaboration of the pattern in cell 17 of Table 6.3.

The diagrams were presented in a booklet, and the child in each case looked at the pictorially presented referential domain while listening to the description of the target object. Four strictly equivalent tasks were later on presented under conditions of *verbal pre-identification*. The target objects were then (1') WHITE dog that is SECOND SMALLEST, (2') LIGHT man with HEAVY work, (3') SECOND SMALLEST number in BIG circle, and (4') SHORT man with SECOND LONGEST way. Blank pages were now inserted between drawings. Thus in each case the child would first listen to the description and then immediately, the moment the last word had been uttered, turn the page and try to identify the referent in the drawing.

TABLE 6.4 Achievements on eight identifying reference tasks.

Achievement	Age 7	$8^1/_2$	N
6 or more correct identifications	5	30	35
5 or less correct identifications	22	14	36
N	27	44	71

A condensed picture of the children's performances is presented in Table 6.4. The latter reveals a considerable (and statistically highly significant) difference between our two age groups. The impact of verbal pre- versus post-idéntification upon ease of identification, however, varies from one task to another (see Tables 6.5 and 6.6). Identification of the particular target combination of heaviness of build and heaviness of work is thus significantly more difficult for our younger children under conditions of verbal pre-identification. Some of them can apparently cope with the two distinctively different elaborations of HEAVY/LIGHT if and only if the intended referential domain of WORK is taken for granted at the moment they listen to the expression. Identification of the target number in a task of type (3), on the other hand, is clearly *less* difficult when it is described immediately before the child is shown the big and the small circles with different typewritten numbers inside them.

We shall briefly return to some of these findings in the epilogue. What had been demonstrated beyond any doubt at this stage of our empirical enquiries, however, was an unequivocal and very strong relationship between *ease* and *nature* of cross-classification. Formally identical tasks were solved by nearly all or only very few children, depending upon whether *orthogonal* or *related* contracts concerning categorization were involved. Failure to establish intersubjectivity could thus in a majority of cases be interpreted as due to an incapacity to cope with two different elaborations of the same, linguistically mediated, abstract draft of a contract, i.e. with one HEAVY/LIGHT categorization of 'body build' and another of 'work', with one BIG/SMALL categorization of 'circle areas' and another of 'numbers', with one

LONG/SHORT attribution to 'body height' and another to 'horizontal distances', etc.

TABLE 6.5   Success (+) and failure (−) on identification of 'HEAVY man with LIGHT work'

	Age groups								
	7 years			8½ years			Both		
Condition	−	+	N	−	+	N	−	+	N
Verbal pre-identification	14	13	27	9	35	44	23	48	71
Verbal post-identification	5	22	27	5	39	44	10	61	71

Thus, only five out of our 27 children in the 7-years group were able to identify 'the one of the SHORT men who has the SECOND LONGEST way to the house' when the target object was described immediately before they were shown the drawing. The failures in this task, moreover, were all of the same kind: ordering of length was obviously performed on ALL distances, not only on those pertaining to the sub-class SHORT men. Coping with two different variants of length thus proved particularly difficult when variant I (body height) had to be attended to in order to single out the proper domain for ordering of variant II (horizontal distance). Deficient operative semantic competence, it seemed, was revealed in diffusion of the domain of the ordering operation (see p. 133).

TABLE 6.6   Success (+) and failure (−) on identification of 'SECOND SMALLEST number in BIG circle'

	Age groups								
	7 years			8½ years			Both		
Condition	−	+	N	−	+	N	−	+	N
Verbal pre-identification	14	13	27	3	41	44	17	54	71
Verbal post-identification	20	17	27	13	31	44	33	38	71

Subsequent studies were accordingly planned with the explicit aim of examining in a more systematic fashion how such diffusion might be affected by spatial arrangement (cell 6 versus cell 5 in Table 6.3), type of cross-classification (cells 5 versus 11 versus 17), options with respect to nature and linguistic encoding of attribute I (variants within cells 11 and 17) and verbal pre- versus post-identification of target object. A number of additional tasks of identifying reference were accordingly constructed and inserted among other problems to be presented to the children in our 8½-year group. In order to eliminate potential effects of sequence of conditions, moreover, approximately half the children were given verbal pre-identifications whereas the other half were given verbal post-identifications of all target objects.

TABLE 6.7   Success (+) and failure (−) on six different identifying reference tasks

| | Verbal identification | | | | | |
| | pre- | | | post- | | |
Task	−	+	N	−	+	N
(1) Cell 6: BLACK cats … SECOND BIGGEST	0	21	21	0	18	18
(2) Cell 5: WHITE dogs … SECOND BIGGEST	3	18	21	2	16	18
(3) Cell 11: LADIES … SECOND LONGEST way	4	17	21	4	14	18
(4) Cell 11: BLACK-clothed men … SECOND SHORTEST way	13	8	21	6	12	18
(5) Cell 17: HIGH men … SECOND SHORTEST way	14	7	21	7	11	18
(6) Cell 17: LOW firemen … SECOND HIGHEST on ladder	18	3	21	7	11	18

There were in all 39 children in the $8^1/_2$-year group who completed all tasks, 21 with verbal pre-identification and 18 with post-identification of the target objects, and the main results from this additional enquiry are presented in Table 6.7. The identifying description was formally identical across all six tasks, and of the form … the one of I that is … SECOND II'est … .

The only essential difference between tasks 1 and 2 concerns spatial arrangement of domain, i.e. random arrangement versus linear ordering of all objects with respect to attribute II. Tasks 3, 4, 5, and 6 are all like task 2 in that respect. The distribution of attribute II, moreover, is such that in every task the target is *not* the SECOND II'est of ALL objects. Failure to attain intersubjectivity on the adult premises is therefore as a rule due to diffusion of the domain of ordering. Thus under conditions of verbal pre-identification the expression 'the one of the SHORT FIREMEN who is SECOND HIGHEST on the ladder' was understood by 18 out of 21 children as referring to that SHORT fireman who is SECOND HIGHEST of ALL on the ladder (see Table 6.4 and Figure 6.3). Only three of those 18 children, however, made that same kind of error when asked to point out 'the one of the WHITE dogs that is SECOND BIGGEST'.

Tasks 3 and 4 are variants within cell 11 of Table 6.3, and the cross-classification involved in identification is of type $(A_1 + B) \times A_2$. The drawing in task 3 showed short female and long male persons standing in line in front of a news-stand, whereas task 4 was about long black-clothed and short white-clothed men approaching the top of a mountain. Moreover, in both cases the redundantly defined sub-set is made known as B rather than A_1, i.e. as LADY rather than SHORT in task 3 and as BLACK-clothed rather than LONG in task 4. There was, nevertheless, a

FIGURE 6.3. 'The one of the SHORT firemen who is second HIGHEST on the ladder'

significant difference in performance on the two tasks under conditions of verbal pre-identification: the *autonomous categorization* 'LADIES' serves to set the sub-set apart, whereas the *sub-class construction* 'BLACK-clothed MEN' makes for diffusion of the domain of ordering.

Tasks 5 and 6, finally, are formally identical. Both require cross-classification of type $A_1 \times A_2$ involving two different elaborations of length. Vertical height, however, is in task 5 made known by a word that is not applicable to horizontal distance, whereas in task 6 both variants (vertical height and vertical position) must be categorized via elaborations of the abstract draft of a contract inherent in the one and the same bipolar pair of adjectives LOW/HIGH. And this is, as we see from Table 6.7, particularly difficult when the target object is made known to the child in the absence of an experientially available referential domain.

Whether intersubjectivity will be achieved in the case of tasks 5 and 6 is thus, in view of the data in Table 6.7, to a significant degree a question of verbal pre- versus post-identification of the target object. Verbal pre-identification, moreover, is in these cases contingent upon mastery of abstract drafts of contracts concerning categorization and/or attribution in anticipation of specific potential elaborations of them. Identification of the target object is achieved the moment such elaborations are 'externalized' as operations upon the visually displayed referential domain. And, we shall argue, the negligible time interval between identifying description and exposure to drawing under conditions of verbal pre-identification may under certain conditions lead to particular taxation of the child's operative semantic competence. What is being referred to by an adult word or expression may thus be perfectly understood if immediately available within the visual field of the child at that very moment of verbal communication, yet incomprehensible if that same entity is talked about immediately before it is seen.

5. Epilogue

Our theoretical and empirical explorations of identifying reference in adult–child communication grew in part out of a discontent with Piaget's notion of words as 'conventional signifiers'. What moreover, seems to emerge as we continue these explorations is evidence of an 'operativity' inherent in language that has been largely ignored—and at times even denied—by Piaget and his associates. Even mastery of a pair of bipolar adjectives such as LONG/SHORT appears, indeed, in view of our enquiries—and contrary to Sinclair-de-Zwart's claim—to be intimately linked to level of 'operativity'. A pre-operational child with one long and two short sticks in front of him may thus certainly achieve intersubjectivity on adult premises when asked to point out 'the LONG stick', yet be entirely at a loss when hearing about a SHORT man who has made many LONG journeys in a SHORT time.

Operative semantic competence, we have argued, must be conceived of as the capacity to achieve intersubjectivity in acts of verbal communication. It is contingent upon mastery of abstract drafts of contracts concerning categorization inherent in ordinary language. The specific elaboration of such drafts into reciprocally endorsed 'actual' contrasts is to a large extent determined by what is taken for granted as an intersubjectively shared HERE and NOW at any given stage of an act of communication. Thus in our identifying reference tasks the child's operative semantic competence is revealed in his attempt to grasp a 'social' (i.e. talked-about) reality and convert it into an 'actual' (i.e. visually displayed) reality. And a failure to achieve intersubjectivity is revealed in his identification of some object other than that presumedly made known to him by the adult.

Verbal pre- versus post-identification constitute different conditions for conversion of 'social' into 'actual' reality and vice versa, and the essential difference between the two conditions may be described in terms of message structure. Which variant of length is intended by the pair of words LONG/SHORT in thus, first of all, conveyed by intralinguistic patterns of dependency of the kind investigated by Wold (in press) (see p. 140), and distinctively different specifications of the general draft are obviously required depending upon whether a MAN or a WAY is being talked about. Under conditions of verbal pre-identification, however, words such as MAN and WAY in themselves merely convey additional drafts of contracts concerning categorization. On the other hand, what is made known by the expressions LONG MAN and SHORT WAY when said about visibly available men and distances is bound to that firmly experientially established HERE and NOW. The ambiguity inherent in LONG/SHORT is thus in the latter case immediately 'disambiguated' in terms of particular perceptual features of the referential domain, whereas 'disambiguation' under conditions of verbal pre-identification is contingent upon a relatively advanced capacity for decentration.

This, we shall argue, is also the reason why so many of the younger children fail to identify 'the HEAVY man with the LIGHT work' when he is verbally described immediately before they are shown the drawing, but succeed in an otherwise strictly equivalent task when they are watching the drawing while listening to the description (see Table 6.5). An expression such as 'LIGHT WORK' is thus at a certain developmental stage of operative semantic competence apparently immediately understood when bound to an experientially available HERE and NOW of some men putting stamps on envelopes and others carrying big sacks, yet incomprehensible in the linguistic context 'HEAVY MAN with LIGHT WORK' when no such referential domain is intersubjectively taken for granted. And incomprehensibility may again most plausibly be interpreted as deficient 'operativity', i.e. as due to centration in particular experiential contingencies. What is involved in HEAVY/LIGHT as a 'conventional signifier' at the level of adult operative semantic competence seems, moreover, to be mastery of a very abstract draft that in specific acts of verbal communication can be elaborated into reciprocally endorsed contracts concerning categorization of WORK, MEALS, TAXES, and DUTIES as well as of STONES and MEN. Some of these categorizations may be considered instances of 'literal', others of 'metaphorical' language use. The expressions HEAVY STONE, HEAVY WORK, and HEAVY DUTY may thus be said to mirror an extrapolation from an initially narrow and sensorimotorically anchored referential domain to successively less 'tangible' though 'actual' human realities. The same seems to apply to BIG/SMALL, however, as a topic such as 'size of material objects' is replaced by, for example, 'numerical value'. The reason why many children seem less capable of identifying 'the SECOND SMALLEST number in the BIG circle' under conditions of verbal post-identification may thus be sought in perceptual interference (see Table 6.6): attendance to a visually salient and in some sense more 'primitive' variant of BIG/SMALL at the moment 'SECOND SMALLEST' is heard may very likely interfere with the intended, far more abstract and possibly not yet firmly mastered, attribution of numerical value.

Ease of identification in our identifying reference tasks is thus apparently determined in a subtle interplay between what is seen and what is said about it, and the interrelationships between operative semantic competence and Piagetian cognitive operations, we shall argue, must be understood as patterns of dependency of the kind encountered in an analysis of message structure. We may thus, if we want to focus exclusively on abstract 'operations of thought', interpret the children's performances on our six tasks of identifying reference in Table 6.7 in terms of *mastery of cross-classification, ordering,* and *class inclusion.* The crucial prerequisites for success in tasks 2, 3, 4, 5, and 6, moreover, are, in view of our findings, clearly the capacities to keep two sub-sets of objects mentally apart and to withstand a 'perceptually induced' diffusion of the domain of ordering. We might hence—on Piagetian premises—expect that the children who succeed in our six identifying reference tasks will also do well in, for example, traditional tasks of class inclusion. A cross-tabulation of individual achievements performed for the verbal pre- and post-identification conditions separately, however, did not confirm such an expectation. The performances of our $8^1/_2$-year-old children on the two presumedly very similar sets of tasks showed no correspondence at all.

Whether a child will withstand diffusion is, as shown in Table 6.7, clearly dependent upon which entities are to be kept apart and which contracts concerning categorization must be endorsed. The dependency upon operative semantic competence, moreover, is particularly transparent when the target object is made known by verbal means before the child is shown the referential domain. Ease of identification is then clearly contingent upon which contracts concerning categorization are involved in the cross-classification: nearly all children succeed in confining the ordering operation to the proper sub-set of objects when cross-classification involves two orthogonal attributes, whereas nearly all of them fail when two different elaborations of the same abstract draft of a contract concerning categorization are required.

Tasks 2, 3, 4, 5, and 6 in Table 6.7 may from such a point of view be said to constitute a scale for assessing mastery of a particular combination of Piagetian cognitive operations at different levels of operative semantic competence. An analysis of individual performances on all six tasks under conditions of verbal pre-identification shows indeed that 19 out of 21 individual patterns of success and failure conform to a strictly ascending order of difficulty from tasks 1 to 6. What has been achieved by our systematic variation of tasks, it may be argued, is thus a specification of what Piagetian researchers frequently—and conveniently—refer to as 'task-specific sources of variance' and/or '*décalage horizontal*'.

Our empirical enquiries so far, however, yield only a preliminary and partial specification. We notice in Table 6.7, for instance, that diffusion of the domain of ordering occurs significantly more frequently in task 4 than in either task 2 or task 3 (under conditions of verbal pre-identification). We do not know, however, whether this is primarily due to the cohesive nature of the superordinate class MEN or to perceptual interference (of visible differences with respect to length *qua* body height upon categorization of length *qua* horizontal distance). This may accordingly be explored by comparing performances on task 4 with achievements in an otherwise equivalent task of type A × B, i.e. a request to single out 'the one of the BLACK-clothed men who has the SECOND SHORTEST way to the house' in a drawing in which all six men approaching the house are equally tall. The impact of purely linguistically mediated contracts concerning categorizations, moreover, may be further illuminated by comparing performances on pairs of tasks in which the very same visually displayed element is made known to the child as, for example, a SNOWBALL or a WHITE circle, a BOY or a SHORT man, etc. (see p. 135). Such modifications and further elaborations of our tasks of identifying reference will hence be attempted in subsequent empirical studies.

A major aim in those studies will be a novel and hopefully more fruitful basis for a dialogue between psychologists who study acquisition of language and those who are primarily concerned with the development of thought. A recourse to *décalage horizontal* in an explanation of data such as those presented in Table 6.7 is, indeed, a symptom of negative rationalism. Much may be gained, therefore, if developmental psycholinguists and Piagetian students of thought become allies in a search for operative aspects of language where on traditional Piagetian premises little more has so far been found than deviance from content-free and formally defined structures of thought.

Acknowledgements

The data reported in this paper were collected by a team of teachers and students. The investigation was a joint venture originating from a research seminar conducted by Karsten Hundeide and the author at the University of Oslo in 1975, and we are grateful to Ingegerd Lindström who had major responsibility for the actual preparation of stimulus material and coding of results.

Notes

1 Our descriptions are literal translations from Norwegian and may for that reason sound somewhat strange in English. The issue of alternative verbal constructions referring to one and the same target object, however, will be discussed in some detail later on.

2 In Norwegian: 'Den av de KORTE personene som har LANG vei til huset.' The adjective pair LANG/KORT is in Norwegian applied to body height as well as to distance.

3 Full isomorphy is achieved only when the two tall persons close to the house are placed side by side on the road to the left and the two short persons are located side by side at the same distance from the house on the road coming from the right. A 'random' arrangement rather than a linear ordering of distances (cells 6 and 15) may be achieved by placing the persons at different distances from the house on roads approaching it from six different directions.

4 'BLACK-clothed' and 'WHITE-clothed' are literal translations of the Norwegian words *svartkledd* and *hvitkledd*.

5 The dependency among operations may in this case be specified as follows: correct identification of the referent of 'the SECOND BIGGEST one' is contingent upon correct identification of the referent of 'the BLACK candles', but not vice versa.

6 The Norwegian word for NUMBER is *tall*, which also has the sense of NUMERAL in English.

150

References

Blakar, R. M., and Rommetveit, R. (1975), Utterances *in vacuo* and in contexts. An experimental and theoretical exploration of some interrelationships between what is heard and what is seen or imagined, *Int. J. Psycholinguistics*, 4, 5–32.

Bruner, J. (this volume), From communication to language: a psychological perspective.

Chomsky, N. (1972), *Studies on Semantics in Generative Grammar*, The Hague: Mouton.

Deese, J. (1962), The structure of associative meaning, *Psychological Review*, 69, 161–175.

Ducrot, O. (1972), *Dire et ne pas Dire*, Paris: Hermann.

Furth, H. G. (1970), On language and knowing in Piaget's developmental theory, *Human Dev.*, 13, 241–257.

Heider, F. (1958), *The Psychology of Interpersonal Relations*, New York and London: Wiley.

Hundeide, K. (1975), Verbalization and discrimination. Mimeo, Institute of Psychology, University of Oslo.

Katz, J. J., and Fodor, J. A. (1963), The structure of a semantic theory, *Language*, 39, 170–210.

Lévi-Strauss, C. (1964), Structural analysis in linguistics and anthropology. In Hymes, D. (ed.), *Language in Culture and Society*, New York: Harper & Row.

Luria, A. R. (1961), *The Role of Speech in Regulation of Normal and Abnormal Behaviour*, Oxford: Pergamon Press.

Marková, I. (this volume), Attributions, meanings of verbs, and reasoning.

Olson, D. (1970), Language and thought. Aspects of a cognitive theory of semantics, *Psychological Review*, 77, 257–273.

Piaget, J. (1926), *The Language and Thought of the Child*, New York: Harcourt Brace.

Piaget, J. (1951), *Judgment and Reasoning in the Child*, London: Routledge & Kegan Paul.

Piaget, J. (1957), *Logic and Psychology*, New York: Basic Books.

Piaget, J. (1972), Language and thought from the genetic point of view. In Adams, P. (ed.), *Language in Thinking*, Harmondsworth: Penguin Books.

Piaget, J. (1973), *The Child's Conception of the World*, London: Paladin.

Piaget, J., and Inhelder, B. (1966), *La Psychologie de l'Enfant*, Paris: Presse Univer.

Quine, W. V. (1972), Methodological reflections on current linguistic theory. In Davidson, D., and Harman, G. (eds); *Semantics of Natural Language*, Dordrecht: Reidel.

Rommetveit, R. (1972), *Språk, Tanke og Kommunikasjon. Ei Innføring i Språkpsykologi og Psykolingvistikk*, Oslo: Universitetsforlaget.

Rommetveit, R. (1974), *On Message Structure. A Framework for the Study of Language and Communication*, New York and London: Wiley.

Rommetveit, R., and Blakar, R. M. (1973), Induced semantic-associative states and resolution of binocular rivalry conflicts between letters, *Scand. J. Psychol.*, 14, 185–194.

Rommetveit, R., Cook, M., Havelka, N., Henry, P., Herkner, W., Pêcheux, M., and Peeters, G. (1971), Processing of utterances in context. In Carswell, E. A., and Rommetveit, R. (eds), *Social Contexts of Messages*, London: Academic Press.

Sinclair-de-Zwart, H. (1972a), Developmental psycholinguistics. In Adams, P. (ed.), *Language in Thinking*, Harmondsworth: Penguin Books.

Sinclair-de-Zwart, H. (1972b), A possible theory of language acquisition within the general framework of Piaget's developmental psychology. In Adams, P. (ed.), *Language in Thinking*, Harmondsworth: Penguin Books.

Strawson, P. F. (1969), *Individuals*, London: Methuen.

Turner, E. A., and Rommetveit, R. (1967), The acquisition of sentence voice and reversibility, *Child Development*, 38, 649–660.

Vygotsky, L. S. (1962), *Thought and Language*, Cambridge, Mass.: M.I.T. Press.

Wold, A. H. (in press), *Decoding Strategies, Word Openness, and the Dimension of Time in Oral Language*, London: Academic Press.

7

THE INTERNAL TRIANGLE: LANGUAGE, REASONING, AND THE SOCIAL CONTEXT

Valerie Walkerdine and Chris Sinha

1. Language and the Piagetian Paradigm

Concern about the problematic nature of the relationship of language and thought has been the subject of considerable attention from both psychologists and philosophers for many years now. Recent work in the field of language development has revitalized the debate and recast its terms along the lines of a search for semantic, and hence cognitive, universals.

As part of the Language Development Project at Bristol University, we began to examine, in an experimental setting, the relationship of the development of some relational terms in language to Piagetian tests of cognitive development. The results which emerged revealed the limitations of a Piagetian view of cognitive development and of the relationship of language to cognition. This chapter is a result of that examination. It seeks to do two things. First, it takes as problematic the universal and a-contextual nature of Piaget's theory of cognitive development and the role of language in the developmental process. Second, it presents an attempt to suggest how an alternative approach to cognitive development might be built up.

The work of Piaget provides the most systematic account to date of the development of *cognition*, and has therefore been a starting point for many theories which postulate a cognitive basis for the acquisition of language. For example, Slobin (1973) attempted to explain language development in terms of 'cognitive prerequisites', while remaining within the framework of transformational grammar. This marrying of the neo-Kantian paradigm of Piaget with Chomskyan Cartesian rationalism is interesting in view of the theoretical disparity between the two approaches. Whereas Chomsky (and, one assumes, Slobin) is prepared to give considerable weight to innate potential, it was his dissatisfaction with such innatist assumptions which first led Piaget to develop his theory of Genetic Epistemology. He believed (in line with the geneticist, Lamarck) that the 'genetic potential' approach to intelligence was misguided because this very genetic potential must itself be the product of an interaction and adaptation between organism and environment. He thus set out to explore the development of the phenomenon we call 'intelligence' in terms of the interaction of individual and environment. Piaget rejected both the Cartesian rationalism espoused by Chomsky and the empiricist tradition which still dominates Anglo-Saxon psychology in favour of a basically Kantian rationalist paradigm. In his model, cognitive development is a teleological process in which the intellect is progressively restructured until it embodies the 'laws of thought' as represented in formal logic systems. Piaget shares the generally accepted view that Western scientific thinking is the highest form of intellectual activity. According to this view, one can extract from an examination of this activity, the fundamental process of thinking which is taken to underlie all science. This process, once isolated, can be expressed in terms of formal logical operations. These operations are open to all because their development is a function of the dynamic interaction of the individual and the environment alone, that is a process in which the contexts in which the development takes place become irrelevant. The nature of the logical operations can be reconstructed by examining the way in which these are structurally built up in the course of the child's actions and interactions. In this way it is possible to understand both the ontogenesis and the phylogenesis of human thought.

Thus, the criteria of Western scientific thinking are superimposed upon our view of cognitive development, which is conceived as progress toward logical thinking, and are established as the pinnacle of a universal developmental sequence. The following statement indicates this line of thinking:

> Whether we study children in Geneva, Paris, New York or Moscow, in the mountains of Iran or the heart of Africa, or on an island in the Pacific, we observe everywhere certain ways of conducting social exchanges between children, or between children and adults, which act through their functioning alone, regardless of the context of information handed down through education. In all environments, individuals ask questions, work together, discuss, oppose things and so on; and this constant exchange between individuals takes place throughout the whole of development according to a process of socialisation which involves the social life of children among themselves as much as their relationships with older children or adults of all ages. (Piaget, 1972, p. 35)

Children the world over are seen as developing through interaction with the environment; but, it is an environment conceived of in 'biological' terms, in the sense that only the 'universal' features of that environment are seen as relevant to development. The child, by acting upon objects in the environment, abstracts principles of operation (logico-mathematical principles) not specific to the objects themselves. The principles of operation finally become the basis of formal, operational thinking in adolescence. Piaget can therefore be said to have a dialetical approach to the relationship of man and environment, but it is a dialectic which maximizes the macro (or bio-physical) features of the environment, while minimizing the micro (or culturally determined) ones.

Piaget views the influence of the social context on cognitive development as important in the macro sense, but does not consider the role of context in terms of the situation as defined by the participants, nor the social and cultural rules operating in the interpretation of the situation by the participants, and in the symbolic mechanisms of interpretation, such as language. Context, in a social or cultural sense, has no role in Piaget's conception of cognitive development, which is characterized only by the development of operating principles resulting from the manipulation of objects.

Piaget's theory is a structural one. He conceives of the process of development only with reference to the structures which characterize thinking at any particular point in development. This structural description is characterized by stages. At around the age of 7 years the child is said to make the transition from being pre-operational (i.e. unable to use operational logic) to the stage of concrete operations, in which he is able to use the logical operating principles on 'here and now' objects. This transition is exemplified by the transition from egocentrism to the ability to decentre, or to take the view of the other. It is by this process that the child enters the category of reasoning beings. To possess operational thinking is to have 'knowledge'. The transition to operational thinking is therefore of paramount importance to Piaget's theory of cognitive development.

Operational principles develop from the manipulation of representations of internalized actions. Representation begins with imitations that accompany action (Piaget's classic example is that of the young child who opens his/her mouth when trying to open a box). Later come private symbols (Piaget cites those in *play* and *dreams* as examples) and public signs (of which those of language are the most important). Systems of representation do not, for Piaget, develop from the structures of *language* but from the structures of action.

The formal system of language is therefore not seen as imposing any constraints upon cognitive development. Language is used in cognition as a system of representation like any other—it reflects cognition. In the interpretation of the child's responses during investigations of cognitive development, therefore, language serves only as a reflection of underlying cognitive competence.

Performance in 'cognitive' tests is therefore believed to be an acceptable criterion by which to judge the level of operative intelligence reached by the child, since neither social or cultural contextual variables nor the formal system of language (the interpretation of which both reflects and structures the social and cultural context in which it is used) are seen as in any way affecting the child's response. A Piagetian model of performance, therefore, largely ignores both the role of context and the mechanisms by which context is defined, one of which is language.

There have been several attempts to investigate further the role of language in cognitive development. Perhaps the best known among these studies is the work of Jerome Bruner and his co-workers undertaken at Harvard during the 1950s and early 1960s. However, there are basic differences between the assumptions of Bruner and those of Piaget. Bruner was originally concerned to explain the Piagetian developmental model. He did so by attempting to chart the development of representation in children. However, by so doing he shifted the emphasis from structure to process; he attempted (Bruner, 1964) to explain Piagetian structure with his process model by reference to three levels of representation, the enactive, seen as a way of representing past events in *motor* responses (for example bicycle riding), the iconic, consisting of the organization of percepts and images, and the symbolic, consisting of a system which is both arbitrary and remote from that which it represents. Such a shift cannot really be said to be explaining Piaget's findings since the latter was concerned not simply with the kind of representation, but with the logical manipulation of relations in operational thinking.

Inhelder *et al.* (1966) have summed up the difference between the Genevan and Harvard positions as follows:

> According to Bruner, cognitive development consists in the acquisition of 'techniques' of information processing. These techniques, through an 'interiorisation' process, form the basis for three information-processing systems: the enactive, the iconic and the symbolic representing different *levels* of cognitive functioning that are presumably correlated with cognitive development. The Harvard project was primarily concerned with the conditions necessary for transition from the *iconic* to the *symbolic* level of cognitive functioning. In the Genevan studies, however, the main preoccupation was clarification of the structuration processes which mediate the transition from one *stage* (in the Piagetian sense) of development to another *stage*. (p. 160).

Even if the assumptions on which the work of Piaget and Bruner is based are different, there is no reason not to take account of Bruner's theory of representation or of his empirical evidence. It has helped to shed new light on the processes involved in many of Piaget's experiments testing for the existence of concrete operational thinking in children. The experiments have also suggested that the role of language in the representation system of cognition changes as children get older.

As we have seen, Bruner's concern with the development of the representational system by which we process cognitive information is different from Piaget's essential interest in the development of *logical ability*. Whereas Bruner saw differences between types of representation, Piaget saw as the central feature of development the move from pre-operational to operational thinking. This led to different concerns for the role of language in the cognitive system. Piaget, stressing the primacy of cognition, tended to minimize the role of language and to assign to it a minor, reflective role. It is seen as only one mode of representation among several. For Bruner, on the other hand, language is *par excellence* the vehicle of symbolic representation. This difference led Bruner and his colleagues to postulate that language tuition could in fact *accelerate* the cognitive functioning of children in the symbolic/concrete operations age group, and consequently led to the formulation of proposals and experiments opposing those of the Genevans. Bruner's experiments sought to examine what happened when children who gave perceptual responses to a conservation test were confronted with the same test carried out behind a screen, so that the child could now rely solely on *linguistic* rather than *perceptual* coding. In one particular study by Frank (reported in Bruner, 1964), conservation-type responses showed a dramatic advance when this screening device was applied.

'Correct responses jump from 0% to 50% among the 4's, from 20% to 90% among the 5's, and from 50% to 100% among the 6's.' In his 1964 paper and in 'Studies in Cognitive Growth' (1966), Bruner cited many more such examples and attempts to *train* cognitive development through language. These were only partially successful.

Such attempts have been frequently criticized by Piaget and his co-workers in Geneva, for example by Inhelder *et al.* (1966). The Genevans claim that since the basis of conservation behaviour lies in the logical system by which the child integrates the operational mechanisms of identity, reversibility, and compensation, and not in the language by which he represents these operations, linguistic training should be ineffective. Since they believed that reversibility was central, the move from egocentric to operational thinking was seen as a transition from *action* reversibility to thought–operation reversibility rather than from iconic to symbolic representation. In this particular paper, they cited two experiments in their attempt to counter Bruner. In these experiments they attempted to provide conditions in which children could *learn* the operational mechanisms rather than conditions in which mechanisms are masked, as in Bruner's experiment. The children were presented with a discrepancy between the expected and actual outcomes. They were also presented with a programmed series of examples designed to yield generalization of an existing elementary structure (for example, from conservation of discrete entities to that of continuous quantities). They were, in addition, taught to use language expressions found to be characteristic of children with conservation concepts in situations of increasing complexity in terms of number, quantities and dimensions.

Their results revealed:

serious objections to the conclusions Bruner draws from the conservation experiment with the screening technique and the limitations imposed on the evocation of alternative responses by the child. The operational structure (as defined by Piaget) underlying the conservation concepts appears to us to be a complex, co-ordinated system that cannot be properly evaluated by rather summary investigations of answers to preselected questions with no exploration of the child's justification of these answers. (Inhelder *et al.*, 1966, p. 162)

In the linguistic training experiments Inhelder *et al.* found two effects. First, after training in the use of 'conservation-terms', children giving partial conservation answers on a pre-test were able to express arguments more clearly on a post-test. Second, many children mentioned the two dimensions, length and breadth, which Piaget took to be central but did *not* achieve conservation (for example, 'There the water goes up higher because the glass is thin; the other is shorter and wider and there is less to drink here').

They conclude that

language training, among other types of training, operates to direct the child's interactions with the environment and thus to 'focus' on relevant dimensions of task situations. Second, the observed changes in the justifications given for answers suggest that language does aid the storage and retrieval of relevant information. However, our evidence offers little, if any, support for the contention that language learning per se contributes to the *integration* and co-ordination of 'informational units' necessary for the achievement of the conservation concepts.

They further suggest that 'language learning does not provide ... a ready made "lattice" or lens which organises the perceptual world' (p. 163).

What Bruner, on the other hand, seems to have been suggesting is that for the young child, perception (or in his terms iconic representation) prevents the use of symbolic representation. In other words, the language contained in the experimental situation is *potentially* helpful but cannot be utilized because of the domination of perceptual coding. Thus, according to this view, perception is seen as preceding language as a tool in the cognitive process, since linguistic forms of representation cannot be ulitized until the child has freed himself/herself from the domination of iconic representation (although symbolic representation does exists from a fairly early age). The iconic level is thus seen as the earlier and stronger form of representation. If this is so, training in words combined with the removal of the perceptual cues, should, as Bruner suggested, help the child to achieve conservation. One problem with this explanation is that of the artificial nature of the situation created when the perceptual input has been removed. It may well be reasonable to suggest that the child is able to use symbolic representation in situations where the perceptual input is blocked out, but how does that carry over to the child's performance in *real* situations where perceptual input remains? Bruner presumably would argue that even if there were no *practical* application of the training principle, it still shows that conservation can occur only when the child learns to place more emphasis on symbolic representation than perceptual input. However, as we have seen, when Inhelder trained children in the use of the vocabulary of conservation without screening out perceptual input, language was seen to help, but did not appear to be a sufficient condition for conservation. Could it be that instead of language (symbolic representation) being essential to conservation it is in fact one of the factors which prevent young children from achieving it? It will be remembered that Inhelder noted that children who could use the lexical items of conservation, but did not conserve, tended to answer along the following lines: 'there the water goes up higher because the glass is thin; the other is shorter and wider and there is *less to drink* here' (our italics).

Could one explanation be that the child fails, not because he/she fails to use linguistic representation, and not because language simply helps him/her to 'give voice to' the cognitive dimensions, but because of confusion over the meaning of the words, leading the child to understand the problem in a way which is different from that of the adult experimenter's interpretation? It could be that the child uses language to focus on particular perceptual dimensions. If this is so, it could explain why screening out the perceptual features of the situation leads the child to a different interpretation or solution.

Certainly there is evidence to suggest that this may indeed be the case. Margaret Donaldson and her colleagues at Edinburgh have examined children's understanding of several words that are commonly utilized in conservation experiments. The word 'less', italicized in the example given by Inhelder, is one such word.

During the Edinburgh Cognition Project, Donaldson and her colleagues investigated the cognitive and linguistic development of pre-school children. Donaldson and Wales (1970) took it as their objective to sample a range of skills which it was felt would be important in later cognitive development. They discovered that all such tests involved a judgement of similarity or difference.

They suggested that interpretation of the word 'same' was by no means a simple task. There exist several possible interpretations which may be used in a variety of circumstances. The first interpretation is in terms of *identity*, 'the identity of an enduring object'. It is an interpretation which has been the subject of considerable philosophic debate. However, when concrete objects are the subject of the judgement, Donaldson and Wales suggest that there are at least three other possible interpretations (1970, pp. 239–240):

(1) Two (or more) objects are the SAME when they are alike with respect to all observable attributes.
(2) The word SAME is used when two (or more) objects are alike with respect to at least one observable attribute, but different with respect to at least one another.
(3) Two concrete entities may be the same in some respect that cannot be directly observed.

It is the third category of similarity which Donaldson and Wales have suggested may be particularly relevant to Piagetian tests. In these tests recognition of sameness may depend on a combination of attributes which, if taken separately, are observably different. Alternatively, the judgement may depend on the subjects' having taken note of an attribute which is not observable at the time of judgement.

They concluded that mastery of 'same' and 'different' appeared to be a very complex task because similarity and difference could be judged in several different ways, depending on the context.

Various tests involving judgements of 'same' and 'different' revealed some of the complexity involved in the mastery of the terms. In one experiment, $3\frac{1}{2}$- to $4\frac{1}{2}$-year-old children were asked to make same/different judgements about two groups of objects. In the first group there were 4 sets of 3 objects; form and colour were coincident in each set. For example, there were 3 blue toothbrushes. In this group any 2 objects were necessarily either the same in all respects, or different in all respects. In the second group there were also 4 sets of objects and 3 colours but in this case form and colour were not coincident. There were, for example, 3 toothbrushes: 1 red, 1 white, 1 yellow. In this group any 2 objects were necessarily either the same in one respect and different in the other, or different in both respects. In each case, the child was either asked to choose an object which was 'the same in some way', or asked to choose one which was 'different in some way' from the stimulus object.

The results overall revealed that the children showed a marked tendency towards 'same' responses. When presented with the first group of objects the children tended to choose the object that was the same in all ways, no matter what the instruction. To the second group of objects, the children nearly always responded 'correctly', that is, their object choices were both the 'same' and 'different' in some way, i.e. the children chose an object which simultaneously satisfied both instructions. The authors interpreted this finding as implying that the children were interpreting 'different in some way' as 'implying a denial of object identity along with the presence of some sort of similarity' (Donaldson and Wales, 1970, p. 250). This would explain why in the second group only 2 out of 30 children picked out an object that was different in all ways under the 'difference' condition. More evidence as to the relative mastery of 'same' and 'different' comes from spontaneous speech data from the same children. Occurrences of 'same' were frequent, but only five occurrences of 'different' were recorded.

In another related investigation, Donaldson and Balfour (1968) provided very similar data on tasks involving the terms, 'more' and 'less'. As with 'same'/'different' they suggested that the interpretation of the terms, 'more' and 'less' varied considerably according to the context of application. They attempted to categorize some of the differences between situations.

The terms 'more' and 'less':
(1) Can apply to discrete units of continuous quantities (mass/count nouns).
(2) May be used in a static sense in the comparison of 2 entities at one point in time, or in situations involving comparison across an interval of time.
(3) May be used when there is a comparison across time in which case one or more entities may be involved.
(4) Can be used where 2 entities and 2 points in time are under consideration, in which 6 comparative judgements are possible in principle.

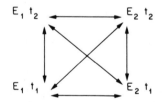

Source: Donaldson and Balfour, 1968, fig. 1.

FIGURE 7.1.

(5) When such comparison across time involves 2 entities, they may or may not be equal at t_1 and they may or may not have changed in quantity at t_2. If they change, one or both may do so. If both change, they may change in different directions.
(6) Where there is change it may be S who makes the change or he may be a passive observer.

Such a categorization suggests that just as the terms 'same' and 'different' were problematic for young children, so may the terms 'more' and 'less be.

Donaldson and Balfour conducted two studies into mastery of the terms.

The first study had the following characteristics:
(1) Discrete units were used.
(2) Both static and changing situations were used.
(3) The entities were sometimes equal and sometimes unequal to each other.
(4) There were always 2 entities in the comparison.
(5) The S sometimes had to make the change himself and sometimes had to judge it.
(6) When the change was made by E only one entity was altered.
(7) The direction of the change sometimes accorded with the final state of the entities relative to one another and sometimes did not.

In the second study the Ss dealt only with one entity and had only to effect a change (in this case to *decrease* quantity).

The children in the first study were aged 3·5 to 4·1 years, and in the second study the same children were used, 6 months later.

In the first study 2 cardboard apple trees were presented. Each tree had 6 hooks in corresponding positions to hold cardboard apples. The trees could be swivelled so that the number of apples could be adjusted by E without S seeing. When the apples were made equal by E, the arrangement of apples was always the same.

The subjects were presented with various situations involving 'more'/'less' judgements and situations in which the subjects had to 'make it so that there are more/less apples ...'.

In the second study there was only one tree and the stimulus situations were all of the form 'make it so that there are less apples on the tree'.

The results of the first study revealed that the children did not appear to differentiate between 'more' and 'less'. They responded in all cases as though all the questions were to do with 'more'. The ability to count did not appear to relate to judgement ability. Additionally, when asked to add or subtract apples the children tended to *add*.

In the second study all children added rather than subtracted apples, though there was some confusion, as though some of the children realised they had made a mistake but did not know how to correct it.

Donaldson and Balfour were not sure how to interpret their results, but felt that they were justified in thinking that the children were treating both 'more' and 'less' as judgements of quantity and thus, by implication, judgements of 'more'.

In a concluding remark, attempting to sum up both the work on 'same'/'different' and on 'more'/'less', Donaldson and Wales (1970) suggested that it might be unwise to attribute these effects to the children's cognitive, as opposed to their linguistic, ability. It might be more helpful to think in terms of an interaction between language and cognition:

An immediate conclusion that may be drawn is that children's failure to respond appropriately in tasks in which they are instructed to perform in accord with such talk as *same as, different from, more than, Is there more here or more here?* and the like, may be as attributable to the structure of the child's language as to other aspects of his cognitive apparatus. Much more work needs to be done before results from such studies become, in any systematic fashion, fully interpretable. To show that similar results may be found when the 'same' tasks are presented 'non-verbally' merely begs the question unless it can be clearly demonstrated that the apparent conveyance of the language performance and other cognitive performance misleadingly reflects two quite unrelated systems of competence. We hold that the simplest interpretation is that the apparent convergence reflects an interaction of the two systems of competence—in a non-circular fashion—because of the apparent need in considering both systems independently, to take account of referential aspects of the situation the child is immediately confronted with, together with what look like the same formal relations some of the time. (p. 265).

It was suggested earlier that Bruner held that the role of language in cognition became central only when the child was able to free himself/herself from the domination of iconic imagery. Inhelder, on the other hand, felt that while language could help in the solution of cognitive problems it did not always make for success. She gave examples of a child's response in which 'conservation' words were used but the child did not attain the concept of conservation. Inhelder is here supposing that the language used by this child *reflected* his cognitive ability. The work of Donaldson and her colleagues suggests at least two points which are relevant to a discussion of the standpoints of Inhelder and of Bruner. First, the mastery of the relational terms used in many conservation problems is by no means a simple task, and in the present state of knowledge of psycholinguistics and in cognitive psychology, it would seem to be premature to suggest that the confusion as to the use of the phrase 'there is less to drink' merely shows that the language is not the mainstay of cognition. Second, it is possible that, instead of language assuming major importance as a tool in cognition only after an iconic stage, it in fact is already interacting with the perceptual apparatus and acting as a focusing tool at a fairly early age. It would seem foolish to ignore the possibility of linguistic coding of relational terms in cognitive experiments even at a stage of development which is supposedly only 'perceptual' in orientation.

The work of Donaldson *et al.* highlighted the complexity of the lexical items used in many Piagetian tests. A child performing in such tests must be able to choose the interpretation of the lexical item (usually a relational term) which best fits the context of the test. An understanding and appreciation of the context in which the experiment occurs may be crucial both for the child in interpreting the experiment and for the experimenter in understanding the child's response.

Although the Genevans have long remained firm in their position that language merely reflects cognition, Inhelder has, more recently, begun to investigate the role of context in the experimental situation discussed by Donaldson and her colleagues, concentrating on what Donaldson and Wales (1970) described as 'referential aspects of the situation' with which the child is immediately confronted. In her investigations into conservation, Inhelder (1972) drew attention to the two kinds of knowledge in the Piagetian structural model, knowledge of the properties of objects, and knowledge of principles of operation (or logico-mathematical knowledge) not specific to the objects themselves, but derived from knowledge of their properties.

Piaget's work has concentrated mainly on logico-mathematical knowledge, paying little attention to knowledge of object properties. Inhelder felt that the interaction of the two knowledge systems was important for an understanding of the developmental process. In a series of experiments on the conservation of number and length, she suggested that Piaget had not really paid enough attention to object properties and that a better understanding of the interaction between the two systems of knowledge could support a process model seeking to explain the development of new structures. She suggested that it is conflict between the two types of knowledge that leads to the onset of a new structural level:

> It is this conflict which will trigger the process leading to the final resolution through reciprocal assimilation of the two subsystems that do not necessarily belong to the same developmental level. The emergence of conflicts can explain the frequently occurring regressions in the subject's overt reasoning—they are only apparent regressions. In fact, they are observable symptoms of an internal event announcing the structuration of a higher order. (Inhelder, 1972, p. 113)

For Inhelder, then, concentration on the process as opposed to the structure which had been Piaget's primary concern, led to a reconsideration of the role of the structural elements, namely, representation and the interaction of the two kinds of knowledge. This new view of process was, however, always intended to be viewed within the existing Piagetian structural model: there was no suggestion that changes in the process model in any way affected the validity of the structural model.

Although Inhelder recognized the importance of 'referential aspects of the situation' in terms of the properties of the objects which feature in the experimental situation, she made no mention of the social context which defines and transmits for the subject those perceptual properties of the objects which are determinant for the culture.

Objects exist in a functionally and experientially defined framework (i.e. the context of the *use* to which the objects are put); function is both *socially* and *culturally* defined.

Apprehension of the properties of objects is not simply apprehension of objects *qua* objects but of objects in socially defined situations. The apprehension of the properties of objects is focused in language. Language is both interpreted within social contexts but also helps to focus attention on particular aspects of the context at hand. This is exemplified by Donaldson *et al.*'s work outlined earlier in which the interpretation of relational terms was seen as a highly complex process, since several possible interpretations of the terms existed and the individual had to know which interpretation best fitted the experimental context.

2. Evidence on the Role of Context

Several investigations carried out under the auspices of the Language Development Project at Bristol have provided data on the developmental sequence in the comprehension of some relational terms in which the interpretation of context, functionally, perceptually, and socially defined, plays a major role.

2.1 The Cup and Ball Experiment

In an experiment 25 2-year-olds and 12 2$^1/_2$-year-olds were presented with a cup which was either the right way up (⊖), or inverted (⊟) . They were asked to put a small rubber ball in/on the cup. If the cup was inverted, it was of course necessary for the child to turn the cup the right way up to put the ball *in* it. Similarly, if the cup was the right way up, it was necessary for him to invert the cup to put the ball *on* it.

Considerable differences were found between the responses of the 2 and 2$^1/_2$-year-olds. At age 2·0, there was a strong tendency either to leave the cup the right way up, or to turn it the right way up if it was inverted. Thus only 5 of the 25 children inverted the cup for *on* with the cup the right way up, but 8 turned the cup the right way up when it was inverted although the instruction was *on*. On the other hand at 2·6 the tendency was to leave the cup where it was. Here, proportionately more children were obtaining correct responses for both 'in' and 'on', but 'in' with cup inverted was found to be more difficult, while all 'on' items except with the right-way-up cup were found to be easier (see Tables 7.1 and 7.2)

TABLE 7.1   Age 2·0; 25 children

| Instruction | | Response | | |
		In	On	Other
⊖	in	25	0(R)	0
⊖	on	18	5(R)	2
⊟	in	20(R)	5	0
⊟	on	8(R)	13	4

(R) = orientation of cup reversed.

TABLE 7.2   Age 2·6; 12 children

| Instruction | | Response | | |
		In	On	Other
⊖	in	12	0(R)	0
⊖	on	10	2(R)	0
⊟	in	2(R)	10	0
⊟	on	3(R)	9	0

(R) = orientation of cup reversed.

These results would suggest the following developmental trend: at age 2·0 years there is still a strong tendency for the child to respond to the instruction by an action seen as appropriate to the unique function of the cup as a container, that is, he responds according to the object-schema *container* and the sensorimotor schema of 'putting the ball *in* the cup'.

At age 2·6, the child is beginning to free himself from this immediate uni-functional apprehension of the object, and is capable of seeing that it may serve other functions in addition to that of a container—for example, when inverted it can serve as a supporting surface. That is to say, he/she has begun to relate the same perceptual properties to alternative functions.

This process can be clearly seen if we examine the *in* item with the cup in orientation 2—inverted. This item is critical, in that if the child is responding in terms of a unique function of cup as container, he/she will place the ball in the cup, after righting it. If, however, he/she is responding to the immediate perceptual properties of the configuration, and recognizing the inverted cup as a potential supporting surface, he/she will respond by placing the ball *on* the cup. In fact the younger children (2·0) took the first course, while at 2·6 children responded in the latter manner. The difference between response distributions on this item at the two ages was highly significant ($p < ·001$ by χ^2).

The hypothesis that children aged 2·0 are responding primarily functionally, and the older age group primarily in terms of the configuration, is supported by the data presented in Table 7.3

TABLE 7.3   Comparison of response styles at ages 2·0 and 2·6

in ⊖ on ⊖	Both Correct ✓	Both 'on'	Both 'in'	Both Wrong ✕	Other
2 years	11	3	7	0	4
2¹/₂ years	1	9	1	1	0

This shows the combined responses of the children at the two ages for the two items, *in* and *on*, in which the cup was inverted. The distributions of response-types are significantly different at the two ages ($p < ·001$ by χ^2). In the first place, it can be seen that the older children make more errors overall than the younger children (though these older children when told to check their responses were all able to correct them).

More interestingly, however, at age 2·0, a large number of children are responding consistently in terms of *function*—i.e. putting the ball *in* the cup in response to both items. At age 2·6, on the other hand, the predominant response was according to *configuration*—i.e. they responded to both items by putting the ball *on* the cup. The distributions of these particular error types were significantly different at the different ages ($p < ·05$ by χ^2).

One possible interpretation could be that young children, rather than responding *functionally*, are in fact responding configurationally, and perceiving the cup as a canonical object: perceiving it in a non-canonical orientation, it may be that they then *righted* it in their minds *before* responding to the actual instruction, and were then inhibited from *again* changing the orientation, so producing an *in* response to both instructions. In fact Tables 7.1 and 7.2, when compared, do indeed show that more 2·0s righted the inverted cup than did 2·6s. However, examination of Table 7.3 shows that (in column 1) no less than 11 children at 2·0 responded correctly to *both* instructions in the inverted condition, whereas only 1 managed to do this at 2·6. The canonical/perceptual hypothesis must assume that a perceptual response bias to 'right the cup' will be triggered *before* the instruction is responded to, in which case one would expect the 2·0s to do this with an *on* instruction as well as an *in* instruction. This was not the case. In fact, the paradox about the whole experiment is the overall superiority of the 2·0s on this condition over the 2·6s. There is no significant performance difference between the two age groups on the cup-upright condition. It would seem then that we cannot account for the 2·0s' performance on the inverted condition by a simple reluctance to operate on a non-canonically oriented object, and a concomitant response-bias to right the cup. This is clear, because when the instruction was *on*, 8 of the 2·0s responded according to this hypothesized response-bias, but 13 did *not*, i.e. they responded correctly. Thus we may conclude that the instruction was responded to directly, and was not mediated through response-biases. We have spoken of only a *tendency* towards 'functional' responding; clearly, for the 2·0s, or some of them at any rate, the *on* instruction can inhibit this tendency by directly eliciting a response of placement, *provided* the cup is already inverted—if it is not, then the action is determined by *function*. The *in* instruction also elicits a placement action, but one which is congruent with function, and hence the child can right the cup. Thus for the younger children, the meaning of the term is located in the schemes ACTION and FUNCTION.

These results taken together with other similar findings (reported in Sinha and Walkerdine, 1974) suggest that children initially understand and use spatial relational terms as a part of the global, undifferentiated functional context of their experiences. They will allocate relational terms to appropriate configurations as long as the perceptual cues signalling the normal functions of the object to which the relational term has been habitually applied in the child's experience, are readily apparent. In this case, perceptual properties of the object serve merely as a recognition device for the activation of a sensorimotor schema. As the child begins to internalize the properties of the objects he operates upon, perceptual properties are isolated as cues signalling an abstract system of potential configurations. The child thus progresses to a concept of the 'abstract object'; from conceiving of the object as unifunctional, he/she begins to conceive of it as potentially multifunctional; having abstracted perceptual features from the immediate function he/she is now in a position to go on—to match these abstract features with the referential fields of words and develop the skill of constructing end-state representations. The range of application of the term then becomes the totality of the contexts in which the child has experienced the use of the term. If, as we shall see in the next experiment, the child is unfamiliar with the context of application he/she is likely to interpret the relational term in a way which is appropriate for another object and context.

2.2 The Locative Orientation Test

In this experiment, 32 $3^1/_2$-year-olds and 30 5-, 6-, and 7-year-olds from a local school were presented with what we have described as the 'Locative Orientation Test'. The intention of the test was to investigate the process of decentring in children's placements of toy vehicles relative to each other on a road. It was suggested that egocentric responses would be made by the younger children and that these would involve the use of themselves as reference points, whereas older children would utilize the axis of each vehicle to guide their responses.

The children were asked to place the car in front of/behind the lorry in the four conditions shown in Figure 7.2.

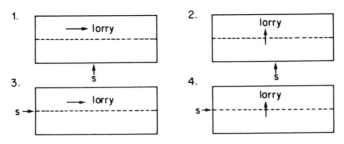

FIGURE 7.2.

It was found that the children do not in fact progress from the use of their own front/back axis to that of the vehicles. The placements made by the $3^1/_2$-year-olds revealed considerable individual variation but, although different from each other, on the whole responses were consistent for each child. It would have been possible to interpret these results as revealing that $3^1/_2$-year-olds were confused over the interpretation of *in front of* and *behind*. However, results from tasks involving placements of objects using a table and a house as reference points suggested that the children did understand the terms in these contexts. What appeared to be happening was that the children had abstracted 'in front of'/'behind rules' from their experience of objects in other contexts. In a situation in which they had not clearly defined for themselves the perceptual properties of the features of the situation governing vehicles, the children used 'in front of'/'behind' rules based on their experience of the use of the terms in other situations. Examples of such placements are given in Table 7.4.

As can be seen, these children appeared to be utilizing 'in front of' and 'behind' rules determined by the abstraction of cues from the situation. It is clear that in a situation in which cues such as 'road' and 'vehicle axis' have no salience for the children they will use only those object cues which do stand out for them. For example, they may successfully isolate a 'front' feature for both vehicles without

TABLE 7.4 Examples of $3\frac{1}{2}$-year-olds' responses on the Locative Orientation Test

(a) Parallel placement strategy (responses given by one child)

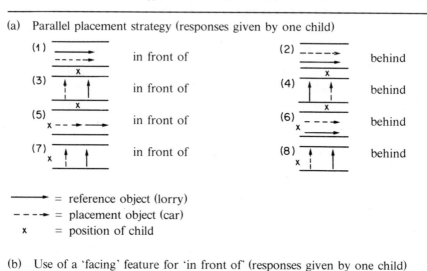

= reference object (lorry)
= placement object (car)
x = position of child

(b) Use of a 'facing' feature for 'in front of' (responses given by one child)

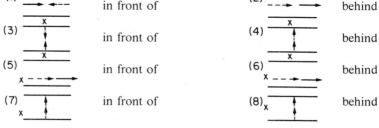

fully understanding its implications for mutual direction of movement. Thus, they could be led to adopt a strategy of placing the vehicles so that they face each other. Indeed this could be seen as an extrapolation of front–back rules governing face-to-face contact by human beings. At any rate, they were evidently not responding to the instructions wholly at random; although a random element may have been involved. Moreover, even when the children were acting according to some rule, they may on occasions have made a mistake in the application of that rule. Responses of older children revealed considerably more consistency in the application of the rules they were using. By the age of about 5, children consistently used the front/back axis and directional orientation of the lorry, regardless of their own position. A few children now use responses based upon the direction of traffic flow along the road. This is something which no children below the age of 5 did, and reflects an increasing knowledge of the rules of road usage. Examples of these types of placements may be seen in Table 7.5.

The results suggest that the growing child is constantly using context (defined in terms of both the functional and perceptual properties of objects and the social/

TABLE 7.5   Examples of Locative Orientation Placements used by children aged 5 years and over

(a)   Consistent use of axis of lorry

(1)   in front of   (2)   behind

(3)   in front of   (4)   behind

(5) x   in front of   (6) x   behind

(7) x   in front of   (8) x   behind

(b)   Consistent use of 'road user' placements

(1)   in front of   (2)   behind

(3)   in front of   (4)   behind

(5) x   in front of   (6) x   behind

(7) x   in front of   (8) x   behind

cultural situations in which they are experienced) to guide his understanding of the world. The child codes his understanding in language, and uses the coding to structure the context in which he interprets a given lexical item. If he is not familiar with the particular context in which the objects are presented (for example, vehicles, roads) the young child is likely to use cues picked up from other experiences of uses of the term to guide his activity. What we are suggesting is that at a fairly early age children understand many relational terms in some context or another. When the $3^1/_2$-year-olds use 'facing' or 'parallel placement' strategies in the Locative Orientation Test, we suggest that they are quite capable of interpreting the terms 'in front of' or 'behind' but that they do so in terms of their limited experience, utilizing 'rules' of placement applicable in other situations.

Evidence from adults in the same test suggests that this phenomenon is by no means restricted to children. Of 16 adults, to whom the test was also administered, only 5 used a 'road usage' strategy, 9 used the axis of the lorry, one used axis of self and one attempted to 'avoid crashes'.

It appears therefore that adults do not perceive the situation in any 'standard' way. The perceived field includes not only the spatial configuration, but also the sum total of what the individual knows about the physical and socio-cultural constraints operating upon the configuration. These constraints constitute the 'rules of the game'. The adult can then proceed to 'operate upon' the organization of elements specified within the perceived framework. Thus, while it *may* be the case that all adults bring the same logical operations to the situation, they do not all perceive exactly the same constraints, since they do not all have precisely the same experience.

If their previous experiences of contexts provides a framework within which both children and adults interpret such relational terms, this would seem to have implications for the kind of interpretations children and adults place on the lexical items in Piagetian tasks—the kind of lexical items already discussed by Donaldson and her colleagues.

In further experiments at Bristol we collected data which suggested that context did indeed play a significant role in the comprehension of 'same'/'different', 'more'/'less' and the consequent interpretation of a Piagetian Conservation of Liquids test.

2.3 Conservation of Liquids Test

It will be remembered that the Piagetian Conservation of Liquids Tests involves judgement of the *equivalence* or *non-equivalence* of the liquid quantities in the two standard beakers and of *identity* or *non-identity* of the liquid which is poured from the standard beaker to the tall, narrow cylinder. In order to perform this task the child has to realize that it is these and only these interpretations of 'same' which are required of him by the experiment. We have already seen (for example, from the work of Donaldson *et al.*) that the word 'same' has several possible interpretations; a child attempting to respond to the instruction in the conservation task is therefore faced with a fairly complex task of interpretation and selection of response according to context appropriateness. We have also seen that, faced with an unfamiliar context, the child may use an interpretation of a relational term based on other contexts within his experience. If this were to happen with the interpretation of 'same' in the conservation of liquids test, then the perception of the nature of the problem and the consequent solution strategy used by the child would most probably be different from that of the adult experimenter. There is evidence from our own data to suggest that this indeed is the case.

The standard Conservation of Liquids Test was presented to the $3^1/_2$-year-olds in the project sample. It was later decided to add a test of compensation as a check of the validity of the 'conservation' response on the standard test. This task involved the S being shown a standard beaker containing orange squash for himself and then presented with a tall, narrow cylinder which was to hold E's drink. The E had a jug of orange squash from which to pour into the cylinder. The Ss were told to shout 'Stop' when 'we've both got exactly the same to drink'.

Of 19 $3^1/_2$-year-olds tested on both compensation and conservation, 14 *failed* conservation but *achieved* compensation. The other 5 children failed both tasks. This result is further complicated by the result obtained when the same children were retested 6 months later at age 4 and then again at $4^1/_2$ (see Table 7.6).

By age 4 the trend to achieve compensation had reversed and the children were now failing both compensation and conservation. This trend continues at $4^1/_2$.

TABLE 7.6   Conservation and compensation: distribution of responses by age

Age	− Comp. − Cons.	− Comp. + Cons.	+ Comp. − Cons.	+ Comp. + Cons.	
$3^1/_2$	5	0	14	0	
4	13	0	3	0	5 'transitional'
$4^1/_2$	8	0	3	0	compensations

Several investigations have revealed 'operational' performance in young children (for a review, see Sinha and Walkerdine, 1977); among these, Mehler and Bever (1967) discovered, too, that this ability apparently 'disappears' as the child grows older. However a school-age sample of children who were also tested by us revealed the expected relationship between conservation and compensation. Space does not here permit an extended interpretation of these particular data. Such a discussion is to be found in the above mentioned review. However, it is suggested that the $3^1/_2$-year-olds achieve compensation because they do not yet properly understand 'same' and 'different'. Such an interpretation is supported by the observation that the children would reply 'Yes' with equal conviction when asked of the two beakers (　　 　), 'Are they the same?', 'Are they different?' This being the case, they were not put off by interpretations of 'same' and 'different' on the compensation task and were able to *remember* the level which the liquid had formerly reached.

By the age of 4 the children were becoming more familiar with the words 'same' and 'different' having met them in a variety of contexts. If the child does use the context to guide his choice of interpretation in relation to his past experience of similar contexts, the perceptual feature of *liquid levels* is likely to be the most salient in this particular context. Piaget would argue that, even so, a child acting operationally should realize that the difference in dimensions of the beakers after the transformation makes for a difference in levels. It is, however, possible that when the 4-year-old is presented with two beakers 　　 　 he chooses the interpretation of 'same' which fits his experience, *logically* proclaiming that the amounts of liquid are 'not the same to drink'. The instruction does not make it clear for a 4-year-old which features he is supposed to regard as salient. For example, the levels are obviously different, and drinking out of a tall beaker is patently not the same as drinking from a short one. The interpretation he has placed on 'same' in this context has altered the nature of the problem to be solved from that which the experimenter thinks he is solving. It is possible, therefore, that the 4-year-old child's failure on the compensation test is, in Inhelder's terms, only an 'apparent regression', announcing the 'structuration of a higher order' (1972, p. 113). Is the child failing to act logically if he applies a different interpretation of 'same' from that which the experimenter expects?

In order to further investigate just how far the terms 'same' and 'different' were indeed leading the child to a different interpretation and hence solution of the compensation problem than that which the experimenter expected, another experiment was devised in which the words 'same' and 'different' were avoided. It was hoped that the use of less problematic lexical items would reveal a different performance on the part of 4- and $4^1/_2$-year-olds.

The testing procedure was as follows. A large toy horse and a small toy dog were placed in front of the S, who was told, 'Here is a big horse, he likes a lot to drink; here is the little dog, he likes a little to drink.' A standard beaker of squash was then placed in front of each animal, the horse's beaker containing more than the dog's. The squash from the dog's beaker was then poured into a tall, narrow cylinder, and the squash from the horse's beaker was poured into another standard beaker. After this operation, the level of liquid in the tall cylinder was higher than that in the standard beaker. The child was then told—'Remember, the big horse likes a lot to drink and the little dog likes a little to drink. Now give them their drinks.'

In this test the language used by the experimenter directs the child not to the perceptual attributes of similarity and differences of the two liquids, but to their actual functional quantities. In other words, the language focuses on the actions to be carried out. While it would be quite inappropriate to claim that this test involving conservation of inequality is functionally the same as a conservation of equality task, it will serve to illustrate any difference in performance in this linguistically different task.

TABLE 7.7   Lot/little test: performance by age

Age	✓	×	Transitional
$3^1/_2$	6	2	1
4	20	1	2
$4^1/_2$	3	6	2

$\chi^2 = 13 \cdot 477$ $p < \cdot 01$

The test was administered to 9 children at $3^1/_2$, 23 at 4, and 11 at $4^1/_2$. It can be seen from Table 7.7 that children are able to give the correct beakers to the animals at $3^1/_2$ and they no longer fail at 4, as in the compensation task. However, it can be observed that on this task children are now failing at $4^1/_2$. At this age, several children spontaneously recorded the liquid quantities in terms of 'big' and 'small' and, becoming confused, assigned the wrong beakers to the animals. It would certainly seem that the interpretation of context in terms of the lexical items in 'Piagetian' tasks has a significant effect on the interpretation and hence solution of the problems. By graphically representing the results of the conservation, compensation, and lot/ little tests the very different developmental patterns of the responses may be clearly seen (see Figure 7.3).

The child's application of logical rules appears, from our experimental evidence, to depend on his prior interpretation of the properties of objects in other real situations. The situation is both definer of the interpretation of lexical items and is itself defined by the interpretation of the lexical items in terms of the child's experiences of other situations.

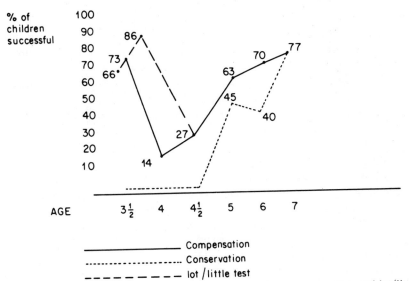

FIGURE 7.3. A comparison of the distribution of conservation, compensation, and lot/little test scores by age

If we combine Piaget's notion of the *symbol* or subjective coding of a representation, with de Saussure's (1959) couple, a sign $= \frac{\text{signified}}{\text{signifier}}$, it is clear that developmental changes take place on both levels of de Saussure's scheme. In this view, language acts as a focuser on aspects of objects and situations in a similar way to that suggested by Vygotsky (1962). A different picture of the Piagetian notion of representation now begins to emerge, in which language acts as a focuser not merely of action-schemes but also of iconic and cultural representational systems.

Context thus defined is part of the solution of logical problems. It is through a coding of the situational context that a child or adult perceives a problem and therefore sets up solution strategies. The formal system of language is one way in which we code the attributes of situations. Language serves to draw attention to features of the situation. A child's or adult's understanding of the referential rules of application coded in a lexical item in a particular situation determines the way attention will be focused, guiding solution-strategies that will be put into operation. This being so, language can no longer be seen as a mere *reflector* of a level of cognitive development, it becomes part of the process of cognitive development itself.

Admitting the role of context as definer of logical problem-solving brings with it problems of the acceptance of 'performance' as a true record of cognitive 'level', since a differential appreciation of the context of the problem can conceivably (and indeed *does* appear to) alter the apparent level at which children perform. The adult experimenter has a very definite idea of the referential interpretation of the lexical items in the experimental situation, but, as we have seen, a different interpretation may lead to a different perception of the task and consequently the utilization of a different solution strategy. The adult experimenter interprets the resulting non-conforming responses as wrong. The child is therefore seen as either not understanding the lexical item (in the case of semantic development) or of not possessing the requisite cognitive capacity (in the case of cognitive development). Development is, in this way, envisaged as a fixed set of performance criteria, which are indicative of a particular level. A 'wrong' response is generally assumed to indicate that the child is at a lower level. But, since the child (or adult) uses strategies which are dependent on his interpretation of the context, and since the interpretation is overlaid by his understanding of the identifying terms, according to the meanings attributed to them, from his previous experiences his performance will, to some extent, reflect the dynamic character of the relationship between cognition, language, and context.

Within the field of recent psycholinguistic and sociolinguistic research there is a growing body of data which can be taken as support for the view that context is central to any understanding of cognitive and linguistic development. There have been several attempts to show that the performance of children in tasks involving elicitation alters considerably if the situation is changed. This approach is exemplified by, for example, the work of Cazden (1970) and of Labov (1970) among others. They argue that what the child *cannot* do should not be taken as indicative of what he *can* do. This position is succintly put by Cole and Bruner (1972, p. 868):

> This view holds that even when attempts have been made to provide reasonable anthropological and linguistic foundations, the conclusions about cognitive capacity from psychological experiments are unfounded because the performance produced represents a complex interaction of the formal characteristics of the experiment and the social/environmental context that determines the subject's interpretation of the situation in which it occurs.

In the field of cross-cultural research in cognitive development, Cole, Gay, Glick, and Sharp (1971) highlighted problems of computing competence from a particular instance of performance in their investigation of the cognitive abilities of Kpelle rice farmers in North Central Liberia. The farmers were found to be inferior to Yale University students in their estimation of some measurements, but far superior in their estimation of amounts of rice. Cole *et al.* point out that it is important not to consider ability as a 'universal manifestation of underlying competence'.

There are also several instances of specific investigations of the role of context in the solution of 'Piagetian' tasks. Gelman (1972) found that young children (aged between 3 and 6 years) were able to display number invariance when the change in number was effected by 'magic', which constituted a change in the experimental condition and therefore the context in the children's eyes.

Similarly, McGarrigle and Donaldson (in press) report data revealing that a change in the perception of the task by children in conservation of length and number tasks substantially altered their ability to conserve. When 50 4–6-year-olds were presented with a standard conservation test only 13 achieved success, but when the transformation happened 'accidentally' as a by-product of an activity directed towards a different goal, all 50 children showed conservation behaviour. McGarrigle and Donaldson conclude in a way similar to that of Gelman: 'Far greater attention must be given to the features of the interactional setting in which the child's knowledge is assessed before any conclusions about the child's competence can be drawn' (p. 11).

Rose and Blank (1974) also point to the a-contextual nature of the Piagetian conceptualization of performance and to the peculiar nature of the questions put by the experimenters, two consecutive judgements being required of the subject, before and after the transformation in the conservation task. Rose and Blank suggest that this experimental requirement may be taken by the child as a cue to confirm a *change* in the initial configuration and relation, and to alter his initial judgement, since in the normal (non-experimental) course of events, one would never ask the identical question twice if a significant change had not occurred in the material that was being observed. The child may thus interpret the second question as implying that a new judgement is necessary, leading him to change his answer.

In their experiments they were able to demonstrate that questioning the child *once* after the transformation as opposed to questioning him twice, once before and once after the transformation, did bring about a significant difference in conservation performance. Lack of attention to context may well, therefore, lead to significant misinterpretation of children's cognitive ability.

In our own data (Walkerdine, 1975) results from a three-term series task of the form:

Put the X in front of/before Y but behind/after Z

(given to children aged $4^1/_2$ to 8 years) suggested that frequency of correct responses was related to the nature of the objects manipulated and to the spatial relationship between the subject and the object array. The objects were variously: toy vehicles on a road, pictures telling a story in a left-right sequence, and three different coloured blocks arranged on a board. The road was easiest, while blocks were by far the most difficult. This result was true of adults as well as children.

Analyses of placements, leading to errors revealed that the mistakes made were of several kinds and suggested that a classical Piagetian classification in terms of presence or absence of a logical ability may be an over-simplification. The responses of both children and adults were found to be related to the contextual cues—or lack of them—present in the experimental situation. For example, in the problem—'Put the red block in front of the blue block but behind the green block', there are no cues presented by the objects (blocks have no intrinsic fronts and backs) and no contextual support by means of which the subject can read *in front of X* except as meaning *between ego and X*. This led to considerable problems so that some adults reported that these difficulties led them to mis-repeat the problem: 'behind the green block' thus becoming 'green block behind'. Few adults achieved success on every problem, while no child above the age of 5 actually failed to achieve success on some items.

These kinds of responses certainly point to an interpretation in which contextual information plays a strategic role in the individual's interpretation of a response to cognitive and linguistic data. (For a fuller account of these complex findings, see Walkerdine and Sinha (1975).)

The kind of data reported in this paper leads the authors to suggest that cognitive development may be considered as a complex interaction of the individual with the social context in which he exists, in which the medium of language plays a central and strategic role. The interaction must of necessity be, to a certain extent, both culture and individual specific, both in the cognitive process itself and in the objects of their application (for example, rice estimation for farmers in Liberia as opposed to the solution of quadratic equations by school children in the West).

It may well seem reasonable enough for Piaget to develop a theory of the cognitive development of the 'abstract epistemic subject', but there are at least two objections to such a model. First, cognition does not function in a vacuum but with real people in real situations. Any definition of the structure of cognition must therefore take account of those situations. Second, Piaget reveals an overriding concern for the development of logic and seeks to equate this with universal cognitive development. By so doing, he puts forward a Western rationalist paradigm as the model of a universal intellect. We should not underestimate the potential inappropriateness of this position with regard to those nations and individuals who do not display that logic. (This point is well made by Cole and Scribner (1974).)

In proposing that cognitive development should be envisaged in terms of the Internal Triangle of language, reasoning, and social context, what features are we suggesting such a theory should possess?

Certainly, the notion of a single developmental pattern becomes problematic as does the concept of stage, as defined by a set of performance criteria. Should we therefore abandon the idea of a developmental sequence altogether? Fodor (1972) has made just such a suggestion. He believes that children's cognition differs from that of adults only in the range of activities to which it is applied; in other words the difference is quantitative and not qualitative. While we would accept that there is an element of truth in such a view, we feel that any account of cognitive development must involve some understanding of other kinds of developmental change. For example, the child's ability to interact with his world depends on his changing ability to perform certain actions such as walking and talking—to give very obvious examples. Such phenomena must mean that the child is simply capable of different activities at different periods of development and, similarly, gradually acquires a range of different experiences. Thus, we suggest that the theory must be developmental—but developmental in a much less rigid way than was formerly envisaged. Luria (1973), for example, offers a very persuasive account of the development of the central nervous system in which he suggests that all the 'higher mental functions' enter into different functional systems at different times during the developmental process. Luria gives one example of the development of writing skills. At first the child's whole attention and effort is put into the formation of each letter. Later the skill becomes 'reflexive' so that hardly any concentration is necessary for the mechanism of letter formation. Thus the mechanisms of attention, selection, and memory, although possibly similar throughout development, will interact differently and for different tasks at different times in the process.

It is clear then that we are advocating some kind of developmental theory. It must be one which sees both 'stage' and 'performance' as problematic. There have been a significant enough number of experiments which have revealed apparently 'advanced' cognitive ability in very young children, to make us wary of suggesting that young children are 'illogical'. Maybe at any rate 'logical ability' as defined in

Piaget's terms should not be considered as constituting a 'turning point' in the developmental process.

If logic develops in response to specific situations there is no reason to deny the possibility that in particular situations children reveal 'logical' behaviour fairly early on, though it is not generalized. Certainly children have been found to reveal 'advanced' characteristics in particular situations, for example, advanced concepts of topology in young high-rise flat dwellers, and of conservation of weight—a condition of survival for children whose homes are built on salt lagoons.

Unfortunately, our quests for evidence of 'advanced development' are usually confined to only a very narrowly defined field of performance, which is usually connected with those pursuits described as academic or intellectual. While we assume that logical ability is revealed in mathematics and science, we give little credit for the application of logical principles in, for example, bookmaking or playing darts. Perhaps the time has come to change our tactics.

Acknowledgements

The authors would like to acknowledge the contributions made by Gordon Wells, Allayne Bridges, and Bencie Woll of the Language Development Project, University of Bristol, in the preparation of this paper.

References

Bruner, J.S. (1964), The course of cognitive growth, *American Psychologist*, 19, 1–15.

Bruner, J.S., Olver, R.R., and Greenfield, P. (1966), *Studies in Cognitive Growth*, New York: Wiley.

Cazden, C. (1970), The neglected situation. In Williams, F. (ed.), *Language and Poverty*, Chicago: Markham.

Cole, M., and Bruner, J.S. (1972), Cultural differences and inferences about psychological processes, *American Psychologist*, 26, 867–876.

Cole, M., Gay, J., Glick, J., and Sharp, D. (1971), *The Cultural Context of Learning and Thinking*, London: Tavistock.

Cole, M., and Scribner, S. (1974), *Culture and Thought*, New York: Wiley.

de Saussure, F. (1959), *Course in General Linguistics*, New York: McGraw-Hill.

Donaldson, M., and Balfour, G. (1968), Less is more: a study of language comprehension in children, *British Journal of Psychology*, 59, 461–471.

Donaldson, M., and Wales, R.J. (1970), On the acquisition of some relational terms. In Hayes, J.R. (ed.), *Cognition and the Development of Language*, New York: Wiley.

Fodor, J. (1972), Some reflections on L.S. Vygotsky's 'Thought and Language', *Cognition* 1, 83–96.

Gelman, R. (1972), Logical capacity of very young children: Number invariance rules, *Child Development*, 43, 75–90.

Inhelder, B. (1972), Information processing tendencies in recent experiments in cognitive learning—empirical studies. In Farnham-Diggory, S. (ed.), *Information Processing in Children*, New York: Academic Press.

Inhelder, B., Bovet, M., Sinclair, H., and Smock, C.D. (1966), On cognitive development, *American Psychologist*, 21, 160–164.

Labov, W. (1970), The Logic of non-standard English. In Williams, F. (ed.), *Language and Poverty*, Chicago: Markham.

Luria, A.R. (1973), *The Working Brain*, Harmondsworth: Penguin Books.

McGarrigle, J., and Donaldson, M. (in press), Conservation accidents, *Cognition*.

Mehler, J., and Bever, T.G. (1967), Cognitive capacities of young children, *Science*, 158, 141–142.

Piaget, J. (1972), *The Principles of Genetic Epistemology*, London: Routledge & Kegan Paul.

Rose, S.A. and Blank, M. (1974), The potency of context in children's cognition: an illustration through conservation, *Child Development*, 45, 499–502.

Sinha, C., and Walkerdine, V. (1974), Spatial and temporal relations in cognitive and linguistic development. University of Bristol. Mimeo.

Sinha, C., and Walkerdine, V. (1977), Conservation: a problem in language, culture and thought. In Waterson, N., and Snow, C. (eds), *The Development of Communication: Social and Pragmatic Factors in Language Acquisition*, London: Wiley.

Slobin, D.I. (1973), Cognition prerequisites for the development of grammar. In Ferguson, C.A., and Slobin, D.I. (eds), *Studies in Child Language Development*, Holt, Rinehart & Winston.

Vygotsky, L.S. (1962), *Thought and Language*, Cambridge, Mass.: M.I.T. Press.

Walkerdine, V. (1975), Spatial and temporal relational terms in the linguistic and cognitive development of young children. Unpublished Ph.D. thesis, University of Bristol.

Walkerdine, V., and Sinha, C. (1975), Object properties, context rules and cognitive structures: the three terms of the three term series. Paper presented at British Psychological Society Developmental Section Annual Conference, York.

8

SPEECH AND THOUGHT

David McNeill

I will contend that to understand the relationship between speech and thought, we must keep constantly in mind that speech is a form of motor activity dominated and co-ordinated by thought processes. Complex actions of all kinds including speech are believed to be co-ordinated through hierarchical or heterarchical arrangements of considerable depth. In these structures the uppermost 'executive' has little or no direct control over the actual motor output, but instead controls a relatively small number of intermediate processes (Bernstein, 1967; Greene, 1972). In speech, the 'executives' in charge seem to be sensorimotor concepts, ideas we may refer to as Action, State, Location, Entity, and others, which can be given a meaning in terms of actions performed on or with objects in the environment (Piaget, 1969).

The same sensorimotor concepts can be detected intuitively in the speech of adults. Such concepts are often condemned as reifications. However, if my argument is sound, they are fundamental in the speech process and indispensable for understanding of the relationship of speech to thought. For example, the sentence *They perceive various possibilities in the law* seems to include at some level an idea of location. This idea can be brought out more clearly by testing the meaning in an explicit locative frame, for example *They perceived various possibilities within the space (boundaries, limits, etc.) of the law*. The success of this frame suggests that the concept of a Location is involved in some way in the meaning of the sentence. (A sentence apparently not involving the idea of Location, despite a locative preposition, is *The Argument went over the King's head*, for? *The argument went through the space (boundaries, limits, etc.) over the King's head*.)

My thesis is that such ideas as Location, which derive ultimately from sensorimotor co-ordinations, are crucial for the organization of speech. Although seemingly insignificant, they play a unique role in speech production, for they have the potential of serving as co-ordinators of movements, including articulatory movements, and at the same time as elements of thought.

Two processes are required. In the first, sensorimotor concepts based on actions in the environment are brought into contact with the integration of speech articulation. This fusion of two schemes (sensorimotor and articulatory) occurs at an early stage and creates the original syntagmas in children's speech. (For discussion of the term 'syntagma', see Kozhevnikov and Chistovich, 1965.) I have discussed this process in an earlier paper (McNeill, 1975). A principal form of evidence for the emergence of syntagmas based on action schemes consists of child utterances ordered so as to correspond to the direction of the relevant action schemes.

The second process, 'semiotic extension', consists of extending sensorimotor concepts to more abstract conceptualizations. According to this view, the intuition of location involved in the abstract meaning of *They perceived various possibilities in the law*, is due to semiotic extension. The sensorimotor concept of Location, which can function as the 'executive' at the apex of a hierarchy of speech programmes, is enriched and differentiated through semiotic extension so as to encompass a more abstract idea.

There is both an *ontogenesis* of semiotic extension, and a *function* of semiotic extension. Ontogenetically, we may speak of the semiotic extension being gradually set up as a child's cognitive growth proceeds. Functionally, there is a semiotic extension during the production of every utterance whenever the literal meaning is not entirely representable at a sensorimotor level. The aim of this chapter is to analyse and compare these two aspects of semiotic extension. To accomplish this, I will make use of the terminology of C. S. Peirce.

The relationship of speech to thought can be understood in terms of the changing sign relations within the sign or symbolic function. These changes reflect variations in the relation of thought to speech. This relationship, expressed in the types of sign it creates, is not homogeneous, but changes from time to time in language development and from point to point in the production of speech. The conception of semiotic extension in terms of changing sign relations thus provides both an account of ontogenesis, from the point of view of temporal change, and an account of the interrelation of signs occurring during the integration of single utterances. The latter account has the task of showing how sensorimotor concepts are aroused from thought processes that are not necessarily sensorimotor, a process in which iconic signs play a crucial role in establishing serial order, and indexical signs in co-ordinating speech action.

1. Iconicity of Speech

The iconicity of speech has been grossly underestimated in earlier linguistic and psycholinguisic discussions. When the question has been considered at all it has been in terms of sensory images, such as sound symbolism or onomatopoeia (for example Werner and Kaplan, 1963), but these kinds of iconicisms truly seem to be of marginal importance. Iconic images of a non-sensory kind, however, can be seen to be fundamental to the process of speaking. The crucial iconicisms are rather more like diagrams. It is upon the diagrammatic aspects of speech that most word order sequences depend. In a perspicacious remark Peirce (2.280) describes sentences as logical icons supplemented by symbolic means: '[I]n the syntax of every language there are logical icons of the kind that are aided by conventional rules.' (References are to the volume and paragraph number in Peirce (1931–1958).) Both in production and ontogenesis there is an interplay and connection of indexical, iconic, and symbolic signs. The process is most easily summarized by describing the ways in which iconic signs are formed, of which, generally speaking, there are two. Each of these methods includes a different form of semiotic extension from the sensorimotor domain of indexical signs, and a distinct relationship to the procedural domain of symbolic signs.

The first is a process in which iconic signs are formed directly with the speaker organizing concepts in specific orientations. (For a discussion of orientation, see Halliday, 1967, pp. 38–51.) For example, thinking of a relationship of location between 'possibilities' and 'law' leads directly to the iconic sign 'possibilities in the law'. That is, the word order of this expression stands as a temporally sequenced sign for the oriented logical relationships between two ideas, (Possibilities) *are-located-in* (Law). With a different orientation of the logical relation, the word order also reverses. Thus, (Law) *is-location-of* (Possibilities), which is referred to by, for example, 'the law contains possibilities'. This direct formation of iconic signs appears at an early stage of ontogenesis. In order to interconnect iconic signs with the sensorimotor level, which amounts to extending a sensorimotor concept semiotically, the speaker can regard the sequence of concepts as specifying the temporal parameters of a speech programme, the programme headed, for example, by Location.

The second method for constructing iconic signs and connecting them with the sensorimotor level is radically different. In this method interrelations of ideas and sensorimotor concepts are created and arranged by means of syntactic procedures. Syntactic procedures thereby *manufacture* a semiotic extension of sensorimotor concepts, concepts which they produce themselves, connecting these with the other ideas also arranged or produced by the procedures, and with other sensorimotor concepts and iconic word sequences formed by the direct method. The result is a greatly enhanced power and flexibility of semiotic extension, possibly one of the reasons why languages have evolved syntactic procedures in the first place.

As an example of a syntactic procedure, the English pseudocleft creates an iconic sequence in which two concepts, both of which have been created by the procedure, are represented as being equated to each other.

What I'm doing (Unspecified (Action))	is	*mowing the lawn.* (Action)
What I'm mowing (Unspecified (Entity))	is	*the lawn.* (Entity)
What this room is (Unspecified(Property))	is	*messy.* (Property)
Where I work (Unspecified (Location))	is	*in my study.* (Location)

The concept of Unspecified and the sensorimotor concepts of Action, Property, Entity, and Location are (in these examples at least) due to the procedure, as is the iconic relationship of (A) *is* (B). The procedure creates these relata in such a way that the conceptual category is the same on both sides of the *be*, even though the concepts and relations internal to these higher concepts may be different. For this reason there must be appropriate nominalizations (for example, *mowing* in the second example, which is a nominalization, as it is unaffected by changes of tense) when the concept is Entity, and a locative prepositional phrase when it is Location. That this concordance is at least partly independent of the subordinate concepts and takes place at a level manufactured by the procedure is shown in a slightly altered sentence, such as,

What I work in	*is*	*my study.*
(Unspecified (Entity))		(Entity)

in which the concordance is between two Entities, with a proportionate shift of the position of *in* relative to *be*, but the subordinate conceptual structure remains the same as in the utterance *Where I work is in my study*. Thus, the procedure plays an active role in the conceptual organization of the utterance.

Both these methods of creating iconic signs and connecting them to the sensorimotor level impose on thought a certain organization. The direct method requires the speaker to think of concepts as related in certain orientations, and as related as well to sensorimotor concepts. These are coherent conceptions, and the speaker must be able to organize his thoughts to make the required relationship possible. For example, having started with 'possibilities' the speaker must conceive of the location as being *is-located-in*, rather than *is-location-of*, a constraint of orientation imposed by speech onto thought. Further, the speaker is compelled to relate these abstract ideas to the concept of a Location. Procedural methods require that the speaker meet certain conditions which translate into demands on thought processes, and impose a pattern of conceptual organization of their own, which must be coherently related to the rest of the conceptual structure. In the pseudocleft, for instance, the relata are identical at the highest conceptual level. This demand may reflect a general law governing equivalence, but it takes a rather peculiar and limited form in this procedure, for it applies only to the part of the conceptual structure that has been manufactured. There can be lack of identity at the lower level—in fact this is typical—so long as it meets the conditions of application for the procedure. (It is just this kind of flexibility that makes the pseudocleft useful for conveying focal information in speech.) Thus the speaker has forced upon him a notion of identical concepts in the face of other concepts that may not be identical, but that still must be related to the equated concepts. Such deterministic effects of language on thought are an important element of speech formation. Without them the integration of signs on which the semiotic extension depends could not take place.

2. The Theory of Signs

According to Peirce every sign involves three elements that are related to each other as a triad. The interrelation of the three elements cannot be reduced to three separate relations of constituent pairs, for no one of these pairs has the quality of being a sign. Only the three elements taken together make possible a sign. The elements of this irreducible triadic relation are what Peirce calls the sign or representamen (which I will call the Sign Vehicle), the Interpretant (anything that is the outcome of interpreting the sign), and the Object. The Sign Vehicle is the word, sentence, sundial, diagram, etc., that conveys the meaning of the sign. The Interpretant is the result of interpreting the Sign Vehicle as referring to the Object. Peirce writes, 'For the proper significate outcome of a sign, I propose the name, the *interpretant* of the sign. The example of the imperative command shows that it need not be of a mental mode of being' (it can be a concrete action) (5.473). The Object is what the Sign Vehicle is interpreted as referring to. The Object might be anything. It is not necessarily a physical object, and might include mental processes and conceptions.

The mechanism of the sign is that the Object–Sign Vehicle relation is duplicated by the Object-Interpretant relation. The Sign Vehicle determines the Interpretant to be related to the Object in the same way as the Sign Vehicle is related to the Object.

A Sign Vehicle is '[a]nything that determines something else (its *interpretant*) to refer to an object to which itself refers (its *object*) in the same way, the interpretant becoming in turn a sign ... ' (2.303).

'A sign is only a sign *in actu* by virtue of its receiving an interpretation, that is, by virtue of its determining another sign of the same object' (5.569).

'A *Sign* is a representamen of which some interpretant is a cognition of a mind' (2.242). And so forth in Peirce (1931–1958).

For example, if the Sign Vehicle is iconic, that is, the Sign Vehicle resembles the Object in some respect, then the Interpretant of this Sign Vehicle, which is an interpretive response, itself resembles the Object. For instance, a diagram refers iconically to its object by arousing a mental representation that also resembles the Object. If the following diagram represents a road from A to B,

$$A \longrightarrow B$$

the Interpretant (an image perhaps) represents the road from A to B in the same way, by resemblance. The Interpretant might be a conception of a spatial orientation that has a certain extent, a beginning and an end—i.e. a conception that results in another iconic sign for the road.

Peirce's theory, then, is that the Sign Vehicle creates or causes the Interpretant to stand in the same relation to the Object as the Sign Vehicle does. This relationship may be iconic, indexical or symbolic, depending on the sign relationships in question.

An important caveat is the following. Signs are often said to perform a certain function with respect to an external and socially shared reference field. For example, a pointing finger may function as an index of an external event for an interlocutor in the same situation. The internal signs resolved here in speech production are functional in exactly the same sense, but there is no external reference field. This field is entirely internal, consisting of mental and other processes. The shift of emphasis does not seem to disturb the logical structure of Peirce's theory. So even Sign Vehicles will be conceived here as being internal. An utterance, viewed as a Sign Vehicle, is internal and not open to direct observation except at the most superficial levels (from which follows an ocean of methodological grief for psycholinguists). In fact, the only truly external signs in the speech formation process as discussed in the present context are final acoustic and muscular effects of the speech programmes. Otherwise the interlocking signs are always internal.

The triadic relationship of Object, Sign Vehicle, and Interpretant can be represented as follows (I am indebted to C. Schmidt for this notation):

Index: O $\longrightarrow$ S $\longrightarrow$ I   a significate outcome is produced in the interpreter's
        real connection   mind by noticing the Object

Icon: O $\longrightarrow$ S $\longrightarrow$ I   a significate outcome is produced in the interpreter's
                                      mind by forming a relationship that resembles the
        resemblance   Object

Symbol: O $\longrightarrow$ S $\longrightarrow$ I   a significate outcome is produced in the interpreter's
        rule   mind by forming a structure that refers to the Object

Peirce casts his discussion of signs in the context of a general epistemological theory in which knowledge is gained through sign interpretations. The glosses above reflect this in speaking of forming a significate outcome in the mind of the interpreter. The function of the sign in the acquisition of knowledge introduces an asymmetry wherein the recognition or interpretation of signs is favoured over the construction and emission of signs. This asymmetry, however, presupposes a corresponding analysis of sign construction. The argument for this conclusion is as follows. Since the Interpretant reproduces the relation between the Object and the Sign Vehicle in interpreting a sign, it is logically required that in producing this sign there is something that is also capable of accomplishing exactly the same thing as a construction. Let us say that this element (to maintain the Peircian flavour) produces a significate input, which I will call the Productant. This Productant as an input duplicates exactly the same relation between the Object and Sign Vehicle that the Interpretant duplicates as an outcome. Thus, we can match the above diagrams for the types of sign with the following which show the relationships involved in sign construction:

Index: P $\longrightarrow$ O $\longrightarrow$ S   a significate input is produced in the producer's mind
        real connection   by noticing the Object

Icon: P $\longrightarrow$ O $\longrightarrow$ S   a significate input is produced in the producer's mind
           resemblance   by forming a relationship that resembles the Object

Symbol: P ——— O ——→ S   a significate input is produced in the producer's mind
         rule   by forming a structure that refers to the Object

The P and I must be related since the I is, as Peirce describes, a reproduction of the
S–O relation (which therefore is the result an an input, the P). Hence the full sign
structure should be represented as

   P ——————— O ——→ S ——————— I

As with the Interpretant the Productant also is a sign of the Object. It differs from the
Interpretant only in being involved in a position logically (not necessarily temporally)
anterior to the Sign Vehicle. For example, with an indexical sign, the sign producer,
by noticing the Object, produces a Productant which is the input for emitting the
Sign Vehicle. It is clear that the Interpretant could not perform this function, for it is
anomalous to say that one produces a sign by interpreting it.

In the case of speech, the Productant of an indexical sign could be a set of neural
commands based on a sensorimotor concept (the Object) that leads into a hierarchy
of processes and to eventual speech co-ordination. With an iconic sign, the speaker
assigns temporal valence to two or more interrelated concepts. This process is a
Productant, the input for forming the Sign Vehicle, a temporally ordered sequence of
concepts, for example (Possibilities) ——→ (Law). (I am indebted to J. Galambos for
raising the issues discussed above.)

If the Productant and Interpretant are merged, if the distinction between
production and interpretation of signs were not important for some purpose, the
diagrams above become the familiar meaning triangle:

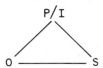

An iconic Sign Vehicle

is a sign [vehicle] which refers to the Object that it denotes merely by virtue of
characters of its own, and which it possesses, just the same, whether any such
Object actually exists or not. It is true that unless there really is such an Object,
the Icon does not act as a sign; but this has nothing to do with its character as a
sign. Anything whatever ... is an Icon of anything, in so far as it is like that
thing and used as a sign for it. (2.247)

Examples of iconic Sign Vehicles are images in painting, maps, diagrams,
metaphors, the bracketing of algebraic formulae, and many word order sequences of
speech. The latter are icons in which likeness is aided by the application of rules.
'[A]n algebraic formula is an icon, rendered such by the rules of commutation,
association, and distribution of the symbols' (2.279). The grammatical organization
of language is iconic in this same sense. To repeat an earlier quote, '[I]n the syntax of

every language there are logical icons of the kind that are aided by conventional rules … ' (2.280). The Interpretant of an iconic Sign Vehicle is the sign perceiver's realization of the arrangement of the parts of the Object that the Sign Vehicle iconically represents. This amounts to a new sign for the Object. It resembles the Object with respect to the arrangement of its parts. For example, understanding the relationship of a road map, the Sign Vehicle, to the layout of a road, the Object, requires forming a mental conception that also resembles the layout of the road, and which is the Interpretant. From the point of view of sign formation, conceiving of such a spatial arrangement results in a Productant. This is a sign which is related to the Object iconically and which causes the Sign Vehicle to incorporate the same iconic relationship to the Object, for example an arrow from A to B.

Oriented pairs of related concepts are what we should call the Objects of iconic word sequences. The Productants of these iconic signs are the processes of interpreting oriented logical relations as having a temporal valence. Temporal concept sequences, when related to sensorimotor concepts, become the temporal parameters of a speech programme, the Interpretant of this iconic sign. The orientation of the conceptual relation is the aspect of the Object of an iconic sign that the word order sequence represents. Interconnected with the sensorimotor level, this temporal sequence specifies an order of speech production.

At an abstract level, the above explanation of word order sequences, for many cases, helps solve the problem of serial order in speech (Lashley, 1951). The serial order is determined iconically, in the first instance, for these cases, from the orientation of the relations between concepts (the Object of iconic word sequences). This process is discussed at length in the work on which this chapter is based.

In terms of the notation given previously, iconic word sequences can be represented as follows:

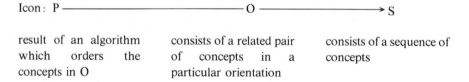

Icon: P ——————————————— O ———————————→ S

| result of an algorithm which orders the concepts in O | consists of a related pair of concepts in a particular orientation | consists of a sequence of concepts |

An indexical Sign Vehicle 'is a sign [vehicle] which refers to the Object that it denotes by virtue of being really affected by that Object' (2.248). Also,

> 'In so far as the Index is affected by the Object, it necessarily has some Quality in common with the Object, and it is in respect to these [*sic*] that it refers to the Object. It does, therefore, involve a sort of Icon, although an Icon of a peculiar kind; and it is not the mere resemblance of its Object, even in these respects which makes it a sign, but it is the actual modification of it by the Object. (2.248).

For example, the sound of a rapping on the door is an indexical sign of someone knocking. There is 'a quality in common' between the blows of this someone and the sound of the rapping, but the character of the sign as an index does not depend on this resemblance. In the same sense there is 'a quality in common' between a sensorimotor scheme which functions as the Object of an indexical Sign Vehicle and the articulatory programmes it co-ordinates, but the indexical relationship lies in the real connection of the articulatory programmes to the sensorimotor engram.

The characteristics of an index (listed in 2.306) are:

(1) No significant resemblance to the Object, although Peirce presumably means to allow 'qualities in common' as described above.

(2) Reference is to an individual existing Object. For example, a rap on the door indicates a concrete single incident of someone knocking. An integrated portion of an utterance similarly indicates an individual existing sensorimotor concept.

(3) The Sign vehicle directs attention to the object by 'blind compulsion'. A pointing finger indicates what it is pointing at, for example, by 'blind compulsion' of attention onto the Object. The relation between the organization of speech action and a sensorimotor concept is likewise one of 'blind compulsion' in which the sensorimotor content of an utterance is sufficient to lead to programming of the utterance. This is a correct analysis given our assumption that there is a real connection between the co-ordination of speech output and the sensorimotor concept; that is, the speech output is a part of the same process initiated and controlled by the concept.

Examples of indices are a symptom of a disease, a sundial, a pointing finger, the deictic pronounds (*I*, *you*, *this*, *that*, etc.), and other signs actually connected with or part of their Objects. The deictic pronouns are connected to their Objects in that they are parts of their Objects; the pronouns are parts of acts of reference and they are signs of these acts. These acts, in turn, denote particular individuals or objects. *I*, for example, is a sign of an act of self-reference, and this act in turn denotes the speaker.

The connections between sensorimotor concepts and speech programmes are more correctly called causal. This relationship of the speech Sign Vehicle to the Object is compositional. It is parallel to the relationship between a disaster and a flood. For example, we can say that a disaster (or speech programme) is caused by a flood (or sensorimotor scheme); and a flood (or sensorimotor scheme) is part of a disaster (or speech programme). Deictic pronouns have become the prototypical indexical signs for many linguistics and psycholinguistics, although their status with respect to the rest of Peirce's discussion and definitions of indices is rather special and limited.

In the integration of speech, sensorimotor concepts, derived from the speaker's organization of thought, become the Objects of indexical signs. The Productant of these signs forms the Sign Vehicles (utterances). It is in this process that sensorimotor concepts are able to fulfil their unique role in speech formation, of being simultaneously the co-ordinators of speech action and signs interpretable by thought. In this sense, speech is action organized on the basis of conceptions. And, due to the interlocking of signs that exists in semiotic extension, speech becomes the ultimate Sign Vehicle for all signs, indexical, iconic, and symbolic.

In terms of the notation used previously, indexical signs can be represented as follows:

Index: P ——————————————————— O ——————————————→ S

| result of 'noticing' the connection between O and S | consists of a sensorimo-tor level concept | consists of a speech action programme (a co-ordinated articulation) |

A symbolic Sign Vehicle 'is a sign [vehicle] which refers to the Object that it denotes by virtue of a law, usually an association of general ideas, which operates to cause the Symbol to be interpreted as referring to that Object' (2.249). A symbol depends crucially on the Interpretant (or Productant). Symbols are signs 'by virtue of being represented to be signs' (8.119). 'A symbol is a sign which would lose the character which renders it a sign if there were no interpretant. Such is any utterance of speech which signifies what it does only by virtue of its being understood to have that signification' (2.304). Examples of symbols are words and sentences, although both also have indexical and iconic aspects. Symbols are related to indices and icons in that symbols tie the individuals indicated by indices to icons that are attached to the symbol (from 2.295).

This description is in fact a prescription for using syntactic procedures in the formation of utterances. The constructed Sign Vehicle of the procedure/symbol contains both indexical (sensorimotor) and iconic elements, which are thus related. There are other parallels as well, and these also support the identification of syntactic procedures as a type of symbolic sign. The manufactured conceptual structure denotes its Object 'by virtue of a law.' It is a sign 'by virtue of being represented to be [a] sign', and depends crucially on the Interpretant/Productant (which are the result of the procedure) for its character as a sign. Peirce clearly intended a wide range of signs as symbolic. Accepting the above identification of syntactic procedures as a type of symbol, however, the term 'symbolic Sign Vehicle' will be used in the present discussion in the specific sense of the outcome of a constructive procedure.

The Object of a symbolic Sign Vehicle in this sense is a conceptualization that may include several internal concepts and the interrelations among them. In the pseudocleft example, the Object includes (a) the idea of two concepts that are (b) connected by a certain relation, and that are (c) regarded as being equal conceptually. All of this (a–c) is part of the Object of this symbolic Sign Vehicle. In addition, there is a co-ordination of the Object of the symbolic Sign Vehicle with other aspects of the conceptual structure achieved via conditions placed on the use of the pseudocleft procedure.

The Sign Vehicle is similarly complex. In the case of the pseudocleft it includes a concept, Unspecified, which underlies the *wh*-term, for example, (Unspecified (Entity)) underlies 'what'; the manufactured *be* relation; the other concept which equals the first; and a manufactured iconic sign (the sequence of these concepts). Note that the Sign Vehicle of this syntactic procedure itself consists of concepts and conceptual interrelations. It thus must interlock with other signs when it becomes the basis of speech organization.

Using the notation employed earlier, a symbolic sign is the following:

Symbol: P ——————————————— O ———————————→ S

| result of applying a procedure | consists of a complex conceptualization | consists of an arrangement of concepts and concept relations manufactured by the procedure |

3. Semiotic Extension in Ontogenesis in Terms of the Theory of Signs

The earliest utterances of children are probably indices of sensorimotor concepts, although it is often difficult to distinguish indexical from primitive iconic formations. Indexical utterances are directly connected to the Objects of the signs, the action schemes upon which the child's cognitive understanding at this stage rests. This is suggested by the close connection of word order sequences with intrinsic directions of action performance, including variations of word order when there is not an intrinsic direction of action, and by the close temporal and spatial proximity of utterances with external objects and actions. (This situation is documented in McNeill, 1975.)

The essential indexical quality of these utterances lies in their fusion with the sensorimotor schemes of the child's cognitive understanding. Given this basis of the syntagma in a fusion of speech actions with sensorimotor action schemes, the process of organizing the utterance itself is part of the meaning of the sign—i.e. both the Sign Vehicle and the Object are assimilated to the same action, the organization of which is the sole form of representation at this stage of development. There is minimal or no gap between speech and thought. Speech is a new form of co-ordinated action, which, in sensorimotor intelligence, *is* thought.

Thanks to these indexical signs, attention to the Object is sufficient to initiate the co-ordinated programming of the utterance. The mental representation of the Object of the sign corresponds to the co-ordinating scheme of the utterance programme.

From an outsider's point of view these early utterances occur rarely, if ever, except in the presence of an action or entity. Later, displacements become possible in which the child produces utterances without the immediate presence of the situation referred to by the sign. From one point of view, these are no longer indices. However, they are true indices if the sensorimotor schemes by which the situation is represented are still the direct basis of utterances. Such utterances can still 'really' be connected with the schemes that represent external situations. I will still call these utterances indices because they do not yet involve any degree of semiotic extension.

As an example of all this, take the action scheme of literally placing a physical object in a certain place accompanied by the word 'up'. This would unquestionably be an indexical use of the expression. So would be merely moving the arms outward without an object and saying 'up'. If the child mentally represents the action of placing an object somewhere and says 'up', but actually does not make the movement, I will call this also indexical, in the slightly stretched sense described above. Similarly, if the child says 'Object-name up', as he might if the action scheme is interiorized, I will still call this indexical.

These purely indexical utterances must be short lived, however, even granting the stretching of Peirce's definitions above. For, small maladaptations of speech and thought soon appear. For example, the child begins to regard the location of objects that cannot possibly be moved, things like messes, in such a way that the syntagmas used for expressing the idea of movement to or from a location can be used also for utterances whose literal meaning is not movement and could not possibly be movement; for example, 'There's a mess in this room'. The evidence reviewed in my earlier paper (McNeill, 1975) showed that some children do not immediately assimilate non-movement locatives to the scheme for movement locatives (non-movement locatives have unstable word orders), but sooner or later this assimilation occurs if the language is one like English which does not have a separate syntactic procedure for non-movement locatives. When there is such an assimilation we may speak of it in terms of the semiotic extension of the sensorimotor conception of movement locatives. A similar statement can be made regarding the extension of alienable possession to inalienable, of the extension of actor—action sequences where actor is ego to other sequences where it is not, etc. Along a wide front, utterances that are originally indexical, and can occur this way, are extended to new meanings that are not signified indexically. There are Productants that are the result of new forms of representation. It is not enough with such utterances to 'notice' a real connection between the meaning and the utterance. A relation of iconic resemblance requiring further capacities of mental representation is necessary as well.

This semiotic extension is equivalent to adding some 'distance' to the indexical signs that were based directly on sensorimotor action schemes. The new sign uses are both iconic and some are even symbolic. Some of the orientations represented by iconic signs are latent in the action sequences which indexical signs would have been based on, but this is not necessarily or always the case. To make the transition to iconic signs, the child must be able to organize mental representations of actions with the appropriate orientations. This would seem to depend on reaching the level of representational intelligence, and would be the initial step of semiotic extension ontogenetically.

Chronologically there does not appear to be a clear-cut sequence of ontogenesis in which one type of sign precedes other types. Apart from the possibility of indexical signs predominating in the speech of some children at a very early point before any semiotic extension has developed, all types of sign including symbolic signs apparently play a part in children's utterances at nearly every stage (we are discussing only patterned speech). However, there does seem to be a sequence in which each type of sign reaches approximately its fullest development. This is an ontogenetic sequence of *terminations* rather than beginnings. Indexical signs are fully developed first, followed by iconic, then symbolic. Empirically, syntactic procedures continue to be acquired for a much longer period than the discovery of the word order sequences in a language takes, (C. Chomsky, 1969, observed some syntactic processes still in acquisition at age 10 years for some children). The picture is something like this:

indices ——
icons ————
symbols ——
cognitive development
——→

The acquisition of symbolic signs is not delayed until iconic signs become possible, though it does continue for a much longer time. The explanation for this sequence of types of sign in part presumably depends on the interaction of linguistic forms with the stages of cognitive growth. The creation of iconic word sequences is possible for a child thanks to his emerging capacity to think by means of mental representations. Some syntactic procedures are also correlated with the early stages of representational thought, for example, the English progressive aspect -*ing* (discussed below).

As Slobin (1973) has pointed out, there is a correlation between the child's intellectual development and its linguistic development which arises because various linguistic forms make different demands on cognitive abilities. The question we can now raise is, Why are there such different cognitive demands among linguistic forms?

At least one factor would be the function performed by each syntactic procedure in bridging a gap that cognitive growth opens between the sensorimotor level of speech output and a new level of thought. As the child's cognitive growth carries him to higher levels of mental functioning, new forms of semiotic extension are needed to maintain contact with the sensorimotor level where speech is co-ordinated. Syntactic procedures come to play an increasingly dominant part in these new forms of semiotic extension. Hence, each procedure will come to be acquired and used when its 'threshold' is reached due to intellectual growth. Before this stage is reached, however, there is no cognitive basis for the procedure, even thought it is modelled for the child in adult speech. Although there is a dependence on cognitive development in determining the order of acquisition of syntactic procedures, there is not a less dependence on the level of sensorimotor integration. It is precisely the gap between the child's mental functioning and the sensorimotor level that establishes the position of different syntactic procedures.

Speech development should take place in a sequence in which initially speech and thought are related as indices. With cognitive growth and semiotic extension, iconic and symbolic relationships very soon come to emerge, with symbolic relationships becoming increasingly important as cognitive growth and the development of semiotic extension continue. This process should be conceived of as a continuous, gradual, but very extensive change in the relation of speech to thought that occurs during ontogenesis. It is here that cognitive development clearly and decisively influences language, its form, function, and development.

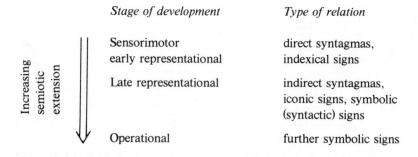

	Stage of development	Type of relation
Increasing semiotic extension →	Sensorimotor early representational	direct syntagmas, indexical signs
	Late representational	indirect syntagmas, iconic signs, symbolic (syntactic) signs
	Operational	further symbolic signs

Recognition of the aspect of language we have called semiotic extension forces us to acknowledge that the relationship between speech and thought cannot be uniform. Cognitive growth detaches thought from action and creates the necessity for semiotic extension in which there is, to use the metaphor of Werner and Kaplan (1963), an increasing 'distance' between speech and thought. The process can be represented as in Figure 8.1.

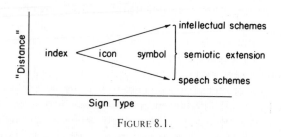

FIGURE 8.1.

From the point of view expressed in this diagram a major aspect of language development consists of discovering how to extend sensorimotor concepts, for it is upon this extension that the co-ordination of speech output depends. New extensions arise when cognitive growth enlarges the distance from the sensorimotor level to the level of the child's mental functioning. There may be constraints on the directions that these extensions may take arising from the organizing principles of cognition itself. For example, the concept of an Entity can be extended to include the relation of *consists-of* but apparently cannot be extended to include the relations of *is-in-state-of*; the latter, if incorporated into an attempted extension of Entity, changes this concept to a State. *(Entity A) consists-of (B)* remains an Entity, but *(Entity A) is-in-state-of (B)* becomes a State. These kinds of transformations of concepts are of basic importance. However, virtually nothing can be said of them. Searching for correlations of the kind suggested might provide some insights into the cognitive restrictions on the forms of semiotic extension.

An example of a syntactic procedure that appears to meet a demand posed at an early stage of representational intelligence, and therefore occurs early in ontogenesis, is the morphological inflection of verbs in English in the progressive aspect *-ing*. Viewed as a symbolic sign, the progressive *-ing* (not the gerund *-ing*) refers to a variety of temporal relationship involving actions in which a performance is, was, or will be in progress at the moment referred to by the utterance. This relationship involves the comparison of a temporally extended action and a reference point (the dot in the diagrams below). For example,

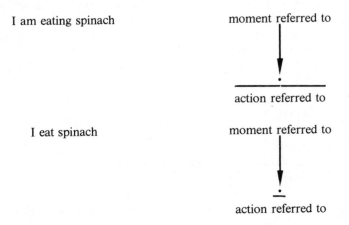

The temporal extension in the progressive tense is not indefinite. That idea is expressed by a generic ('tenseless') verb,

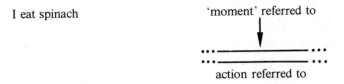

If we grant certain assumptions about the meanings of these tenses, it seems that the idea of a temporally extended action could arise along with the development of representational thought, due to the interiorization of sensorimotor action schemes (Piaget, 1969). As action schemes are differentiated from actual action performances, the child comes to be able to represent the distinction between actions and intentions to act. Previously, this distinction would have been only implicit; from the point of view of the child's representations, intentions and actions based on intentions would have been indistinguishable. Once these distinctions are clearly established, however, independent references are possible to intentions, actions, or both, and these could lead to the progressive, simple present, and (possibly) generic tenses as follows. The present progressive represents the situation in which a moment of time relates to an intention (which is inherently extended in time). Thus stative verbs, such as *know*, to which the notion of an intention is inapplicable, do not appear with the progressive (*_I am knowing the rules of chess_ is odd because it invites us to think that knowing is a matter of intending to know). The simple present tense represents the situation in which a moment of time relates to an action (which is inherently momentary). Thus it is the 'simple' tense, so called, because it refers to behaviour not necessarily interpreted as intentional. (For the same reason, it appears with stative verbs.) The generic tense seems to represent the situation in which there is not a moment of time but where intentions relate directly to momentary actions (the latter understood as repetitive). Thus the generic tense has a meaning of habitual or otherwise motivated action, in which an action is explained by reference to an intention. (This explanation does not account for the appearance of the generic tense with stative verbs, as in *he knows Chicago well*. It may be that the explanation in terms of intentions is too narrow.)

Before there is interiorization of action schemes, none of these situations could be represented differently by children; but after interiorization, there would be a basis for semiotic extension involving the tense system, including the progressive inflection *-ing*. Further semiotic extension would then be necessary to use these tenses when the performers or agents are inanimate things that do not have intentions. (Cf. Brown, 1973.)

An example of a later developing syntactic procedure, associated with more advanced levels of intellectual functioning, is that of marking temporal reversals between two time points in speech, such as present–past time points ('I know you did it', etc.). The inflectional complexity in this case does not seem to be greater than that with the *-ing* inflection, but these temporal reversals do not reliably occur until 4 years of age (Cromer, 1968). This result is plausibly due to the cognitive thresholding of such a procedure at the onset of concrete operations, when the representation of reversals becomes possible.

Above the sensorimotor level, then, concepts and interrelations arise from the kind of mental functioning which is separated from the sensorimotor level on which speech output is integrated. The resulting semiotic extension of the sensorimotor ideas within an utterance results in an assortment of iconic signs, indices, and symbolic signs created by various syntactic procedures. This network of signs embodies the speech–thought relation in adult utterances.

It would be misleading to say that each utterance is an ontogenesis in miniature, because that suggests a succession of stages, whereas the steps of the production process may often be conducted in parallel, but the aphorism expresses one valid point, namely, that the stages of ontogenesis leave traces in the formation of semiotically extended utterances. Corresponding to the chart given earlier for the changing speech–thought relations during ontogenesis, there is the following chart for the manifold thought–speech relations during the production of utterances.

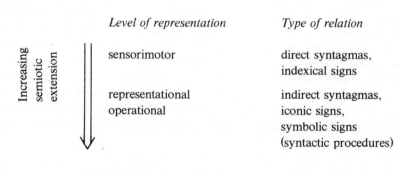

	Level of representation	*Type of relation*
Increasing semiotic extension	sensorimotor	direct syntagmas, indexical signs
	representational operational	indirect syntagmas, iconic signs, symbolic signs (syntactic procedures)

Putting the three types of sign together into a single representation involves producing the different types of sign in such a fashion that they interlock. This takes the following form: the Sign Vehicles of iconic and symbolic signs become the Objects of indexical signs. In this way, speech programmes are activated through the interpretation of sensorimotor ideas as iconic or symbolic signs of more abstract ideas. Semiotic extension plays an essential role in setting up the sign relationships with sensorimotor content which make this interpretation possible. For it is through semiotic extension that the iconic and symbolic signs are organized. The semiotically extended sensorimotor content, in turn, is the input to the Productant of the indexical Sign Vehicle (which is the activated speech programme). Thus the link is completed between abstract thought and speech output.

In the pseudocleft example used before, the procedure creates two concepts, for example Entity, and a *be*-relation between them. This comprises the production of the symbolic aspects of the pseudocleft structure, using the word 'symbolic' in the specific sense mentioned earlier. At the same time, the speaker forms interrelations among concepts on the level at which the speaker's thinking processes have a reasonably direct effect. Converting these relations into temporal sequences corresponding to orientation, comprises the production of the iconic aspects of the utterance. Again, simultaneously and interdependently, the sensorimotor level concepts either syntactically or directly produced may be 'noticed'—regarded as schemes for co-ordinating the movements of the articulatory process.

4. Linguistic Determinism of Thought

Semiotic extension creates an unavoidable form of linguistic determinism of thought during speech production. It is necessary for the speaker to organize his thinking in specific ways in order to produce word sequences and to make use of different syntactic procedures. A child discovers 'ways of organizing ideas' in forming iconic word sequences. From the earliest stages of ontogenesis there is a kind of linguistic determinism of thought, a necessity if there is to be semiotic extension of sensorimotor ideas which contact more abstract ideas.

This description of linguistic determinism requires reconsideration of the opposition between linguistic and cognitive determinism as it is usually stated. Usually these potentialities are regarded as mutually exclusive (Bruner, 1966; Piaget, 1970; Cromer, 1974). But in fact they are intimately related and comprise two aspects of the same underlying lack of direct adaptation of speech to thought; their opposition is purely superficial. The child's cognitive growth determines the course of the development of semiotic extension, but it is the structure of language and its requirements that force a distinctive pattern of thought during the production of speech. It is thus possible to see how the two hypothese of linguistic and cognitive determinism relate to each other.

During ontogenesis new syntactic procedures emerge to meet the demands for further semiotic extensions created by the process of cognitive growth. Here, clearly, one can speak of a cognitive determinism of language. Cromer in a statement of this view has written as follows:

It may be recalled that the Sapir–Whorf hypothesis, in its strong form, claimed that the way we view the world, the way we process and understand reality, is almost totally determined by the language we speak. With increasing research on language acquisition, however, the pendulum has begun to swing in the other direction. We have seen that in his very first words, the child is not merely imitating the language he hears about him; he is creating a set of categories to make reference to particular relations. Piagetian theorists have argued that the child begins his language acquisition process only when the cognitive processes of the sensori-motor stage have been completed. At slightly later ages, evidence has been quoted which seems to indicate that each new acquisition is made possible only through particular cognitive advances. We have seen how the earliest operations of verbs code only a specific set of cognitive meanings. We have also seen that the acquisition of prepositions depends on the advancing understanding of spatial relationships. In addition, we have noted the differentiation and addition of different types of negation as the child grows older. We have seen that a number of grammatical relationships are lacking until the child is cognitively able to free his viewpoint from an egocentric point in the flow of time. Evidence has also been reviewed that even more advanced linguistic techniques must await particular cognitive developments such as those formulated in the Piagetian stage of operational thinking. It would appear, then, that a position directly the reverse of that put forward by the Sapir–Whorf hypothesis is indicated, and we can call this the 'cognitive hypothesis'.

To parallel Whorf's wording of the hypothesis of linguistic determinism, the cognitive hypothesis might possibly be phrased like this: we are able to use the linguistic structures that we do largely because through our cognitive abilities we are enabled to do so, not because language itself exists for all merely to imitate. Cognitive processes differ not only at different ages but in how they enable the individual to break down the language that he hears to secure the elements which he can understand and produce. (Cromer, 1974, p. 234). Copyright © Brian Foss and contributors, 1974. Reprinted by permission of Penguin Books Ltd.

However, such a hypothesis must be related to the hypothesis of linguistic determinism rather than opposed to it. Both cognitive and linguistic determinism arise from the same lack of direct adaptation of speech to thought that creates the necessity for semiotic extension. Cromer's citation of the Sapir–Whorf hypothesis, therefore, may be inappropriate, at least for Sapir's views (of which more below), since this hypothesis, no less than the so-called 'cognition' hypothesis, flows from the same underlying lack of direct adaptation of speech to thought. Separating and opposing these hypotheses is quite arbitrary and artificial.

An example of a deterministic effect of speech on thought is the coupling of conceptual orientations with the occurrence or non-occurrence of certain syntactic procedures. The direct object of a verb in English must be oriented in the Operative direction unless a syntactic procedure such as the passive is used. Equivalently, to make use of the English passive procedure it is necessary for the speaker to organize the conceptual relation between the object and verb Receptively. The organization of thought in this instance interacts with the syntactic procedure employed.

In other languages, Japanese, for example, if one uses the neutral form, it is necessary to organize the conceptual relation between an object and verb Receptively, as follows,

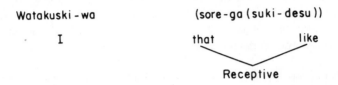

whereas the Operative orientation is obtained via a syntactic procedure of nominalization or relative clause formation, for example,

$$(((\text{Watakuski-no suki na-no)wa) are desu})$$

my   liking   one   is   that

Operative

With respect to Japanese, therefore, the Receptive relation, which is neutral in this language, is forced by English into linkage with the syntactic procedure of passivization. And with respect to English, the Operative relation, which is neutral in it, is forced by Japanese into linkage with the syntactic procedure of nominalization.

For this reason, fluent speakers of these languages should constantly organize their thinking in somewhat different patterns as they produce Operative or Receptive relations. Operativity, in Japanese, is associated with the characteristic meaning and pragmatic uses of nominalization or equivalent devices. Receptivity, in English, is associated with the meaning and pragmatic uses of the passive or its equivalents. In the sense of meeting different cognitive demands in the different languages, the hypothesis of linguistic relativity would seem to be valid for those points of organization where the orientation of the languages differ.

5. The Sapir–Whorf Hypothesis

In a passage presenting his views, Sapir declared that 'thought may be defined as the highest latent or potential content of speech, the content that is obtained by interpreting each of the elements in the flow of language as possessed of its very fullest conceptual value'. Moreover, 'thought may be no more conceivable, in its genesis and daily practice, without speech than is mathematical reasoning practicable without the lever of an appropriate mathematical symbolism' (Sapir, 1921, p. 14).

At least two types of linguistic determinism should be distinguished, however, although neither Sapir nor Whorf seem to have noticed the equivocation. (Nor has anyone else to my knowledge.) There is, on the one hand, the immediate form of linguistic determinism described above, that arises inevitably from the process of speaking. On the other hand, there is an enduring effect of language on 'habitual thought'. One type of determinism might occur but not the other.

Sapir seems to have meant the immediate form of determinism when he wrote that thought is the 'content that is obtained by interpreting each of the elements in the flow of language as possessed of its very fullest conceptual value'. Whorf (1941), however, clearly envisioned an enduring kind of determinism, when he wrote, in a well-known passage, that in a culture as a whole there is 'a vast amount that is not linguistic yet shows the shaping influence of language':

> By 'habitual thought' and 'thought world' I mean more than simply language, i.e., than the linguistic patterns themselves. I include all the analogical and suggestive value of the patterns ... and all the give-and-take between language and culture as a whole, wherein is a vast amount that is not linguistic yet shows the shaping influence of language. In brief, this 'thought world' is the microcosm that each man carries about within himself, by which he measures and understands what he can of the macrocosm. (Whorf, 1941, p. 84)

Such enduring effects of linguistic determinism may involve a contemplative or interpretive attitude toward the deterministic effects that arise immediately in the 'flow of language'. The Operative orientation of the verb–object relation in English, for example, except when linked to orientation-changing syntactic devices, could create the idea in the mind of an English-speaking thinker that actions have some sort of logical priority over objects. This would be a conclusion whose entire basis is a form of language. In Japanese, with Receptive orientations except when linked to orientation-changing syntactic devices, the deterministic conclusion might be that objects are logically prior to actions, i.e the opposite of English and again a conception that depends on a form of language.

Given the distinction between immediate and enduring deterministic effects from language, we should expect that children would show effects of the first kind almost immediately in ontogenesis, but that the second, in so far as it depends on a metalinguistic awareness, would emerge only later.

The determinism described in the Sapir–Whorf hypothesis can be seen to depend on semiotic extension in the following way. When Sapir wrote that 'thought may be described as the highest latent or potential content of speech' he could only mean the most extreme extension of speech to the realm of thought, encompassing all that thought that is potentially expressible with particular speech forms. Likewise, when Whorf wrote, 'I include all the analogical and suggestive value of the patterns' in the influence of language on thought, he apparently meant the same range in the realm of thought, that thought that is potentially expressible in the given speech form. Thus, the full effects that Sapir and Whorf describe depend on there being semiotic extensions of the basic speech mechanisms.

Acknowledgement

Based on material in a book to be published by L. Erlbaum and Associates, Hillsdale, N.J. The preparation of this paper was supported by funds from the Guggenheim Foundation, the Sloan Foundation, the National Institute of Mental Health, and the University of Chicago.

References

Bernstein, N.A. (1967), *The Co-ordination and Regulation of Movements*, Oxford: Pergamon.

Brown, R. (1973), *A First Language: the Early Stages*, Cambridge, Mass.: Harvard University Press; London: Allen & Unwin.

Bruner, J.S. (1966), On cognitive growth I, II. In Bruner, J.S., Olver, R.R., and Greenfield, P.M. (eds), *Studies in Cognitive Growth*, New York: Wiley.

Chomsky, C. (1969), *The Acquisition of Syntax in Children from 5 to 10*, Cambridge, Mass.: M.I.T. Press.

Cromer, R. (1968), The development of temporal reference during the acquisition of language. Thesis, Department of Social Relations, Harvard University.

Cromer, R. (1974), The development of language and cognition: the cognition hypothesis. In Foss, B. (ed.), *New Perspectives in Child Development*, Harmondsworth: Penguin Books.

Greene, P.H. (1972), Problems of organization of motor systems. In Rosen, R., and Snell, F.M. (eds), *Progress in Theoretical Biology*, vol. 2, New York: Academic Press.

Halliday, M.A.K. (1967), Notes on transitivity and theme in English, Part I, Journal of Linguistics, 3, 37–81.

Kozhevnikov, V.A. and Chistovich, L.A. (1965), *Speech: Articulation and Perception* (translation of *Rech: Artikulyatsiya, i Vospriyatiye*), Washington, D.C.: National Technical Information Service, U.S. Department of Commerce (JPRS # 30,543).

Lashley, K.S. (1951), The problem of serial order in behavior. In Jeffress, L.A. (ed.), *Cerebral Mechanisms in Behavior*, New York: Wiley.

McNeill, D. (1975), Semiotic extension. In Solso, R. (ed.), *Information Processing and Cognition*, Hillsdale, N.J.: Lawrence Erlbaum Associates.

Peirce, C.S. (1931–1958), Hartshorne, C., and Weiss, P. (eds), *The Collected Works of Charles Sanders Peirce*, Cambridge, Mass.: Harvard University Press.

Piaget, J. (1969), *The Child's Construction of the World*, Totowa, N.J.: Littlefield, Adams.

Piaget, J. (1970), *Genetic Epistemology*, New York: Columbia University Press.

Sapir, E. (1921), *Language, an Introduction to the Study of Speech*, New York: Harcourt, Brace.

Slobin, D.I. (1973), Cognitive prerequisites for the development of grammar. In Ferguson, C.A., and Slobin, D.I. (eds), *Studies of Child Language Development*, New York: Holt, Rinehart & Winston.

Werner, H., and Kaplan, B. (1963), *Symbol Formation: an Organismic Developmental Approach to Language and the Expression of Thought*, New York: Wiley.

Whorf, B.L. (1941), The relation of habitual thought and behavior to language. In Spier, L. (ed.), *Language, Culture, and Personality*, Menasha, Wisc.: Sapir Memorial Publication Fund. Reprinted in Carroll, J.B. (ed.) (1956), *Language, Thought, and Reality*, New York: Wiley; Cambridge, Mass.: M.I.T. Press; London: Chapman & Hall.

9

ATTRIBUTIONS, MEANINGS OF VERBS, AND REASONING

Ivana Marková

Some philosophers and linguists have argued recently that to ask for the meaning of a word or sentence or other linguistic form is misleading, because such a question erroneously implies the existence of some entity called 'meaning', an entity which has an inner structure than can be established by linguistic analysis (Fillmore, 1971; Putnam, 1975).

Fillmore (1971, p. 274) suggests instead that we should turn our attention to 'what ... I need to know in order to use this form appropriately and to understand other people when they use it'. But this question poses another problem as it is by no means clear what exactly it is to know how to use a linguistic form. Alston (1963), for example, expressed concern that no serious attempt had been made to show in what sense meaning could be interpteted as use. He listed the numerous different senses of 'use' and pointed out that we have been left with a number of alternatives as to the conditions under which it is applied.

However, irrespective of which sense of 'use' we might have in mind, the main point is that the appeal to use in theories of meaning always implies reference to *contextual* aspects of language, which distinguishes these theories from those which consider meaning to be an entity which can by analysed in its own right into semantic components. The consideration of contextual aspects of language in general and of meaning in particualr entails focusing on language as a means of interpersonal communication. And such an approach to the meaning of words or, rather, to the meaning potentialities of words, will be applied in this chapter. We shall make the following assumptions:

(1) Words and sentences only coexist with interpersonal communication; they only *are* words and sentences when intended as such by a speaker and understood as such by a listener, and without interpersonal communication are only so many marks on paper or so many vocal sounds. To use words is not simply to transplant dictionary meanings to communication situations. Rommetveit (1974) has pointed out that what is conveyed by a linguistic form is substantially determined by the communication situation within the temporarily shared social world of the

participants. He shows, for example, that the dictionary meaning of the word 'pot' is not very helpful in interpreting the cryptic dialogue of middle-aged parents worrying as to whether their son is smoking pot. The meaning of such a cryptic dialogue, consisting perhaps of a simple word, is, however, fully understandable when it is evaluated against the established social reality of the parents at the moment of speech (Rommetveit, 1974, p. 29).

(2) Our choice of words is not, however, determined solely by the context of the communication situation. The meanings we can attach to a word, and therefore the uses to which we can put the word, are limited by our acquired cognitive categories and attributions. In fact, our participation in a temporarily shared social world *presupposes* our acquistion of public strategies of categorization and social rules of attribution. For example, unless we master the categories GOOD/BAD, MALE/ FEMALE, or acquire the rules according to which we attribute SUCCESS/ FAILURE, RESPONSIBILITY/NON-RESPONSIBILITY, we are unable to comprehend and use the words associated with these categories and attributions. But to know the categories and attributions commonly associated with a certain word is only a necessary and not a necessary and sufficient conditon of the appropriate use and comprehension of the word: these categories and attributions only provide what Rommetveit calls 'drafts of contracts', our actual communicative semantic competence depending on our ability to elaborate these general schemes in particular social contexts:

> What is involved in HEAVY/LIGHT ... seems, moreover, to be mastery of a very abstract draft that in specific acts of verbal communication can be elaborated into reciprocally endorsed contracts concerning categorization of WORK, MEALS, TAXES, and DUTIES as well as of STONES and MEN. Some of these categorizations may be considered instances of 'literal', others of 'metaphorical' language use. (this volume, p. 147)

We all differ, however, with respect to the complexity and boundaries of our categorization and social attributions. For example, the child's categorizations may appear very simple from the point of view of an adult. Thus for the child the difference between 'hope' and 'fear' may be limited by the boundaries of categorizations such as GOOD/BAD. The poet or philosopher, on the other hand, might have very subtle systems of categorizations and attributions. For example, Marcel (1967) argues that in order to understand what 'hope' means we have to consider it in relationship to 'desire'; that it is not 'hope' and 'fear' which stand opposed, but 'desire' and 'fear'. He contrasts 'desire' and 'hope' on the basis of distinctions between impatience and faith, active and passive waiting: 'it is precisely here, in this relation to Time ... that the essential difference lies between Desire and Hope. The latter involves, indeed, a waiting, and we will have to recognize the existence of a *range* which goes from inert waiting to active waiting' (Marcel, 1967, p. 280).

The purpose of this chapter is to consider some psychological prerequisites of the mastery of verbs. As verbs represent actions and relationships, their use and comprehension is bound to mastery of the rules of attribution necessary to understand those actions and relationships. In the first part of this chapter we shall therefore deal with the attributional analysis of action and its relevance to the mastery of the meaning potentialities of verbs. In the last part of the essay we shall be concerned with *how* social attributions built into the meaning potentialities of verbs may determine partly the way a sentence containing such a verb is interpreted. In particular, we shall be concerned with the effect of dispositions and episodes in the interpretation of premises in conditional reasoning.

1. Attribution Theory

Attribution theory examines the processes by which people explain the changes or events taking place in their environment, particularly those involving human action. The primary assumption of attribution theory, based on Heider's (1958), 'naive' psychology, is man's striving for order and meaning in his experience, and his capacity for finding such stability results in a subjectively established, predictable, and controllable world. Part of this striving takes the form of a search for *dispositional* properties, which, according to Heider, are 'the relatively unchanging structures and processes that characterize and underlie phenomena' (Heider, 1958), p. 80). Dispositional properties are manifested in specific kinds of phenomena displayed when specific conditions obtain. They are found both in the physical world and in man's behaviour. For example, the thermal conductivity of copper is displayed by the rise of temperature of one end of a bar of that metal when the other end is placed in contact with a source of heat; the brittleness of glass is displayed by the fracture of a sheet of glass under a sharp blow. In human beings dispositions are such properties as personality traits, abilities, attitudes, emotions. The friendliness of a person is displayed by helping his fellow man and by a smile.

Dispositional properties, therefore, because they are perceived as representing stable features of the world, play an essential role in the explanation of events and actions. But explanation also depends upon proper consideration of all the relevant factors involved, and our interpretation of the outcome of an action depends upon our evalutaiton of the contribution of these different factors. Let us take Heider's example of a person sitting in a boat lying on the surface of a lake, and moving the oars with a rowing action. The outcome of this action can be interpreted in a number of ways:

He is trying to row the boat across the lake
He can (i.e. he has the power and ability to) row the boat across the lake.
He wants to row the boat across the lake.
It is difficult to row the boat across the lake.
Today is a good opportunity for him to row the boat across the lake.

It is sheer luck that he succeeded in rowing the boat
across the lake.

It is clear from these examples that an event involving human action, such as the movement of a boat across a lake, is determined partly by the person rowing it, and partly by the environment, for example the wind, the current, and the resistance of the water. Heider therefore talks, in the Lewinian tradition, in terms of *effective personal force* and *effective environmental force*. The actual direction of the boat will depend on the relative strengths of the two forces, and observers will attribute the cause of its motion accordingly. The coincidence of the attempt with a temporary reduction of environmental force can increase the chances of success. Correspondingly, the result of an action can be affected by changes in personal force through the influence of personality traits, moods, fatigue, and so on.

Effective personal force is itself seen as the resultant of 'can' and 'try'. 'Can' is mainly a dispositional concept concerning a person's abilities to control his environment. The perception of 'can' depends upon a person's success or failure in performing a particular kind of action. If the environmental force is very great, so that very few people can perform the task, success is attributed to the person, whereas if anyone can do it success is attributed to the ease of the task. 'Try' in the naive analysis of action is divided into intention — *what* a person is trying to do — and exertion —*how hard* he is trying to do it. We may discover whether a person intended a particular action, or what his intention was, in a number of ways, for example, from his own statement, from our knowledge of the person in question or of people in general, or, where different means are being used in attempting to achieve some end, by perceiving where the lines of action converge. Exertion can be discovered by direct observation of the effort applied or from the variety of means tried in attempting to perform the task, or it can be inferred from one's knowledge of the person and the difficulty of the task. Our cognition of intention and exertion plays an important role in our judgement of a person's responsibility for some action. If someone is struck by a stone, our judgement of the thrower's action will depend upon our knowledge of his intentions. Similarly, the degree to which a person exerts himself is evidence for the genuineness of his intentions. The level of responsibility we attribute to a person will differ according to our perception of his intentions, according to our perception of the care or carelessness of such a person, and will depend upon our judgement as to the extent to which such eventualities could have been foreseen.

Thus the outcome of an action is explained by referring to the motives, intentions, dispositions, and so on of the actor, or by identifying an interplay between personal and environmental factors. Hence we can conceive of 'space of action' as compounded of causality, intentionality, dispositionality, and so on, in much the same sort of way as we conceive of physical space as compounded of lengths and areas and volumes (Rommetveit, 1974, p. 119). In order to grasp the nature of physical space it is necessary to master the rules of length, area, and volume. Similarly, in order to make sense of the space of action, it is necessary to master the rules of attribution. Consequently, just as Euclidean ideas are built into our concepts of physical objects, so Heiderian attributions are built into our interpretations of actions. Just as the words 'thread' and 'field' are comprehensible only in terms of length and area, so expressions identifying actions, for example HE ROWS THE BOAT can be interpreted appropriately *only* when we have mastered the rules of attribution. Actions may be conceived of as performances of tasks, and

> The word 'easy' … is … comprehensible if and only if … [John] is considered as part or aspect of some action or task [(do)Y]. What is conveyed by either 'eager' or 'can', on the other hand, can only be made known if John is attended to as a potential actor, i.e. as X in [X(do)]. The word 'eager', moreover, makes sense if and only if said about *motivational aspects* rather than his *ability* as a potential actor. (Rommetveit, 1974, p. 116)

2. Rules of Attribution in the Development of the Child

We know from Piagetian studies that unless a child has mastered certain cognitive operations, for example can attend to several pieces of information at the same time and relate them together, he is unable to perform certain cognitive tasks. A child must be able to focus on both length and density in the task of conservation of number, if he is to solve this type of problem, or to focus on the transformation of things, for example on changes of shape, or on the breaking up of things into pieces, if he is to solve the task of conservation of substance.

Similarly, unless a child has mastered the rules of attribution, he cannot assess an event or an action in the adult way. But while in order to cope with transformations of *physical* reality the child must realize that objects have properties and forces which are not dependent on his own will, in order to cope with *social* reality the child must realize that people are not only sources of forces like physical objects, but can also express their *own* wishes, needs, and feelings. The child thus has to learn to consider not only his own interests but also the interests of others, and he has to learn to follow social rules. Acquisition of social concepts, therefore, is determined not only by the child's cognitive maturity, but also by his social maturity. Consider, for example, the concept of responsibility. Attribution of responsibility may differ according to the type of situation and relative contribution of personal and environmental forces (Heider, 1958). First, the situation may be one in which the person is merely associated with the act or state of affairs. For example, responsibility may be attributed to a person for something in which he has not been involved personally, such as blaming him for something done by the political party of which he is a member. Second, responsibility may be attributed to a person for the outcome of an action rather than for what he actually intended. Thus Piaget has shown that young children judge morality according to the outcome of an action rather than according to the intentions of the actor. A little girl who wanted to help her mother and accidentally broke ten cups was judged as naughtier than a girl who broke one cup intentionally (Piaget, 1932). Third, a person might be held responsible for after-effects which were not part of his own goal. Fourth, a person is seen as responsible only for what he intended to do. And last, a person may be seen as only a product of environmental forces and therefore not responsible for his actions at all.

It has been shown both in Piagetian and Heiderian types of research that a child proceeds in his development from the type of responsibility in which a person is judged only according to the outcome of an action, to those types in which environmental forces and actor's intentionality are both taken into account in the evaluation of an action (Shaw and Sulzer, 1964; King, 1971). In our own research into the psycho-social effects of chronic physical disability, we have found that a child's perception of responsibility is associated with his social background and with the degree of severity of his disability. Children with a middle-class background attribute more responsibility to actors than children from working-class families, and children with physical disability attribute less responsibility to actors than non-handicapped children (Murray, 1976). Perception of responsibility is also associated with social relationships: popular children attribute bad outcomes of an action to chance rather than to bad intentions, while unpopular children attribute them more to bad intentions (Aydin, 1976).

Mastery of the rules of attribution is also reflected in the communicative competence of a child. Words expressing the dispositional qualities of people and interpersonal relationships appear in a child's language much later than words expressing immediate and directly observable events. Early child utterances are comments on actors and their actions, and on objects and their appearances and disappearances. Studies concerning the child's perception of other people show that a young child originally describes other people in terms of their physical characteristics (he is tall, she is pretty, he lives near my house) rather than in terms of personality characteristics and social attributions. Although evidence of dispositional attribution is to be found in kindergarten children's descriptions of other people (Peevers and Secord, 1973), the complexity and subtlety of dispositional characterization increases until adulthood. Attribution of *negative* dispositions, however, is expressed in the child's language much earlier than attribution of positive dispositions (Marková and Lockyer, 1976; Aydin, 1977), Also the appearance of verbs in the child's language reflects the process of increasing decentration and consideration of the points of view of other people. Carol Chomsky in her study of the acquistion of syntax in children (1969) made the interesting discovery that sentences with the verb 'promise' are at first interpreted in the same way as sentences with 'tell' and only at the age of 8·0–9·0 do children interpret such sentences correctly. Chomsky argues that learning a word in one's language encompasses two processes: first, the process of acquisition of semantic knowledge, i.e. of knowledge of the concept attached to the word, and only second the process of acquisition of syntactic knowledge, i.e. of the grammatical constructions into which the word may enter:

> A complete knowledge of the word includes both this semantic knowledge and all the syntactic knowledge relating to the word. For a word like *promise*, where there is a particular difficulty attached to the syntactic aspect of the word, we see that the child first acquires semantic knowledge, and later progresses to full syntactic knowledge. (Chomsky, 1969, p. 5)

Such a claim, however, does not seem to be justified. It presupposes that semantic and syntactic knowledge are independent of one another. There are no grounds for this supposition. It is more likely that syntactic development is dependent upon semantic knowledge and the grammatical rules attached to the word 'promise' may be difficult for a child because of his slow progress in the comprehension of its meaning. The verbs 'to tell' and 'to promise' differ as to the extent to which personal relationships are built into their semantic potentialities. Unless the child learns the rules of procedure connected with promising, and understands the consequences of breaking the rules, the consequences of his personal commitments, and of the power relationships involved in such procedures, he is unable to distinguish 'promise' from 'tell' or, possibly, 'promise' from 'threaten'. And mastery of such rules is, until a certain stage of his cognitive and social development, beyond the capacities of a child.

3. Attributions and Verbs

We have maintained that in order to understand action and in order to make inferences beyond immediate perceptual experience we have to master the rules of attribution. We can now investigate from this point of view the extent to which attributions are built into the meaning potential of verbs. While in most of our everyday conversation we use words quite unaware that interpersonal communication is always laden with knowledge and rules of attribution, it is only when the words are not used in accordance with such knowledge and when commonly shared rules are broken that we become aware of them. Let us consider this subject with respect to those attributions which we have already discussed in sections 1 and 2, namely causality, dispositions and episodes, and intentions and responsibility.

3.1 Causality

Let us imagine that someone asks you:

What are you doing?

and you answer:

> I am holding a gun with my hand and pressing the trigger with my finger until the hammer is released and the bullet flies out,

instead of saying briefly:

I am shooting.

Clearly the single word 'shooting' is a substitute for the whole description given above because the whole description of the action and also the form that an explanation of the action must take (for example, to cause damage) are built into the meaning potentialities of the word 'shooting'. Only if a person comes from a different culture and does not know what shooting is (if there is such a culture) is it necessary to describe the bodily movements involved in using a gun, and to explain the purpose of such movements, both in terms of the immediate consequences (for example, killing) and the why of these consequences (for example, killing as a sport, for food, in defence, and so on). And, indeed, to be pedantic in our description, the words 'gun' and 'bullet' at least would also have to be replaced by lengthy redescriptions.

Words, however, differ as to their descriptive and explanatory power. Hanson (1958) points out that while some words express nothing but sense-data, for example 'disappearing', 'bitter', 'red now', 'in a pure sense-datum language causal connexions could not be expressed. All words would be on the same logical level: no one of them would have explanatory power sufficient to serve in a causal account of neighbour events .... Causal connexions are expressible only in languages that are many-levelled in explanatory power' (p. 59–60).

Most of our communication, however, is concerned with more complex issues than the expression of sense experience in terms of sense-data, and most words, therefore, have built into them more categories and attributions than those of mere sense experience. The majority of words are 'theory-loaded', carrying reference to existing knowledge and carrying implications that go beyond whatever is given in sense experience. This theory-ladenness of words may take different forms. For example, the same word (or essentially the same word) may embody attributions which differ according to context. Thus adjective predicates are passive, for example colours, and verb predicates are active, like 'shine' and 'glitter'. Moreover some predicates may take either the active or passive form, for example colours in Slav languages. A Czech folk song says: the meadow greens ... (zelená se louka ...) and the Russian romantic poem by Lermontov starts: The lonely sail whites ... (beleet parus odinokij ...).

Or, words can embody causes in some contexts, and effects in others:

Diagnoses, analyses, prognoses, are built into [words]. That is why in certain contexts they explain scars, clumsiness, rough surfaces and death; why it is natural to refer to the wound as the cause of the scar, to the scar as the cause of clumsiness, to the crater as the cause of uneven surface reflexion, to volcanoes or meteors as the cause of the crater, and to poison as the cause of death. (Hanson, 1958, p. 57)

Because words differ as to their descriptive and explanatory power and some are richer than others, some words both presuppose and imply more knowledge than others. While the verb 'to move', itself, when used intransitively (for example, the sun moves) may be considered to be a sense-datum verb, particular verbs of motion differ as to the complexity of the categories which they embody, as several psychologists concerned with the semantic structure of this group of verbs have shown; they may express direction (come, go, ascend, climb), speed (run, crawl), the specific environment in which the movement is accomplished (fly, swim, walk), and so on (cf. Miller, 1972; Levelt, Schreuder, and Hoenkamp, 1976).

Perhaps we could say that the less the explanatory power of a word, the more the situations to which it may refer can be found. Thus 'to move' would refer to more situations than 'to run', and 'to run' would refer to more situations than 'to chase', as the first verb would refer to all situations in which motion is present, the second would refer to situations where motion is relatively fast, and the third would refer to situations of fast motions with intention to reach someone. What it shows, however, is not that the meaning of 'run' can be decomposed into semantic components 'move' + 'speed', and 'chase' decomposed into 'move' + 'speed' + 'goal', etc. It only shows that there are aspects of situations which can be characterized as 'movement', 'speed', etc. Controlled systematic changes of such aspects of situations might enable us to find the minimum conditions under which these situations could be labelled as 'running', 'chasing', etc. An ingenious technique for this purpose has been introduced by Johansson (1973) and adapted by Levelt *et al.* (1976). Johansson attached light spots to the joints of people and then made film recordings in the dark so that the films consisted only of moving lights. These were immediately recognized by viewers as human gait. Levelt *et al.* asked an actress to perform movements (stroll, trip, limp, hop, race, etc.) so that again only moving lights were seen by subjects. The film recordings can then be modified by the experimenter any desired way by altering individual frames. A similar effect could be obtained with the co-operation of a film cartoonist. Labelling a certain situation by a certain word may be very subtle, as pointed out by Hanson when considering the attributions embodied in 'stretch'. While we talk about stretching rubber, elastic bands, springs, shrunken clothing, etc., we do not, on the other hand, talk about stretching butter on a scone, stretching seed in the garden, nor about gas stretching from the cooker into the atmosphere, or a cloud stretching when caught by the wind. But, ponders Hanson (1958, p. 57),

Perhaps these are all cases of stretching; there are times when these might be natural ways of speaking. Still, there are differences between stretching rubber and springs on the one hand and stretching butter, sand and gas on the other. In the former cases, when we stop stretching, the body returns to its original shape; but this is not so with butter, sand or gas.

From physical motion we can take a step further and consider the explanatory power of verbs labelling complex human actions and relationships. Such verbs embody the rules of social attribution of intentionality, responsibility, dispositionality, and others.

3.2 Dispositionality and Episodicity

Just as we interpret an event or action either as a mere episode or as the manifestation of a disposition, so verbs may be episodic or dispositional in character (Ryle, 1949). 'Know', 'believe', 'conduct electricity' are all dispositional verbs; we say that a man is skilful or knows something, that glass is brittle and sugar dissolves in water, irrespective of whether these dispositions are actually being displayed. But dispositions such as skill and knowledge are mental qualities, and for Ryle this is all part of the dogma of the ghost in the machine that he is concerned to exorcise. For Ryle, therefore, skill and knowledge become potentialities which, indeed, have no real existence between the episodes in which they are displayed. Statements concerning them are to be construed as conditionals, stating what occurs and what we may expect to occur whenever certain conditons are fulfilled.

What, then, distinguishes the possession of a disposition from its non-possession? We need not follow Ryle in insisting that the possession of a disposition makes no difference except at the time that it is displayed. Brittleness in glass and conductivity in copper are held to be due to permanent features of crystal and electronic structure, and it seems reasonable to suppose that mental dispositions are permanent or relatively permanent qualities in people which are displayed in various ways when circumstances so demand. Nevertheless, we can follow Ryle in the account he gives of the differences between those episodes which are merely chance occurrences, and those which are exercises of dispositions. Clumsy people are constantly tripping and tumbling, and so are clowns, but only a clown is displaying any skill. The skill, however, is not *part* of an act; it is something about the act, the manner and circumstances in which it is performed, that distinguishes it from the act of a clumsy person. Similarly, what enables us to distinguish an assertion from an identical statement pronounced in parrot fashion lies in the context of the former. Observation of repeated episodes in all their variations and differing contexts are therefore fundamental to the discovery of these distinctions.

As we shall see later, the dispositionality and episodicity of verbs are contextually dependent. Nevertheless we can distinguish between strongly dispositional and strongly episodic verbs. Among strongly dispositional verbs are 'cognitive' verbs, such as 'know' and 'understand', and verbs expressing feelings and emotions, such as 'hate', 'avoid', 'like', 'love', 'admire', and so on: if I understand something it is usually interpreted as a more or less stable feature of the mind, not changing from 'yes' to 'no' and back over a period of time. Other dispositional verbs include verbs expressing tendencies and habits, such as 'buy', 'play', 'drive', etc.; the question 'do you drive?' is concerned with one's ability to drive rather than with what one is doing at the moment: and verbs expressing physical properties are very often dispositional, for example 'dissolve'—'whenever sugar is put into water it dissolves', and 'melt'—'whenever the temperature is above zero snow melts'.

Strongly episodic verbs are: all classes of performative verbs, as analysed by Austin (1962) (verbs are performative when saying something also means doing something, for example, by saying 'I order you' I am not only saying something, but also performing an act); and verbs such as 'promise', 'accuse', 'apologize', 'thank'. Other episodic verbs include: all verbs in which a disposition or ability is actualized, such as 'buying', 'baking', 'avoiding', as in 'Mother is baking a cake', 'I am avoiding a sharp corner', etc.; verbs of motion, such as 'go', 'throw', and verbs denoting exchange of property, for example 'take', 'give', 'borrow', etc.; and finally achievement verbs, such as 'succeed', 'fail', 'wake up', 'arrive'. This is not intended to cover all verbs, only to show what is meant by dispositionality and episodicity and to give a few examples of each.

The English language seems to distinguish strongly dispositional verbs by not using them in the present continuous tense; we do not usually say 'I am hating', 'I am loving', 'I am knowing'. Strongly dispositional verbs also seem to be resistant to conjunction with verbs of immediate change, such as 'advise', 'decide', 'order', 'become', 'remember', but go naturally with verbs expressing gradual change, such as 'learn' or 'begin'. Thus 'learn to hate' and 'begin to understand' are perfectly natural combinations, whereas if the context gives no other clue, 'remember to love' and 'decide to understand' sound distinctly odd.

Although some verbs are specifically dispositional *or* episodic in character, and therefore display their dispositionality or episodicity when used *in vacuo*, others may be interpreted in various ways when used in sentences *in vacuo*. Let us take, for example, the sentence

Mary reads the newspaper

and consider it as an answer to two particular questions. First, it could be an answer to the question

What does Mary do?

In this case the answer 'Mary reads the newspaper' would be related to certain episodes in her life; she may be reading the newspaper now, in the afternoon, she may read it from time to time, often, seldom or sometimes. These actions, of course, may be performed for different reasons: Mary might be reading the newspaper because she is bored and has nothing better to do, or she might be interested in politics, in sport, in advertisements, and so on. These actions are not, however, necessarily expressions of any habits or personal interests, but may simply be the way Mary occupies her time. Further evidence might lead us to suppose that her actions reflect some genuine interest, but knowing only that there is a certain person, Mary, and that this person has been reading a newspaper, would we be prepared to predict that she will continue reading a newspaper in the future, for example, go and buy it when it is not available at home, when she goes on holiday and so on? Probably not.

Second, let us consider 'Mary reads the newspaper' as an answer to the question

What sort of person is Mary?

In this case the reply, 'Mary reads the newspaper' is specifically related to Mary's personality traits, such as her habits, interests, mental capacities, and so on, rather than to certain episodes in her life. The sentence is not concerned with her actions at any moment; it tells us, however, about Mary's disposition to read newspapers. Although we might not know what personality traits underlie this disposition, i.e. whether she likes reading, whether she is interested in politics, sports, the women's page, and so on, we might still be prepared to predict that she will continue reading newspapers, irrespective of her future circumstances. For her to stop reading newspapers would be for her to lose her interest or no longer have access to newspapers, and so on.

3.3 Intention and Responsibility

In order to understand the meaning potentials of verbs such as 'kill', 'murder', 'execute', 'assassinate' we must understand the differences between the intentions underlying the actions in question and the social settings and roles of the persons involved. A person may be killed in a car accident or by a falling stone or by a disease, but he can be murdered, executed or assassinated *only* by another human being. Moreover, the difference between them lies in the character of the of the intention, murder having the goal of revenge or personal gain, assassination having a political aim, and execution being killing as a punishment for some criminal act. Although in all cases we are faced with the death of a person, our judgement of such an act of killing is determined by the WHY and our social attributions of the killing. While murder is always a case for criminal law, execution is part of criminal law. If we say, however, about an executed political prisoner, 'he was murdered', we might mean different things: the execution itself might have been a criminal act; or we might just be expressing our judgement of an act of execution, thus communicating our disagreement with the criminal law, or with the judgement of the act for which the person was executed, or with capital punishment as a whole.

Similarly understanding of the differences between 'say', 'promise', 'swear', 'threaten', and 'warn' is determined by understanding of social power and other social relationships. The sentence

The father said he would do it

does not on its own express a threat or promise or warning, and may be just a statement of the father's intention to do something. Its meaning can only be disambiguated by the context in which it is used. On the other hand, the sentences

The father promised he would do it

The father threatened he would do it

express both the father's power and his intention to act in such a way that his action would have certain consequences for other people. While promising involves an obligation to fulfill what is said, swearing on oath involves a *moral* obligation and not fulfilling it gives other people (or God) the right to punish. Intention in all of these cases is not a purely private matter, it has social significance in the sense that threatening or promising have consequences for other people. Hence words of intention can be used properly only after the individual has learned the social relationships that underlie them. Similarly the *language of judging* expresses our understanding and interpretation of acts in which people are involved as victims and defendants. The understanding of such roles as victim, defendant, and so on presupposes the understanding of human relationships involving intention to harm, to benefit, to be responsible, to have moral obligation. We mentioned earlier that the notion of responsibility may refer to different types of responsibility (p. 203). Although in language and communication we are not usually aware of making these differences in attribution of responsibility, we do distinguish between them by using certain verbs rather than others. The responsibilities connected with 'indict', 'accuse', 'impeach', 'blame', 'criticize', and plain 'say' are different types of responsibility: 'indict' applies to the formal accusation of a person, while 'impeach' is limited to the formal accusation of a high political figure, probably only the head of a state. 'Accuse' presupposes certain power relationships and would have *no effect* at all if the 'judge' were unable to administer moral judgement and punishment. At least such a punishment must involve changed attitudes toward the accused and therefore accusation should make him feel worse, embarrassed, ashamed. 'Accuse' involves the moral type of responsibility and we attribute morality to people and not to inanimate objects, while the responsibility in, for example, 'blame' or 'criticize' encompasses also other senses of responsibility. We blame the environment, we blame inanimate objects as well as people, but we usually criticize only those objects which are somehow connected with man's actions. We blame a factory and criticize a factory, but only blame and do not criticize a stone. While the accused, if he proves to be guilty, deserves punishment, the one who is criticized does not necessarily deserve punishment, and criticism is often understood as a sort of help.

4. Attributions and Conditional Reasoning

In the remainder of this chapter we shall consider how attributions, namely dispositions and episodes, built into the meaning potentialities of verbs, may affect the way a sentence is interpreted. To do so, we shall explore the field of conditional reasoning.

The psychology of conditional reasoning has for many years been based on assumptions borrowed from propositional logic. The subject is presented with premises and his task is to draw or evaluate inferences from such premises: the problem is defined by the experimenter in terms of the logical structure of the propositional or predicate calculus and the subject is assessed as to his ability to draw logically correct conclusions from the problems defined for him. The psychologist's effort has, therefore, been focused on *pure reasoning*, understood as reasoning abstracted from context and freed from all subjective and intersubjective human factors; and the main task for him has been the investigation of deviances from the ideal of pure reasoning as determined by the laws of thought. Accordingly, in reasoning tasks with conditionals it has been presupposed that 'if ... then' is or should be interpreted in only one way, i.e. the way defined by the propositional calculus, while the content of the task has been thought to be irrelevant, and therefore has not been considered at all.

But experiments with conditionals have failed to obtain results which would conclusively demonstrate either that people think according to the propositional calculus or that some other rules guide the inferences which people draw. Matalon (1962) and similarly Peel (1967) found that children read 'if ... then' predominantly as a biconditional. Wason (1968) found that even highly intelligent undergraduates were unable to draw 'logically correct' inferences when the negation of the consequent was given together with the conditional sentence. Taplin (1971) reached the conclusion that 'No truth-table function exists for conditional sentences which is common to all individuals' (p. 224). Wason introduced the notion of a defective truth-table in which 'no truth-value [is] specified for those cases where the antecedent is false' (Wason and Johnson-Laird, 1972, p. 90).

It is a commonplace among logicians that truth-functional logic is only a partial representation of natural language. I.M. Copi, for instance (1961), points out that there are several kinds of implication, so that the meaning of the horseshoe (or arrow) symbol cannot be regarded as *the* meaning of the expression 'if–then'. It is a component common to all of them, but only, therefore, *part* of the meaning of any of them. And the same applies to the other connectives. Mates (1965) makes a similar claim: after pointing out that the formalized language L of formal logic is modelled on natural language, and that the sentences of L are intended to be 'counterparts' of sentences of the natural language (in a somewhat vague sense of 'counterpart'), he goes on to note that although we may read '.' as 'and' and 'v' as 'or' and '→' as 'if ... then', 'serious confusion will result if one takes these readings to indicate some sort of synonimity ... since such words as 'or', 'and', 'if ... then' are not always (if ever) used truth-functionally in everyday language, their representation by the connectives of L is always more or less questionable' (pp. 41, 74). He illustrates this by an interpretation of L having the set of all the characters in *David Copperfield* as its domain, and considers the sentence

If Barkis is willing, Peggoty will marry him

as an interpretation of Wb→Mpb (Mates, 1965, p. 68). The sentence in the natural language contains an appropriate reference to time, whereas that in L does not. The effect of this difference comes out when we consider the equivalent sentence in L, − Mpb→ − Wb. The corresponding sentence in the natural language is

If it is not the case that Peggoty will marry Barkis, then Barkis is not willing,

which would *not* be considered equivalent to the former. There is also a *causal* connection involved (Mates, 1965, p. 69).

Mates also points out that while for any given interpretation any expression of L always has exactly the same meaning, the meaning of an expression in natural language is not fixed in this way, but depends heavily on context. But in what way may context influence the interpretation of a sentence? One possible way is suggested by the discovery of the generalizing power of the verb by Abelson and his students (Abelson and Kanouse, 1966; Gilson and Abelson, 1965). According to them, the persuasiveness of messages may be due to the function of the verb: some verbs can produce a very high degree of generalization although the evidence is weak or even contradictory.

If political regime A executes two peasants, it seems reasonable to say, 'Regime A executes peasants'. But if political regime B earns the respect of two peasants, it seems bizarre to conclude 'Regime B earns the respect of peasants'. (Abelson and Kanouse, 1966, p. 173)

The generalizing power of the verb is attributed by Abelson to different *implicit quantifiers* tacitly attached to the subject or object of unquantified sentences. Although Abelson is uncertain as to *why* different implicit quantifiers are attached to certain types of verbs, he indicates one possible line of investigation of the nature of the verb effect, drawing attention to the differences between 'observable and reportable' actions and those states of affairs which cannot be directly reported or observed as they are usually *feelings* which can be concealed. Thus if 'someone *has* (buys, produces, steals) X's', it cannot mean that one has *all* X's, and so on. Generalization to 'someone has X's', etc., should therefore be fairly easy, since such sentences are not interpreted as having the universal implicit quantifier. On the other hand, one can well like, avoid, hate, understand all X's, so that sentences such as 'one likes X's' can well carry the universal implicit quantifier (Gilson and Abelson, 1965). However, just because they can, negative instances will count against the acceptance of such sentences. Kanouse (1972) proposed that verbs are associated with low implicit quantifiers 'if and only if, the relation described by the verb limits either the availability of the object or the resources of the subject' (p. 126). If a person has a thing, no one else can have it, so the value of the implicit quantifier is low, that is 'John steals books' is interpreted as 'John steals some books'. On the other hand, another person's disliking or liking something does not reduce one's own ability to like or dislike it, and the value of the implicit quantifier is high, for example 'John dislikes books' is interpreted as 'John dislikes most books'. However, if we look more closely at the data of Abelson and his students we find that the correspondence between the implicit quantifiers and the generalizing power of those verbs is not particularly good (Marková and Farmer, in press). The hypothesis of implicit quantifiers, therefore, only yields a partial explanation of generalizing power, and we must accordingly search for a more basic explanation. Searching for such an explanation and enquiring at the same time whether the effects of verbs observed by Abelson appear in reasoning with conditionals as well, we have designed simple experiments in which subjects were presented with conditional tasks and asked to draw conclusions from such tasks. Each conditional task consisted of two premises and a question:

Premise 1: A conditional sentence of the 'If p then q' type.

Premise 2: p or q was either affirmed or denied: $(p, q, \bar{p}, \bar{q})$

Question: Does subject–verb–object?

All sentences were similar in form to Abelson's type of sentence: the object in the antecedent was a class name and the object in the consequent of the conditional was the name of a sub-class of the antecedent's class. Six of Abelson's verbs were used: 'buy', 'have', 'understand', 'avoid', 'hate', 'ignore'.

For example:

If John avoids French books he will avoid *Madame Bovary*.

John avoids French Books.

Does John avoid *Madame Bovary*?

If John buys French books he will buy *Madame Bovary*.

John does not buy French books.

Does John buy *Madame Bovary*?

We found that subjects' answers were determined by the interaction between the verbs and logical forms of the tasks in such a way that 'buy', 'have', and 'understand' were grouped together and 'ignore', 'avoid', and 'hate' were grouped together. The strong interaction effect between verbs and logical forms could not be accounted for in terms of the dichotomies of the propositional and predicate calculus. Further investigation and interviewing of the subjects suggested, however, that attributions built into the meaning potential of verbs determine the way the reasoning task was interpreted by the subject, in this particular case depending on whether the verb was interpreted as *dispositional* or *episodic*.

The sentences 'John ignores French books' and 'John does not ignore French books' are, without additional context to tell us otherwise, probably associated with dispositions; at least this is what we could infer from our subjects' responses and their interviews. Similarly, 'John does not buy French books' seems to be associated with a disposition rather than an episode. 'John buys *Madame Bovary*', on the other hand, is episodic. We can see why this is so if we consider the way in which the word is commonly used. It is associated with a number of actions, such as John going to the bookshop, talking to the shopkeeper, paying for the book, and so on. The association of 'buying *Madame Bovary*' with an action, together with the knowledge that *Madame Bovary* is a French book, makes it quite acceptable to the subject to infer 'John buys (a) French book(s)', understood as a sequence of actions.

If we now return to our previous discussion of Abelson's and his colleagues' work, their attempt to account for verb effects in terms of the tacit use of the quantifiers of formal logic may be conceived of as a first step towards an explication of more complex strategies of attribution. The terms 'every', 'some', and 'all', it appears, may be further analysed into tacit presuppositions concerning *how often, in what capacity*, and *why* some action is performed. Dispositionality and quantification, however, are not logically tied, as a person's dispositions can be revealed by information about an action he performs only once. Thus 'John buys French books' or 'John goes to church' may be dispositional even though the event were observed only once. But this is nothing more than what we already know about inferring dispositions from actions. For example, Sue's mother knows very little about Sue's fiancé, John, and thinks that he has no intellectual interests or religious inclinations. She asks Sue: What kind of man is John? Sue's answer 'John buys French books' and 'John goes to church' is not primarily concerned with how often John does these things but with his intellectual and religious dispositions. The notion 'implicit quantifier' may thus be misleading giving the impression of some more or less stable relationship with a verb, rather than a relationship which only externally expresses much deeper tacitly induced assumptions concerning the topic and the why of communication (Rommetveit, 1974).

Verbal reasoning cannot thus ignore the meaning potentialities of words because, as we have seen, the logical structure of the reasoning task may be determined by attributions built into the meaning potential of words. The subject's interpretation of the problem is necessarily bound to the social context and to the subject's mastery of natural language in everyday discourse. Only when we know the effect of these factors on the meaning attributed to a problem can we decide whether the subject's logic operates in accordance with the meaning which he attributed to the problem, or whether his logic is defective. The strategies of categorization and rules of attribution must therefore always be taken into account in our consideration of any human activity involving language and communication.

Acknowledgements

The work reported in this paper was supported by an SSRC research grant. I wish to thank Colin Wright for commenting on drafts of the paper and for his help in clarifying my ideas.

References

Abelson, R. P., and Kanouse, D. E. (1966), Subjective acceptance of verbal generalizations. In Feldman, S. (ed.), *Cognitive Consistency*, New York and London: Academic Press.

Alston, W. P. (1963), Meaning and use, *Phil. Quarterly*, 13, 107–124.

Austin, J. L. (1962), *How to Do Things with Words*, Oxford: Clarendon Press.

Aydin, O. (1976), Perception of intentions by popular and unpopular children, Paper read to the BPS Social Section, York.

Aydin, O. (1977), The description of peers and the perception of intentions by popular and unpopular children. Unpublished Ph.D. thesis, University of Stirling.

Chomsky, C. (1969), *The Acquistion of Syntax in Children from 5 to 10*, Research Monograph no. 57, Cambridge, Mass.: M.I.T. Press.

Copi, I. M. (1961), *Introduction to Logic*, New York: The Macmillan Company.

Fillmore, C. J. (1971), Verbs of judging: an exercise in semantic description. In Fillmore, C. J., and Langendoen, D. T. (eds), *Studies in Linguistic Semantics*, New York and London: Holt, Rinehart & Winston.

Gilson, C., and Abelson, R. P. (1965), The subjective use of inductive evidence, *Journal of Personality and Social Psychology*, 2, 301–310.

Hanson, N. R. (1958), *Patterns of Discovery*, Cambridge: Cambridge University Press.

Heider, F. (1958), *The Psychology of Interpersonal Relations*, New York and London: Wiley.

Johansson, G. (1973), Visual perception of biological motion and its analysis, *Perception and Psychophysics*, 14, 201–211.

Just, M. A., and Clark, H. H. (1973), Drawing inferences from the presuppositions and implications of affirmative and negative sentences, *Journal of Verbal Learning and Verbal Behavior*, 12, 21–31.

Kanouse, D. E. (1972), Language, labeling and attribution. In Jones, E. E., Kanouse, D. E., Kelley, H. H., Nisbett, R. E., Valins, S. and Weiner, B. (eds), *Attribution: Perceiving the Causes of Behavior*, Morristown, New Jersey: General Learning Press.

King, M. (1971), The development of some intention concepts in young children, *Child Development*, 42, 1145–1152.

Levelt, W. J. M., Schreuder, R., and Hoenkamp, E. C. M. (1976), Structure and use of verbs of motion. Paper read at the conference on Psychology of Language, University of Stirling.

Marcel, G. (1967), Desire and hope. In Lawrence, N., and O'Connor, D. (eds), *Readings in Existential Phenomenology*, Englewood Cliffs, N. J.: Prentice-Hall.

Marková, I., and Farmer, J. (in press), On problems of context and attribution in verbal reasoning, *European Journal of Social Psychology*.

Marková, I., and Lockyer, R. (1976), Peer relations in haemophilic children. Unpublished report, University of Stirling.

Matalon, B. (1962), Étude génétique de l'implication. In Beth, E. W., Grize, J. B., Martin R., Matalon, B., Naess, A., and Piaget, J., *Études d'épistémologie génétique*, *16. Implication Formalisation et Logique Naturelle*, Paris: Presses Universitaires de France.

Mates, B. (1965), *Elementary Logic*, New York: Oxford University Press.

Miller, B. (1972), English verbs of motion: a case study in semantics and lexical memory. In Melton, A. W., and Martin, E. (eds), *Coding Processes in Human Memory*, Washington, D.C., Winston.

Murray, M. (1976), Attribution of responsibility in asthmatic children. Paper read to the BPS Social Section, York, September 1976.

Peel, E. A. (1967), A method for investigating children's understanding of certain logical connectives used in binary propositional thinking, *The British Journal of Mathematical and Statistical Psychology*, 20, 81–92.

Peevers, B. H., and Secord, P. F. (1973), Developmental changes in attribution of descriptive concepts to persons, *Journal of Personality and Social Psychology*, 27, 120–128.

Piaget, J. (1932), *The Moral Judgment of the Child*, London: Paul, Trench, Trubner.

Putnam, H. (1975), *Mind, Language and Reality*, Philosophical Papers, vol. 2, Cambridge: Cambridge University Press.

Rommetveit, R. (1974), *On Message Structure*, New York and London: Wiley.

Rommetveit, R. (this volume), On Piagetian cognitive operations, semantic competence, and message structure in adult–child communication.

Ryle, G. (1949), *The Concept of Mind*, London: Hutchinson.

Shaw, M. E., and Sulzer, J. L. (1964), An empirical test of Heider's levels in attribution of responsibility, *Journal of Abnormal and Social Psychology*, 69, 39–46.

Taplin, J. E. (1971), Reasoning with conditional sentences, *Journal of Verbal Learning and Verbal Behavior*, 10, 218–225.

Wason, P. C. (1968), Reasoning about a rule, *Quarterly Journal of Experimental Psychology*, 20, 273–281.

Wason, P. C., and Johnson-Laird, P. N. (1972), *Psychology of Reasoning: Structure and Content*, London: Batsford.

10

LANGUAGE AND INTERPERSONAL RELATIONS

Guy Fielding and Colin Fraser

1. Introduction: Language, Participation, and Relationships

In this chapter we shall be concerned with several social psychological questions regarding relations between the extra-linguistic setting of communication, and the language used in conversation. Our primary focus will be on the social relationships existing among and between participants in conversation. We shall begin by outlining some of the thinking which informed our initial investigation of the language correlates of dimensions of interpersonal relations. An exploratory but relatively complex empirical study based on these conceptions will be described. The most interesting of the findings from that study can be formulated in terms of a general pattern of choices—a nominal–verbal stylistic dimension—within the language system, and we shall attempt a first characterization of the linguistic nature of this dimension and point to a diverse set of studies which appear to have been concerned with the same set of choices. We shall then propose a social psychological basis for this particular pattern of linguistic choices in terms of the speaker's focus of concern in the conversation.

Sociolinguistics is concerned with the relations between systems of communication, especially linguistic systems, and the social situations in which they are used. The social situation is frequently analysed in terms of the first three components of Hymes's (1972) mnemonic SPEAKING, i.e. settings, participants, and ends (or purposes). The 'setting' locates the interaction, for instance as in an office or a restaurant, but also as an interview or after-dinner conversation, and as formal or casual–personal (see Joos, 1962). 'Participants' specifies the characteristics of those taking part in the interaction, for instance as male and female, but also as husband and wife, and as friends or enemies. 'Ends' refers to the intended objectives or actually achieved outcomes.

This analysis tends to see the participants as static individuals rather than as actors in a dynamic social relationship. Information about a participant as an individual may indicate what conversational resources he brings to the encounter. Information about the participants' relationship tells us what use will be made of those resources.

A language device may be used consciously in order to create a particular impression of the speaker. Other linguistic choices may be made of which the speaker is not aware, but whose effects form part of his deliberately managed self-presentation. Other aspects of his conversational performance may be thought of as 'leakage' (Ekman and Friesen, 1969), unintended features which he attempts to eliminate when he becomes aware of them. Consciously selected features are a function of the speaker's attitudes to his listener. These selections from among the possibilities open to him reflect the existing relationship and indicate the relationship he wishes to create. Those features of which he is unaware also reflect the existing relationship, and to the extent that his listener is affected by them are also responsible for altering that relationship. In the study of non-verbal behaviour considerable attention has been paid to these processes of impression management and unintended leakage. The experiment reported in this chapter examines the verbal correlates of differing social relationships.

Social relationships in a dyadic conversation may be described in terms of social roles specified at a cultural-institutional level or as personally negotiated relationships specified in terms of interpersonal attitudes. A number of studies have investigated the linguistic correlates of roles and role relationships. In a well-known series of studies Brown and his colleagues (Brown and Gilman, 1960; Brown and Ford, 1961) showed that the form of address used by a speaker was a function of the role relationship between him and his listener. More recently more general features of language style have been studied. For example Berko-Gleason (1973) has described the speech of mothers to their children; Candlin et al. (1974) have described that of doctors; and Torode (1976) that of teachers in the classroom. However, role relationships do not completely determine the selection of particular conversational behaviours. Indeed, it is the existence of choice which allows the individual to express particular meanings by selecting a 'marked' form rather than the expected, socially prescribed form. This element of individual choice and the consequent apparent unpredictability led Blom and Gumperz (1972) to suggest that deterministic analyses of the speech event should be abandoned in favour of purely interpretive models. Sankoff (1972) modified this suggestion, proposing a model which was predictive with respect to appropriate, unmarked speech styles, but which was merely interpretative with respect to the apparently less predictable forms. In Sankoff's model features of the speech event at the cultural level of analysis, for example role relationships, were predictive, while unpredictable usages were interpreted in social psychological terms, for example interpersonal attitudes. This can be illustrated by reference to Brown's studies of terms of address. Brown (1965) suggested that the choice of address forms, referential pronouns and greetings, etc., could be understood in terms of the operation of the 'solidarity' and 'power' semantics. These terms originally specified the dimensions underlying different role relationships. That is, speech selections were seen as determined by the role relationship between speaker and listener. However, in order to account for the full detail of the data it became necessary to invoke the social psychological analysis of interpersonal attitudes. This can be seen most clearly in the case of changes in forms of address. When 'Mr Jones' becomes 'Fred', this is likely to be a consequence not of an altered role relationship but of a changed personal one; the role relationship may continue to be one of employer-employee, but the change occurs because the interpersonal attitudes have become more positive. If the analysis were limited to a consideration of role relationships, this change in the form of address would be unintelligible. Examination of the personal relationship renders it meaningful and predictable.

It was our assumption that differences in interpersonal attitudes could account for variations in speech forms which are inexplicable when the analysis is at the level of role relationships. This assumption is open to examination since the structure of interpersonal attitudes can be specified rigorously, and independently of the structure of role relationships. The influences of interpersonal attitudes upon speech behaviour can then be investigated empirically.

Analyses of both the objective and subjective structure of interpersonal relations have converged upon a description of two, bipolar, orthogonal dimensions, for example Foa (1961). These two dimensions have been consistently identified but variously labelled. Lorr and McNair (1963, 1965) and Leary (1957) described them as the *affection–hostility* and *dominance–submission* dimensions. The affection–hostility dimension appears to correspond to the love–hostility dimension extracted by Schaefer (1959), to the associative–dissociative factor identified by Triandis *et al.* (1966) and to Osgood *et al*'s (1957) evaluative dimension. The dominance–submission dimension resembles the control-autonomy dimension identified by Schaefer (1959), the superordinate–subordinate factor of Triandis *et al.* (1966), and Osgood *et al*'s (1957) potency dimension.

These dimensions have appeared in studies of both interpersonal attitudes and of interpersonal behaviour. In both types of study they emerge as important and reliable components of the relationship. It was, therefore, decided to examine the linguistic correlates of variations in these two dimensions. In addition the effects of interpersonal familiarity were also studied. Several theories of face-to-face communication suggests that familiarity, either defined behaviourally in terms of the extent of previous interaction, or cognitively in terms of participants' knowledge of each other, is an important aspect of the speaker–listener relationship. For instance, Mead's (1950) concept of 'taking the role of the other' implies that certain types of communication can only be successfully achieved if the speaker knows a great deal about his listener.

Empirical support for the selection of these three aspects of interpersonal relationships as important determinants of conversational style was provided by a series of studies performed by Wish and his associates (Wish, 1973, 1974; Wish *et al.*, 1973; Wish and Kaplan, 1974). In these studies subjects were presented with descriptions of various speech events. The purpose and topic of the conversation were specified, and the participants were described in terms of social roles. Subjects were then asked to judge the similarities between the events in terms of the expected conversational behaviour of the participants. When subjected to multidimensional scaling analyses subjects' responses consistently identified four dimensions. These were described as (1) 'Cooperation, friendliness and harmony *vs.* competition, hostility and conflict'. This is equivalent to the dimension we will refer to as 'liking'.

(2) 'Democracy and equality *vs.* autocracy and inequality'. If it is remembered that Wish's analysis deals with dyadic behaviour whereas we have considered our dimensions as individual attitudes, then this corresponds to the dimension we will refer to as 'superiority'. (3) Intense *vs.* superficial'. This was related to the participants' familiarity and the salience or appropriateness to them of the topic being discussed. It corresponds to the dimension we will label 'familiarity'. The fourth dimension, which was described as 'Personal and informal *vs.* impersonal and formal', appeared to be primarily a function of the topic or purpose of the conversation rather than of the participants. In the experiment reported below this dimension was explored by studying a number of different conversational tasks.

2. An Exploratory Experimental Investigation

The experimental procedure was designed to gather samples of speech from speakers having particular, specified relationships with their listeners. These relationships were defined in terms of the speaker's liking of her listener, her feelings of superiority or inferiority with respect to that listener, and her familiarity with her listener. These speech samples were analysed to determine whether systematic speech variations were associated with differing interpersonal attitudes, and whether distinct speech styles were associated with particular interpersonal relationships.

2.1 Design and Procedure

The participants were 24 female, first-year non-psychology undergraduates at the University of Bristol who had volunteered to take part in our research. The study was carried out in the moderately spacious, comfortable, cluttered, slightly seedy room of the second author. The main part of the study involved each participant addressing someone she knew who was in a particular relationship to her in terms of liking, superiority, and familiarity. Each of the three dimensions was represented by only two values, i.e. like and dislike; superior and inferior; familiar and unfamiliar, the systematic combination of the three dimensions producing eight different types of speaker-listener relationships, for example someone who was liked, superior, and unfamiliar, or someone who was disliked, superior, and familiar, etc. In advance of the study, each participant was randomly assigned to one of the eight types of relationship. The problem then was to find a person having such a relationship to the participant.

This was accomplished by asking each participant to provide an exhaustive list of acquaintances, casual as well as close. Using a sorting procedure, all the acquaintances were then classified in terms of the three dimensions, which had been described to the participants in a mixture of cognitive, affective, and behavioural terms. From the set of people who conformed to the assigned relationship, for example liked, superior, unfamiliar, the participant was asked to indicate the female person who best typified that particular relationship. Only then was the participant told that this person would be the addressee in the series of communication tasks which were to follow. Analyses of a subsequent questionnaire assessing liking, superiority, and familiarity between speakers and addressees provided good validation of our sorting method's success in locating addressees bearing the desired relationships to the speakers.

Prior to addressing the selected person each participant performed two preliminary tasks in which she addressed the experimenter. In the first of these tasks she described a close male friend and this speech sample was used to provide 'baseline' measures for use in convariance analyses. In the second of these tasks she described the person she would address in the principal tasks. This description required the participant to consider the key characteristics of the addressee and her relationship with her. It was intended that, by making these characteristics salient, performances in the principal tasks which followed would be easier and more realistic. Following these initial tasks, each participant recorded messages or discussions which she assumed would be heard and, where appropriate, acted upon by the selected addressee. There were five tasks, during which the experimenter withdrew to work at a table at the far end of the room, and the participant recorded the messages in response to written instructions for each task, using a hand-held dictaphone.

The selection of the five communication tasks was not guided by a systematic framework for the analysis of topics, but was intended to sample a wide and contrasting set of speech genres and communication problems. The tasks were performed in the same order by all participants, an order which began with the most structured task and progressed to less clearly defined, but more intimate and conversational-like tasks. The tasks and the order in which they were performed were as follows: (1) The speaker described, in succession, six abstract line drawings in such a way that the listener should be able to identify each drawing from a larger array of similar drawings. This task involves the speaker's role-taking ability *vis-à-vis* the cognitive skills of the listener and is primarily concerned with the transmission of objective, referential information. The materials were derived from those used by Krauss and his colleagues (see, for instance, Krauss and Glucksberg, 1970) and this task will be referred to as the 'Krauss task'. (2) The speaker was asked to persuade her listener to become a blood donor. (3) The participant was given several cartoons and asked to describe them so that her listener would appreciate their humour. (4) The speaker was asked to discuss her leisure interests. (5) The speaker was asked to describe to her listener her relationship with her parents. Jackson *et al.* (1971) had found this topic to be interesting and salient for participants similar to ours, and it was more intimate (Jourard, 1971) than any of the preceding topics. This fifth task will be described as the 'Parents task'.

Of the five main tasks only the Krauss and Parents tasks will be reported in this paper. Preliminary analyses indicated that speech in the other three tasks was very similar to that in one or other of these two strongly contrasting tasks.

Because of the exploratory nature of the study we did not test any specific hypotheses. Instead our analysis attempted to provide an overall description of the speech samples. Calculation of measures of syntactic, lexical, and physical features was computer-assisted using programmes developed for the analysis of conversation (Fielding, 1976).

The syntactic analysis was based on the immediate constituent grammar of Fries (1952), as developed by Jones *et al.* (1963) for use in the statisitical analysis of spontaneous speech using computer-assisted identification of word classes. Jones *et al.* claimed that their classification of word types was relatively free from the need for decisions based upon contexts of use, that inconsistent and arbitary classifications were avoided, and that the categories established were statistically reliable. Our analysis identified five 'content' classes (nouns, verbs, adjectives, quantifiers, and adverbs) and eight classes of 'function' words (auxiliaries, pronouns, indefinites, relatives, conjunctions, prepositions, articles, and interjections). These corresponded roughly, but could not be equated with, the parts of speech of a traditional grammar. The analytical scheme is described in detail in Jones *et al.* (1963).

A number of common lexical statistics were calculated. Measures of productivity (total number of words, or tokens), diversity (total number of different words, or types) and proportionate usage of each syntactic word-class were calculated for each speaker on each task. Finally, a variety of 'conversational devices' were identified. These formed three clusters of measures. The first consisted of features reflecting a speaker's encoding difficulties, for example hesitations (see Boomer, 1965; Lay and Paivio, 1969) and uncompleted words. The second cluster included devices for indicating anxiety or expressing uncertainty, for example ritual phrases (Lalljee, 1972), conditional sequences (Cook-Gumperz, 1973), and 'markers of uncertainty' (Johnson, 1947). The third cluster included devices for structuring the conversation and the addressee's involvement, for example emphasis regulators (Cook-Gumperz, 1973), and tag sequences (the ego-referencing phrase 'I think' and the alter-referencing phrases 'you know' and 'you see').

2.2 Results and Discussion

Two strategies were possible when analysing and presenting the outcomes of the multiplicity of indices just described. One was to test each measure individually for significant differences between experimental conditions on each task, thus minimizing the chances that a significant association between speech and interpersonal relationship would go undetected. This strategy does, however, have certain shortcomings. One problem is that the large number of tests of significance makes it likely that some spuriously significant results would be contained among those reported. A second problem is the difficulty of integrating and presenting the lengthy and complex set of resultant findings. Therefore we adopted an alternative strategy. Factor analyses were performed enabling us to combine the data in such a way as to reduce the number of significance tests and facilitate the synthesis and understanding of the results.

Factor analyses revealed four main dimensions which appeared as factors in the experimental tasks (the Parents and Krauss tasks) and in the covariance task. The least important of these dimensions consisted of factors which reflected the speaker's pre-planning, as opposed to post-editing of her performance. One pole of the dimension consisted of hesitations, i.e. filled pauses and what we will refer to as 'automatic phrases', such as 'sort of' and 'you see'. These indices are associated with uncertainty and verbal planning. The other pole consisted of measures which indicated an absence of pre-planning and/or subsequent revision and correction, for example uncompleted words. In the experimental tasks these factors accounted for only a small proportion of the total variance, but they did distinguish between speakers as a function of their relationship with their listeners. Speakers showed more evidence of pre-planning when addressing listeners whom they felt were superior to themselves (Krauss task $F = 4\cdot 61, p < \cdot 05$; Parents task $F = 10\cdot 90, p < \cdot 01$). Broen and Siegel (1972) showed that speech errors are reduced when speakers are aware of being evaluated. If a speaker admires and respects her listener, and describes her as superior, then it would be expected that the salience of evaluation would increase. Greater attention would then be paid to speech resulting in a more careful and more fluent performance.

A 'qualification' factor emerged in all three tasks. It was defined by indices such as the ratios of substantive tokens (nouns and verbs) to qualifier tokens (adjectives, quantifiers, and adverbs), and the similar ratios of substantive types to qualifier types. A series of indices describing the proportion of different kinds of qualifiers used loaded significantly and positively on these factors; adverbs loaded most highly, followed by adjectives, approximate quantifiers, and then all quantifiers. The use of qualification was associated with the use of semantically empty filler phrases such as 'sort of' and 'in fact'. This probably related to the need for increased planning (Boder, 1940). Although the dimension accounted for a significant proportion of the total variance on each task, analysis showed that there were no significant differences as a function of the speaker-listener relationship. One possible basis for the dimension might be stable characteristics of the individual speakers. The dimension appears to be related to the adjective-verb ratio (Busemann, 1925, cited Boder, 1940; Rorschach, 1964). Busemann proposed that the ratio reflected the relative importance of action and qualitative concerns, and that this ratio was characteristic of an individual. Evidence presented by Cope (1969) and Poole and Field (1971) supports this view and suggests that qualification is a component of the overall degree of linguistic elaboration.

The two most important dimensions extracted were factors which we labelled 'productivity' and the 'nominal-verbal' distinction. The indices which loaded significantly on the productivity factors were the total number of tokens produced, the number of different types, and the simple type-token ratios of different word classes, which vary as a function of sample size (Carroll, 1964). In the experimental tasks the productivity factors accounted for 15 per cent (Krauss task) and 12 per cent (Parents task) of the total variance. In all tasks a number of other measures which were not directly functions of sample size also loaded significantly on the productivity factors. These additional indices suggested that increased productivity might be associated with task ambiguity (Siegman and Pope, 1972) and/or concreteness (Gillie, 1957).

The nominal-verbal factors were defined in terms of the ratios between the number of nouns and verbs, and between the number of nouns and pronouns, and by the proportions of parts of speech associated with the nominal (for example nouns, adjectives, and articles) and verbal (for example verbs, auxiliary verbs, and adverbs) aspects of the language system. In the Parents and Krauss tasks the nominal-verbal factor was the first factor extracted, and accounted for approximately 15 per cent of the total variance in each task. In addition to measures related directly to the nominal-verbal distinction other indices associated significantly with this dimension suggest that the 'verbal' pole indicated a more spontaneous, informal, and personal style. For instance, personal pronouns referring to the speaker and listener were more frequent, as was the use of the ego- and alter-referencing sequences 'I think' and 'you know'. This noun versus verb distinction, together with its related word classes, represents a fundamental and perhaps universal grammatical distinction (Robins, 1952). Similar factors were found in studies by Cope (1969) and by Carroll (1960). Listeners' responses to the two styles were discussed by Wells (1960) and examined empirically by Carroll (1960).

Analyses of variance performed using speakers' scores on the productivity and nominal-verbal factors produced interesting and unexpected results. When the productivity dimension was examined there were no significant main or interaction effects due to differences in the speaker-listener relationship in either the Parents or Krauss tasks. The absence of significant effects, particularly with respect to familiarity and liking, was quite unexpected. A considerable number of studies suggest that a speaker's productivity is related to his liking for his listener (Potashin, 1946; Back, 1951; Howeler and Vrolyk, 1970; Kelly, 1973). These studies all report that people talked longer to listeners they liked. Similarly, a number of studies have reported that speaker-listener familiarity affects the length of speech samples (for example Krauss and Weinheimer, 1964; Lowenthal, 1967). As familiarity increased, the speaker reduced the duration of his speech. We considered the possibility that the lack of significant effects in the present study might have been due to the marked individual differences between speakers and the consequently large error variance. Therefore, analyses of covariance were performed on the single index, total number of tokens, using as a covariate the number of tokens produced in the standardized covariance task. These analyses took into account each participant's characteristic level of productivity, and also controlled for any bias in the assignment of speakers to the different experimental conditions. These covariance analyses confirmed the earlier analyses, no significant differences in productivity being found.

These results suggested that, despite its ease of measurement and its frequent use, productivity may not be a particularly useful dependent measure in the study of speech style and interpersonal relationships. A number of theoretical treatments of the communication process suggest that different interpersonal relationships allow, or require, different message structures to be used, and these message structures will, among other differences, be of varying length. For instance, Rommetveit (1974) sees communication as a process of nesting what is new and to be made known onto what is already known. He points out that in the case of very closely shared social realities a great deal can be conveyed by very brief, cryptic expressions. When the context of communication is not perfectly and mutually understood the elaboration of these 'elliptical' expressions is necessary in order to communicate effectively. However, it is clear that message length is epiphenomenal and that an understanding of the relationship between communication processes and interpersonal attitudes is dependent upon consideration of features other than the mere amount of activity. Williams (1972) reached a similar conclusion. In a study of the stylistic correlates of interpersonal attraction he concluded that 'the most successful measures appear to be those which utilize the semantic or syntactic content of the transcript ... rather than those which rely purely on the physical attributes of the transcript (i.e. amount of speech)' (Williams, 1972, p. 14).

Analyses of variance performed on the nominal-verbal factor scores showed that differences in speakers' liking for their listeners had a significant main effect in both experimental tasks. In the Parents task speech to liked listeners was significantly less nominal than was speech to disliked listeners ($F = 8.30$, $p < .05$). A significant familiarity by liking interaction was evidently due to the unfamiliar dyads. Speech addressed to a familiar, liked listener did not differ significantly from that addressed to a familiar, disliked other. However, speech addressed to an unfamiliar, liked listener was significantly less nominal than that to an unfamiliar, disliked listener. In the Krauss task speakers addressing a liked listener were similarly less nominal than those talking to a disliked listener ($F = 6.55$, $p < .05$). Although the familiarity by liking interaction was not statistically significant, in the Krauss task as a whole speech to a familiar addressee was significantly less nominal than that to an unfamiliar listener ($F = 6.41$, $p < .05$).

3. The Nominal-Verbal Distinction

In this section we will consider in greater detail the objective and subjective characteristics of the nominal-verbal dimension. We will then consider how the results reported above may be understood in terms of the association of interpersonal relationships, interpersonal processes and linguistic choices. Finally we will propose a general basis for the nominal-verbal distinction in social psychological terms, namely a distinction between the ideational and interpersonal concerns of the speaker.

Consider a situation which might have been discussed by one of the participants in the Parents task. Her family has bought a new washing-machine. The ensuing events might have been described in terms such as:

The automatic washing-machine was delivered by the store. After the departure of the installation engineer my mother and father had, for the first time, an opportunity to have a proper look at their purchase.

Alternatively, the following might have been said:

They delivered it, and after the engineer had left, well, then it was the first time they looked at it properly.

The first sentences are predominantly nominal whereas the second, a paraphrase of the first, is a 'verby' sentence. It contains relatively more verbs and pronouns, and relatively fewer articles and nouns. These examples also illustrate some of the other differences likely to be associated with the nominal-verbal distinction. The noun/ verb choice is not syntactically minimal. For instance, in nominal constructions extensive use is made of non-finite rather than finite verb forms, modification is adjectival rather than adverbial, the construction is likely to be longer than the equivalent verbal structure, and the variety of structures allowed is rather restricted (Wells, 1960).

These objective differences are associated with subjective differences. The nominal style is likely to be more monotonous, less personal, and more formal. It appears to be a carefully considered and closely monitored production. The verbal style, on the other hand is characteristic of spontaneous, unreflective speech. It is immediate, informal, and varied. Carroll (1960) found that nominal passages were described by judges as impersonal, remote, and rational while verbal passages were felt to be personal, intimate, and emotional.

These subjective characteristics associated with the two different styles provide one possible explanation of the results of the present study. This explanation assumes that the speaker will exploit the listener's response to the two styles in order to manipulate the speaker-listener relationship. When addressing a listener she likes, the vivid, personal, and varied qualities of the verbal style (Wells, 1960; Carroll, 1960) would be appropriate. However, when addressing a disliked listener, the impersonal, unemotional, formal characteristics of the nominal style would be preferable.

This account can be extended to provide an explanation of the familiarity by liking interaction found in the Parents task. This showed that the most nominal speech was addressed to unfamiliar, disliked listeners and the least nominal to unfamiliar, liked listeners. Differences between speech addressed to familiar liked and disliked listeners were smaller and not significant. When addressing a liked but unfamiliar listener, a participant in our study would have been creating a relationship. She would have attempted to indicate her liking for her listener and to have generated a favourable impression of herself. In dyads where the listener was liked, but well known to the speaker, the tasks of establishing and furthering the solidarity of the relationship would already have been performed. Only the maintenance and marking of the stable relationship would have been necessary. Thus, although the verbal style was appropriate in both conditions, a more extreme style might have been expected in the unfamiliar condition. In the familiar speaker-listener dyads future meetings were likely to be as frequent and numerous as past meetings. In the dyads where mutual liking existed these future meetings would have been welcomed. However when dislike existed further meetings would have been problematic and were likely to occur only because of unavoidable external constraints. In such circumstances the members of the dyad would have concealed the true nature of their attitudes towards each other. Taguiri (1958) showed that such dissemblance does occur, for while people in his study could accurately identify those who liked them, recognition of the people who disliked them was significantly less accurate. This is partly because of self-deception on the perceiver's part, but is also a function of the behaviour of the perceived. In the present study members of the familiar but disliked relationships needed to maintain a reasonable degree of co-operation in order to accomplish the goals which necessitated their participation in those relationships. As socialized members of the speech community they were also aware of normative pressures which demanded that other people should not be hurt by the communication of negative evaluations. Tesser and Rosen (1975) have identified a norm of this kind, which restricts the transmission of information which causes distress to others. These pressures to dissemble were particularly strong in the established, continuing relationships. In the unfamiliar speaker-listener relationships, future interactions, both sought and imposed, were unlikely. The effectiveness of social and, particularly, individual pressures to disguise feelings of dislike were therefore much reduced. Thus speech to an unfamiliar disliked other would be markedly more nominal than that to a familiar disliked other. The largest nominal-verbal difference is found when speech to the unfamiliar liked listeners is compared with speech to the unfamiliar disliked listeners. This is understandable, for in the first condition there is a positive desire to indicate liking, and in the other few pressures to conceal the lack of attraction, or actual dislike.

These patterns of impression management appear to be the most likely explanation of the nominal-verbal differences found in the Parents task which we have just been discussing. The relative attractiveness of the styles to the listener and the differing involvement of the speaker accord well with the individual requirements and social demands imposed by the various experimental conditions. If, however, we turn our attention to the Krauss task, it becomes evident that some further explanation is required. The Krauss task is markedly more nominal than the Parents task. In the Krauss task the noun-to-verb and noun-to-pronoun ratios, and the proportion of nouns, articles, adjectives, and prepositions, were significantly higher. In the Parents task, on the other hand, verbs, auxiliary verbs, adverbs, pronouns, and conjunctions were all significantly more frequent. Observation of participants' performances suggested that these differences reflect the very different communication problems set by these two tasks. The Krauss task imposed a clear structure upon the speaker's performance, which was dictated by the immediate context of physical objects. Effort was concentrated upon the transmission of objective information, the performance being adjusted in terms of the listener's competence. In the Parents task the task and the topic were loosely specified, the choice of material and treatment being left to the speaker. In this task the speaker was concerned with the problem of describing her attitudes and emotions, and her relationship with her parents. When discussing this topic her listener's own attitudes, etc., would have been more relevant than her competence. The focus of attention in the Krauss task was primarily 'ideational' while that in the Parents task was principally 'interpersonal'.

Halliday (1970) argued that these two functions (together with a third, the 'textual') are the basic concerns of language and that they are associated with, or realized by different language structures or 'models of language' (Halliday, 1969). The ideational language model expresses the speaker's observations and interpretations of states in the objective world. It constitutes the representational content of utterances. The interpersonal language model reflects the speaker's concern to establish, maintain, and modify social relationships. It represents his understanding of, and reactions to, these subjective relationships.

The ideational versus interpersonal distinction implies not only the exploitation of different models of language, but also the speaker's adoption of different roles with respect to the speech event. When the focus of the speaker's attention is ideational he observes, describes, analyses, and interprets the phenomena under discussion. The speaker adopts the role of 'observer' (Halliday, 1975) and uses the ideational language model to identify and assign attributes to the things talked about. When the focus of his attention is interpersonal, he adopts a more active role. Not only is the nature of the existing relationship reflected in the speech event, but he also modifies it as a consequence of his involvement in the event. The interpersonal model of language implies action rather than description. Through it the speaker operates in, and acts upon, the subjective, social world. Halliday (1975) refers to the speaker in this role as an 'intruder'. The interpersonal language model expresses the speaker's involvement with the listener, the ideational model involvement with the conversational topic.

The structural correlates of the two models have not been specified systematically, but the noun and nominal group are the principal means of representing naming and attributive propositions, and the verb the principal means of representing actions and relationships (particularly the system of mood, see Halliday, 1970). If for the time being we accept the equation of the ideational function with the greater elaboration of the nominal system, and the interpersonal function with the greater elaboration of the verbal system, we can usefully apply this distinction in order to understand the results of the present study.

In the Krauss task the speaker's attention was concentrated upon stimulus objects in the real world and she would therefore have been expected to use the 'ideational' model of language. Speech in the Krauss task should therefore have been more nominal, as in fact it was. Variations in speech style within each task can also be understood in terms of differential emphasis upon the ideational and interpersonal functions. In the Krauss task the immediate problems of describing the task stimuli to unfamiliar listeners probably demanded that attention be biased towards ideational concerns, whereas when addressing a disliked listener a strategy of deliberately avoiding interpersonal issues may have been chosen as a means of coping with the conflicting individual attitudes and social norms presented by the situation. Within the Parents task, where the interpersonal function was the primary focus of attention, the active creative nature of the 'intruder' role was most appropriate when speakers addressed a liked, but unfamiliar listener, less so when addressing an unfamiliar and disliked listener where the process of objectification and the impersonal role of observer would again have been the preferred strategy.

Some independent empirical evidence exists to support this account. For instance, it seems that speakers are aware of, and consciously employ the conversational strategies described above. Wish and Kaplan (1974) found that people described conversations in which relationships were co-operative and harmonious as personal and informal. Conversations which involved overt or potential conflict (for example between political rivals or bitter enemies) were described as impersonal and formal. A number of studies provide support for the hypothesized relationship between the nominal-verbal and ideational-interpersonal distinctions. In an experiment reported by Moscovici (1967) subjects were shown a series of pictures and asked to (1) describe them, or (2) make up a story using the pictures, or (3) animate the story, using dialogue and indicating the action. These tasks varied in the extent to which the speaker was personally involved as an actor rather than being an objective observer. Moscovici found that the descriptive task contained the highest proportion of nouns, and the animated story the greatest proportions of verbs, personal pronouns, and function words. In an earlier experiment by Moscovici and Plon (1966) the seating positions of subjects in conversing dyads were varied. The seating arrangements were (1) face-to-face, (2) face-to-face but separated by a screen, (3) side-by-side, and (4) back-to-back. Moscovici's (1967) analysis of these conditions suggests that the face-to-face conditions emphasized interpersonal conditions whereas in the other two conditions ideational concerns were more important. Utterances in the interpersonal conditions contained a higher proportion of verbs and function words, whereas utterances in the ideational conditions were significantly more nominal. Back and Strickland (reported in Back, 1961) conducted a study in which small groups of subjects were given the task of writing a pamphlet under instructions which either emphasized group co-operation and co-ordination or emphasized individual competence and endeavour. The 'group' condition would seem to have emphasized interpersonal concerns whereas the 'individual' condition would have led to a concentration upon ideational concerns. Communications in the 'individual' condition contained significantly higher proportions of nouns and adjectives and were structurally less varied.

These quite dissimilar experiments provide indirect support for the hypothesized relationship between the nominal-verbal and ideational-interpersonal distinctions. A direct test of this hypothesized relationship might be to study the speech of task and socio-emotional leaders in small discussion groups. Descriptions of these two types of leader (Bales and Slater, 1955) suggest that the roles they play within the group would lead them to adopt, respectively, the ideational and interpersonal model of language. It would therefore be expected that the speech of task-orientated leaders would be more nominal and less verbal than that of the socio-emotionally orientated leaders.

In this chapter we have argued that the nominal-verbal dimension is an important and general aspect of language style. This structural distinction appears to reflect the relative emphasis the speaker places upon the ideational and interpersonal functions of language. The nominal-verbal dimension described in this chapter is a rather rough and ready, empirically derived specification of this functional distinction. A more sensitive and detailed description of both of these aspects of the language system is obviously needed. The development of these descriptions, and the empirical exploration and testing of the links between them, would seem to provide a fruitful approach to the continued study of language and social relationships.

Acknowledgements

The research for and preparation of this paper was supported by SSRC Grants HR1821 and HR3608/1 held by the second author. Most of the work reported in this chapter was carried out while both authors were members of the Department of Psychology, University of Bristol.

References

Back, K.W. (1951), Influence through social communication, *J. Abn. Soc. Psychol.*, 46, 9–23.

Back, K.W. (1961), Power, influence and pattern of communication. In Petrullo, L., and Bass, B. (eds), *Leadership and Interpersonal Behaviour*, New York: Holt, Rinehart & Winston.

Bales, R.F., and Slater, P.E. (1955), Role differentiation in small decision-making groups. In Parsons, T., and Bales, R.F. (eds), *Family, Socialisation and Interaction Process*, New York: Free Press.

Berko-Gleason, J. (1973), Code switching in children's language. In Moore, T.E. (ed.), *Cognitive Development and the Acquisition of Language*, New York: Academic Press.

Blom, J.P., and Gumperz, J.J. (1972), Social meaning in linguistic structures; code-switching in Norway. In Gumperz, J.J., and Hymes, D. (eds), *Directions in Sociolinguistics*, New York: Holt, Rinehart & Winston.

Boder, D.P. (1940), The adjective-verb quotient: A contribution to the psychology of language, *Psychol. Rec.*, 3, 309–343.

Boomer, D.S. (1965), Hesitation and grammatical encoding, *Language and Speech*, 8, 148–158.

Broen, P.A., and Siegel, G.M. (1972), Variations in normal speech disfluences, *Language and Speech*, 15, 219–231.

Brown, R. (1965), *Social Psychology*, New York: Free Press.

Brown, R., and Ford, M. (1961), Address in American English, *J. Abn. Soc. Psychol.*, 62, 375–385.

Brown, R., and Gilman, A. (1960), The pronouns of power and solidarity, In Sebeok, T.A. (ed.), *Style in Language*, Cambridge, Mass.: M.I.T. Press.

Busemann, A. (1925), *Die Sprach der Jugend als Audsruck der Entwichlungorhythmik*, Jena: Fischer.

Candlin, C.N., Leather, J.H., and Burton, C.J. (1974), English language skills for overseas doctors and medical staff. Mimeo: Progress Reports 1, 2, 3, and 4, Department of English, University of Lancaster.

Carroll, J.B. (1960), Vectors of prose style. In Sebeok, T.A. (ed.), *Style in Language*, Cambridge, Mass.: M.I.T. Press.

Carroll, J.B. (1964), *Language and Thought*, Englewood Cliffs, N.J.: Prentice-Hall.

Cook-Gumperz, J. (1973), *Social Control and Socialisation*, London: Routledge & Kegan Paul.

Cope, C.S. (1969), Linguistic structure and personality development, *Counselling Psychol. Monogr.*, 16, 1–19.

Ekman, P., and Friesen, W.V. (1969), Nonverbal leakage and clues to deception, *Psychiatry*, 32, 88–105.

Fielding, G. (1976), Lexcan: a user's manual for a programme to analyse conversation. Mimeo: School of Human Purposes, University of Bradford.

Foa, U.G. (1961), Convergences in the analysis of the structure of interpersonal behaviour, *Psychol. Review*, 68, 341–353.

Fries, C.C. (1952), *The Structure of English*, New York: Harcourt, Brace & World.

Gillie, P.J. (1957), A simplified formula for measuring abstraction in writing, *J. Applied Psychol.*, 41, 214–217.

Halliday, M.A.K. (1969), Relevant models of language, *Educ. Review*, 22, 26–37.

Halliday, M.A.K. (1970), Language structure and language function. In Lyons, J. (ed.), *New Horizons in Linguistics*, Harmondsworth: Penguin Books.

Halliday, M.A.K. (1975), *Learning How to Mean: Explorations in the Development of Language*, London: Arnold.

Howeler, M., and Vrolyk, A. (1970), Verbal communication lengths as an index of interpersonal attraction, *Acta Psychol.*, 34, 471–515.

Hymes, D. (1972), Models of the interaction of language and social life. In Gumperz, J.J., and Hymes, D. (eds), *Directions in Sociolinguistics: the Ethnography of Communication*, New York: Holt, Rinehart & Winston.

Jackson, R.H., Manaugh, T.S., Wiens, A.N., and Matarazzo, R.D. (1971), A method for assessing the saliency level of areas in a person's current life situation, *J. Clin. Psychol.*, 27, 32–39.

Johnson, W. (1947), *People in Quandaries*, New York: Harper & Row.

Jones, L.V., Goodman, M.F., and Wepman, J.M. (1963), The classification of parts of speech for the characterisation of aphasia, *Language and Speech*, 9, 94–107.

Joos, M. (1962), The five clocks, *International Journal of American Linguistics*, 28.

Jourard, S. (1971), *Self Disclosure: an Experimental Analysis of the Transparent Self*, New York: Wiley.

Kelly, F.D. (1973), Paralinguistic indicator of patient's affect: attitudinal significance of length of communication, *Psychol. Reps.*, 32, 1223–1226.

Krauss, R.M., and Glucksberg, S. (1970), Socialisation of communication skills. In Hoppe, R.A., Milton, G.A., and Simmel, E.C. (eds), *Early Experiences and the Processes of Socialisation*, New York: Academic Press.

Krauss, R.M., and Weinheimer, S. (1964), Changes in reference phrases as a function of frequency of usage in social interaction: a preliminary study, *Psychonom. Sci.*, 1, 113–114.

Lalljee, M. (1972), Units of ritualised speech and situational anxiety, *Proceedings of B.P.S. Conference on Nonverbal Behaviour*, Oxford.

Lay, C.H., and Paivio, A. (1969), The effects of task difficulty and anxiety on hesitation in speech, *Can. J. Behav. Sci.*, 1, 25.

Leary, T. (1957), *Interpersonal Diagnosis of Personality*, New York: Ronald Press.

Lorr, M., and McNair, D.M. (1963), An interpersonal behaviour circle, *J. Abn. Soc. Psychol.*, 67, 68–75.

Lorr, M., and McNair, D.M. (1965), Expansion of the interpersonal behaviour circle, *J. Pers. Soc. Psychol.*, 2, 823–830.

Lowenthal, K. (1967), The development of codes in public and private language, *Psychonom. Sci.*, 8, 449–450.

Mead, G.H. (1950), *Mind, Self and Society*, Chicago: Chicago University Press.

Moscovici, S. (1967), Communication processes and language. In Berkowitz, L. (ed.), *Advances in Experimental Social Psychology*, vol. 3, New York: Academic Press.

Moscovici, S., and Plon, M. (1966), Les Situations colloques; observations théoriques et expérimentales, *Bull. Psychol.*, 19, 702–722.

Osgood, C.E., Suci, G.J., and Tannenbaum, P.H. (1957), *The Measurement of Meaning*, Urbana, Ill.: University of Illinois Press.

Poole, M.E., and Field, T.W. (1971), Social class and code elaboration in oral communication, *J. Speech Hearing Research*, 14, 421–427.

Potashin, R.A. (1946), A sociometric study of children's friendships, *Sociometry*, 9, 48–70.

Robins, R.H. (1952), Noun and verb in universal grammar, *Language*, 28, 289–298.

Rommetveit, R. (1974), *On Message Structure. A Framework for the Study of Language and Communication*, New York and London: Wiley.

Rorschach, H. (1964), *Psychodiagnostics*, New York: Grune & Stratton.

Sankoff, G. (1972), Language use in multilingual societies; some alternative approaches. In Pride, J.B., and Holmes, J. (eds), *Sociolinguistics*, Harmondsworth: Penguin Books.

Schaefer, E.S. (1959), A circumplex model for maternal behaviour, *J. Abn. Soc. Psychol.*, 59, 226–235.

Siegman, A.W., and Pope, B. (1972), The effects of ambiguity and anxiety on interviewee verbal behaviour. In Siegman, A.W., and Pope, B. (eds), *Dyadic Communication*, Oxford and New York: Pergamon.

Taguiri, R. (1958), Social preference and its perception. In Taguiri, R., and Petrullo, L. (eds),

Person Perception and Interpersonal Behaviour, Stanford, Calif.: Stanford University Press.

Tesser, A., and Rosen, S. (1975), The reluctance to transmit bad news. In Berkowitz, L. (ed.), *Advances in Experimental Social Psychology*, vol. 8, New York: Academic Press.

Torode, B. (1976), Teachers' talk in classroom discussion. In Stubbs, M., and Delamont, S. (eds), *Explorations in Classroom Observation*, London: Wiley.

Triandis, H.C., Janaka, Y., and Shanmugam, A.V. (1966), International attitudes among American, Indian and Japanese students, *Int. J. Psychol.*, 1, 177–206.

Wells, R. (1960), Nominal and verbal style. In Sebeok, T.A. (ed.), *Style in Language*, Cambridge, Mass.: M.I.T. Press.

Williams, E. (1972), The results of analyses of transcripts from the pilot experiment on communication medium and interpersonal attraction. Unpublished report of the Communications Study Group, University of London.

Wish, M. (1973), Individual differences in perceptions of dyadic relationships, *Proceedings of the 81st Ann. Conv. of A.P.A.*, Quebec.

Wish, M. (1974), Dimensions of interpersonal communication, Proceedings of the 18th Ann. Conv. of the Human Factors Society, Huntsville, Alabama.

Wish, M., and Kaplan, S.J. (1974), Situational and relational aspects of interpersonal communication, Mimeo, Murray Hill, N.J.: Bell Lab.

Wish, M., Kaplan, S.J., and Deutsch, M. (1973), Dimensions of interpersonal relations: preliminary results, *Proceedings of the 81st Ann. Conv. of A.P.A.*, Quebec.

AUTHOR INDEX

SUBJECT INDEX